TWO FLAGS

Return to the
Warsaw Ghetto

TWO FLAGS

Return to the Warsaw Ghetto

MARIAN APFELBAUM

gefen publishing house
JERUSALEM • NEW YORK

Originally published in French as *Retour sur le Ghetto de Varsavie* (Paris: Editions Odile Jacob, 2002), in Polish as *Dwa Sztandary: Rzecz o powstaniu w getcie warszawskim* (Cracow: Wydawnictwo Literackie, 2003) and in Hebrew as *Bekhazara Legeto Varsha: Hitkomemut Ha'igud Hatzvai Hayehudi* (Jerusalem: Yad Vashem, 2004).

Typesetting: Jerusalem Typesetting
Cover Design: S. Kim Glassman

ISBN 978-965-229-356-5

Edition 1 3 5 7 9 8 6 4 2

Gefen Publishing House, Ltd.
6 Hatzvi Street, Jerusalem 94386, Israel
972-2-538-0247
orders@gefenpublishing.com

Gefen Books
600 Broadway, Lynbrook, NY 11563, USA
516-593-1234
orders@gefenpublishing.com

www.israelbooks.com

Printed in Israel

Send for our free catalogue

In memory of
Mieczyslaw Dawid Apfelbaum
and Irena Apfelbaum
who died in the fighting
during the Warsaw uprisings

ACKNOWLEDGMENTS

To Chaya Lazar, for her help in documentary research in Israel.

To Sylwia Szymanska, for her help in documentary research in Poland.

To Malgorzata Maliszewska, for her help in translating and organizing the bibliography.

To my wife Laurence, for her support and patient rereading of the manuscript.

On one of the concrete buildings someone had unfurled, like a call to battle against us, two banners – the Jewish and Polish flags.

We understood the moral and political importance of this act and took the flags very seriously. Flags and national colors are a weapon of combat on the same order as a rapid-fire cannon, or even a thousand of them.

– General Jürgen Stroop,
in charge of crushing the Warsaw ghetto[1]

1. Jürgen Stroop, *The Stroop Report: The Jewish Quarter of Warsaw Is No More* (New York: Pantheon, 1979), p. 5. This is the Stroop report on the liquidation of the Warsaw ghetto in 1943, written at Himmler's request and meant for him. Three copies were made of this report, one each for Himmler, Krüger and Stroop himself. The daily communiqués making up this report appear as appendix 3.

CONTENTS

FOREWORD

This book was born of another book, and that one was born from a debt.

The debt can be traced back to the years 1943–44. My father was in charge of the cardiology department at Czyste hospital in the Warsaw ghetto. Refusing to desert his post, it took the murdering of all of the patients by the Germans to relieve him of his duties.

It was not until early 1943, after the first ghetto revolt, that my parents and I left the ghetto through the sewers. It was a long and arduous journey. My teenage sister was involved in the resistance movement and had refused to flee the ghetto and the further fighting that was to come.

The only way, as a Jew, to survive on the "Aryan" side of the wall was to live in hiding, and that meant an apartment, money to pay off the inevitable blackmailers, and then a new place to stay to put an end to the blackmailing; and then the whole cycle would resume once more. A single blackmailer could ruin the lives of many people, ultimately causing deaths, but it took a wide network of people to save a single Jew or a Jewish family. Great strength of character was required to take part in such efforts, because any aid to, or even contact with, a Jew was punishable by death; and it was not only the "guilty" person whose neck was on the line – the person's family, servants, concierges, and even the neighbors would have to pay the heavy price for such "treacherous" deeds.

In short, we survived thanks to the help of admirable people who risked their lives to save ours. Throughout my whole professional career, as a professor of nutrition, it has been my wish not so much to repay that debt as to express my gratitude through a firsthand account of their actions. But as a matter of personal preference and training, I prefer study to testimonials, the objective to the subjective. I felt that my expression of gratitude would have to take a more objective, impersonal form.

In the course of my efforts to do so, I met Teresa Prekerowa, the author of an historical study entitled *Zegota*, after the Polish name of the Commission for Aid to the Jews, which saved my life, among countless others.

Not once – not in her book on Zegota, her other publications, nor in the great many sessions where we worked together – did Teresa mention that she herself had been a heroic defender of the Jews, and for this had been awarded the title of Righteous Gentile. Her example could only spur me on in my preference for history over a personal account. We worked on this book about Zegota together and translated it. Teresa died soon after she had finished reading the proofs, and the book was published four years ago by Editions du Rocher. That marked the fulfillment of my initial plan.

But in an entirely unexpected fashion, as a result of my voyage through English-language books and a few in French, the Warsaw archives in particular, I was presented with a new problem. The reality of the ghetto uprising, from the preparations to its actual unfolding, was far less monolithic, and more complex, than the image portrayed in Western literature. As I read and reread the material, I became convinced that not only was this image oversimplified, but that an important part was missing – because it had been erased. That erasure, that discrepancy between the image and the real story, is the subject of this present book.

Aside from a few quotations taken from Western sources cited in counterpoint, this book is comprised, to a large degree, in the main body of the text, the footnotes and the appendices, of long translations from Polish sources, some of them contemporaneous with these events and others written later by those who took part in or witnessed them. The bulk of this material has never been published before. Some of it has been extracted from Polish publications considered confidential at the time of publication, and afterwards forgotten and never translated. I was aided in these long efforts (long because the archives in Poland were opened up little by little after the fall of the Communist regime in 1991 and are still to this day not well catalogued, with hardly any computerization) by Sylwia Szymanska, a young Polish historian.

I have opted for full citations, and for presenting some documents in their entirety, so as to avoid the danger of any tendentious editing (even involuntarily) that would distort or change the authors' original meaning. Most of these events are recounted by a number of different sources. In some cases, the eyewitness accounts confirm one another; in others, there are discrepancies which I have striven to highlight and, where possible, explain. When uncertainty remains, I have indicated that.

I have maintained a clear and unambiguous separation between these accounts and my own opinions on the events and my hypotheses regarding the differences between sources. Thus I have chosen to present the documents themselves, even at the cost of making this a more difficult "read" than it might have otherwise been.

I lived through the events of the ghetto as a child and was therefore neither a participant nor an active observer. The fact that members of my family took part in the ZZW's (Jewish Military Union) actions was one of the reasons I went back to the archives.

I am aware of the iconoclastic character of this book. After all, it amounts to accusing the extensive and venerable literature on the Warsaw ghetto insurrection of not only lying, but lying by omission. All I can ask is that the reader judge the contents of this book on its own merits, sparing no indulgence for the author because he was supposedly once a victim, but also sparing no indulgence for those who, because of now-obsolete ideologies, have distorted the truth since the time of the uprising itself, and deliberately persisted in this error ever since.

In the course of writing this book, I was faced with a moral problem regarding the rabid anti-Semitic opinions expressed after the war by Tadeusz Bednarczyk, one of the witnesses to whom I frequently refer. Despite his opinions, I decided to retain his narrative concerning the ghetto for two reasons:

1) The first is that, according to very numerous sources, Bednarczyk was involved in helping the Jewish underground, a task that had been officially assigned to him by the Polish underground.
2) The second is also confirmed by all sources: he was the only Pole cooperating with the Jewish underground who was authorized, because of his professional status, to enter and leave the ghetto on a daily basis – from the beginning of the ghetto to the end.

In light of the above factors, his anti-Semitic postwar opinions ultimately seemed to me to be of minor importance.

CHRONOLOGY

September 1, 1939	German invasion of Poland
September 28, 1939	Surrender of Warsaw
December 1939	Foundation of the ZZW (Jewish Military Union)
November 1940	Ghetto walled in
June 1941	Germany attacks USSR
July 22–September 12, 1942	The major "transfer"
December 2, 1942	Foundation of the ZOB (Jewish Fighting Organization)
January 18–21, 1943	First ghetto revolt

April 19–May 16, 1943	Ghetto Uprising (dates as given in the Stroop Report)
September 1943	End of the Uprising
August 1944	Warsaw Insurrection
January 1945	Liberation of Warsaw
May 8, 1945	Germany surrenders

CHAPTER 1

FRATERNAL ENEMIES

Two organizations of more or less the same size fought in the Warsaw ghetto uprising, the ZOB (*Zydowska Organizacja Bojowa* – Jewish Fighting Organization) and the ZZW (*Zydowski Zwiazek Wojskowy* – Jewish Military Union). However, the ZZW has all but disappeared from the history books. This book, based on quotations from participants and eyewitness accounts, describes the actions of the ZZW and discusses the reasons for its disappearance.

Thus, the highly official *Polish Military Encyclopedia* says of the ZZW:

> At the initiative of the OZ (*Organizacja Zbroja Wyzwolenia* – Liberation Military Organization), and with the participation of a group of Jews, including former officers in the Polish army and members of the right-wing Jewish organization Betar, an underground Jewish military organization was founded in Warsaw in December 1939. The commander was Captain M. Apfelbaum, known as "Kowal." The ZZW worked closely with the OW-KB (*Korpus Bezpieczenistwa* – Security Corps) and maintained contact with the AK (*Armia Krajowa* – Home Army), which provided it with arms and instructors. Armed units of the ZZW took part in the fighting in defense of the ghetto on January 18–21, 1943, the liquidation and sabotage actions carried out in April 1943, and the ghetto uprising. Many dozens of

> ZZW members were evacuated through the sewers by special units of the OW-KB and the AK.[1]

Two of the main leaders of each of these two Jewish organizations survived the war: Marek Edelman, deputy commander-in-chief of the ZOB; Icchak Cukierman, coordinator of the ZOB political committee; Henryk Iwanski, a captain in the Polish Resistance and main supplier of aid and arms to the ZZW; and Kalmen Mendelson, a lieutenant in the ZZW and its deputy commander-in-chief.

We will let Iwanski speak first. Below is a letter he wrote in 1956, while living in poverty and neglect in Poland, to Lywia Lubetkin, at the Ghetto Fighters' Kibbutz in Israel where she and her husband were treated as exemplary heroes:

> My dear colleague Lywia.[2] I was very sick and could not write; now I am better and so I'm writing. I want to clear up the following matters for you and the others: In October 1939, General Sikorski decided to form a number of clandestine platoons, one of them meant to support the Jews. This platoon was organized in Warsaw. It was to be commanded by a man with experience in fighting the Germans, and I had fought in all the battles against the Germans in Silesia [battles fought to determine the newly independent Poland's western border at the end of World War I]. My platoon was part of the OW [Military Organization]. I had a meeting with Jewish friends and we constituted the *Zydowski Zwiazek Wojskowy* [the ZZW, Jewish Military Union]. Those were my orders. Before, during and for a short time after the Ghetto Uprising, I furnished the ZZW with arms, ammunition and grenades, food and medicine constantly; no one ever took a penny and in these actions my son and my brother lost their lives, and I myself was seriously wounded in the head with

1. Dan Kurzman, *Mala encyklopedia wojskowa*, vol. 3 (Warsaw: Wydawnictwo Ministerstwa Obrony Narodowej, 1971), p. 648.
2. Lywia is Liwia (or Ziwia in Hebrew) Lubetkin, alias Celine, a former member of the ZOB general staff and wife of Cukierman. In their publications on the ghetto uprising, neither of them has ever mentioned the ZZW.

long-term consequences to this day, including the paralysis of the left side of my body. My wife, who cleaned, treated and fed wounded and sick Ghetto refugees during and after the Insurrection, came down with tuberculosis, from which she still suffers, and because of all that, you, Anitka [affectionate diminutive for Lywia] and the other Ghetto fighters owe us a letter from time to time – we ask for nothing more, and as for the fact that my wife and I were linked to the ZZW and not the ZOB, perhaps that does not make us guilty.

We wanted to help the people of the Ghetto in any way we could and I think we did our best – for that cause we gave the lives of our closest loved ones and our health – and that the ZZW people fought bravely and behaved as honorably as the ZOB people is not our fault. You and Antek[3] and all of you in the ZOB should forgive my wife and I, and not forget that all that time our apartment was used as a hiding place and infirmary for the Jews, that my wife and I never made any distinction among you: the wounded, starving and mistreated people of the Ghetto, according to politics or which combat organization they belonged to; I took as many of you out of the Ghetto as I could and put them in the hands of my wife and the organization's doctors, and thanks to that, there are many people still alive today in Warsaw, elsewhere in Poland and the world who were treated and protected under my orders.

When it comes to the dead, one should only speak well of them or say nothing at all, and I know that a great many people died in the Ghetto, arms in hand, fighting against the Nazis, and they were members of the ZZW. Today all that is history, and beloved friends of the ZOB, the whole world knows that yours is the greater merit, and for that reason please speak well of them as well and write to us because we hold the warmest feelings for *all* of you [the only underlined word in this letter].

Our warm greetings to you and all of your kibbutz.

---

3. "Antek": Icchak Cukierman, a ZOB leader, its deputy commander and its representative to the AK. This name is also often spelled "Yitzhak Zuckerman."

Henryk[4] and Wictoria Iwanski, 8 x 1959.[5]

Now let us listen to Marek Edelman, speaking in Poland in the spring of 2000 to the journalist Anka Grupinska, who compiled a collection of memoirs by survivors of the uprising:

– [...] Marek, can we begin by talking about the ZZW?
– The ZZW? Why do you care about them? Why do you want to talk about the fascists?
– But seriously, Marek, there are many memoirs of the Warsaw ghetto written by both Zionists and non-Zionists and none of them mention the ZZW.
– That's because there's nothing to talk about.
– You yourself often talked about it in Poland.
–...about the ZZW?
– No, and that's my point. You talked about the insurrection and never mentioned the ZZW. Perhaps we should look at the facts.
– But what facts? There were no facts!
– [...] Marek, do you really mean to say that no one in the ghetto belonged to the ZZW?
– Except for that house on Muranowska Street,[6] no one.
– Did you know Dawid Wdowinski?
– No. Who's he?
– Doctor Wdowinski. He was a doctor in the ghetto and chairman of the ZZW Political Council. He survived and wrote a book about the ZZW published in the United States.[7]
– I haven't heard about it. Because they had a political council? Ah! People can write anything. Don't make too much of them, they were disgusting.

---

4. Other documents concerning Henryk Iwanski can be found in appendix 1.
5. Warsaw Ghetto Files, Jabotinski Institute, ch7b-1/20.
6. In Polish, all nouns have a gender. Thus, for example, since "street" is feminine, the name of the street is feminine and takes an *-a* ending (Muranowsk*a* street); since "square" is a masculine noun, the name of the square is masculine and takes an – *i* ending (Muranowsk*i* square). The distinction is made throughout this book.
7. David Wdowinski, *And We Are Not Saved* (New York: Philosophical Library, 1963).

– Why disgusting?

– They thought they were the most important because they had gotten a few weapons from the nationalists, it seems.

– Do you know from who?

– People say that it was from people who belonged to *Plug i Miecz* [Plow and Sword, a marginal and caricaturally anti-Semitic far-right Polish organization].

– In 1991, I talked with a man who used the name Jozef Grynblatt in the ghetto and Bednarczyk after the war. He gave me quite a few details about the ZZW. He said he belonged to the military council himself.

– I never heard that they had a military council.

– Ringelblum describes visiting their headquarters at 7 Muranowska Street [see chapter 5].[8]

– So? They were a bunch of porters, smugglers and thieves. They shut themselves up in that house, let off a few shots and then ran away the same day. There's nothing to talk about. It's possible that they were the ones who hung that flag.

– There were two flags flying, it seems.

– That's possible.

– When was the ZZW founded? Some people say 1942.

– Certainly not! Much later.

– January 1943?

– Later, probably. And anyway, I don't know. I'm an old man and I don't remember.

– Didn't you meet with them? You, Antek [Icchak Cukierman] and Anielewicz?

– Yes. Their commander Frenkiel came with two other men.

– Leon Rodal?

– I don't know.

– And they came to that meeting armed.

– So did we.

---

8. Emmanuel Ringelblum, *Polish Jewish Relations during the Second World War* (New York: Howard Fertig, 1976), p. 169–70.

– And they brandished their weapons and demanded that you put yourselves under their command…
– We brandished our weapons too.
– What do you still remember about that meeting?
– Nothing, nothing important. They wanted to be in charge. They said they didn't want to argue about it, that they would shoot us. So we told them that we had arms too. But all that didn't matter.
– Where did you meet with them? At their place on Muranowska Street?
– No, somewhere in Nalewki, in our hideout.
– Was that after the January action? [January 1943, date of the first ghetto revolt.]
– Of course. Just before the insurrection. A week or two…I can't tell you exactly. And they demanded that we let them be in charge because they were a military organization! And because they had contacts. They really did have contacts. And plenty of weapons. Compared to us, they had a lot more. In other words, percentage-wise, they had much more. […][9]

I have chosen Iwanski's scathing irony and Edelman's denials to sketch the background to a fratricidal struggle, although not a bloody one; a struggle which, up until now, has been lost by the ZZW, to the extent that this organization has totally disappeared from the pages of Hebrew or English literature – or rather, never made an appearance there at all.[10]

9. Anka Grupińska, *Ciągle po kole: Rozmowy z żołnierzami getta warszawskiego* (Warsaw: Wydawnictwo Twój Styl, 2000), pp. 273–75.
10. To be noted: Chaim Lazar Litai, *Masada shel Varsha: HaIrgun HaTzevai HaYehudi BeMered Geto Varshah* [The Masada of Warsaw: The ZZW in the Warsaw Ghetto uprising] (Tel Aviv: Jabotinsky Press, 1963), and its English version *Muranowska 7: The Warsaw Ghetto Rising* (Tel Aviv: Massada-PEC Press, 1966), and Wdowinski, *And We Are Not Saved.*

CHAPTER 2

THE FOUNDING OF THE ZZW

The German army entered Warsaw on October 1, 1939. Three days later, on October 4, the Germans formed a Jewish Council (Judenrat) made up of 24 members, a similar number of alternate members and a chairman, Adam Czerniakow, formerly the vice-chairman of the Warsaw Jewish Community. Jewish governments called Judenrat, with extensive powers, were set up all over Nazi Europe, especially in the ghettos.

FOUNDING MEMBERS

Shortly afterwards, among the many administrative measures prepared in advance and now rapidly implemented was the publication of an order for all Polish military officers to report on December 14 for internment in special camps. Of course, a great many of them, Polish Catholics as well as Jews, chose not do so. This meant they had to go underground. Lieutenant Mieczyslaw Dawid Apfelbaum, a well-off and cultured Polish man who was my cousin, explained his decision to Captain Henryk Iwanski, who had been the commanding officer of his battalion. This is how Iwanski recalled that conversation:

> One day in November 1939, four Jewish men came to see me at Saint Stanislas hospital at 37 Wolska Street where I was working

> then. Among them were Maurice Apfelbaum, a lieutenant in the Polish army, Second Lieutenant Henryk Lipszyc, [...] Bialoskora and Kalmen Mendelson.[1]
>
> I knew Apfelbaum well. He had fought in my regiment during the siege of Warsaw. "Captain Iwanski," he said, "we don't want to go to the Oflag [German camp for officer prisoners of war]. Help us organize the Jewish youth and train them to fight the enemy. We have dark days ahead of us. The Jews are being subject to prohibitions and discriminatory measures; the campaign against them has already begun. We can't just stand back and watch this oppression be imposed on us. We have to act."
>
> "First of all, forget the name Iwanski," I replied. "From now on, my name is Bystry. And before we get down to practical matters, I just want to say that anyone who wants to fight the Germans is our brother. It's a fact that you Jews are on the frontline. We can't waste any time; get organized and ready for battle. We'll help you as much as we can."
>
> The four men left my room with four Vis 9 mm semi-automatic pistols, each with a spare ammunition clip. Compliments of the KB for our comrades-in-arms.[2]

The KB, or rather the OW-KB, had just been founded itself. On September 9, after the first big reversals suffered by the Polish army, but before the surrender of Warsaw, General Sikorski made two announcements during a meeting with political and military leaders. First, he had decided to leave the country in order to continue the fight (he was to serve as both prime minister and commander-in-chief, first in France and then, after the French surrender, in

1. Tadeusz Bednarczyk, who was not present at the meeting, mentions Apfelbaum, Lipszyc and Bialoskora but omits Mendelson and adds Rodal; in any case, all five of them were to become leaders of the ZZW. See Bednarczyk, *Zycie codzienne warszawskiego getta.*
2. As told to Chaya Lazar in 1962. See Chaya Lazar, "The Jewish Military Organization (ZZW) in the Warsaw Ghetto Uprising: Fifty Years since the Uprising 1943–1993," *Publications of the Museum of the Combatants and Partisans* 7, no. 77 (April 1993): 20. Also see a very similar account in Henryk Iwanski, "*Czy mozna bylo ratowac ludzi...? Mowi major 'Bystry,'*" *Kultura* 6, no. 16 (April 21, 1968): 254.

Britain, until his death in 1943). Second, he announced the foundation, effective immediately, of a Military Organization (OW), of which the OW-KB was a constituent part from the beginning. The political orientation of this movement was centrist. It distanced itself from the extremely reactionary right-wing government then in power (since the death of Marshal Pilsudski, whose government was centrist) and even more from the very small Communist Party (dissolved by Stalin shortly before the war), which it rejected as an ally of the Soviets who had just invaded the eastern half of Poland. The OW's program was simple: resistance against the occupier and support for the future government in exile headed by General Sikorski.

Captain Iwanski was a member of OW-KB, and the ZZW was a part of that organization, from the day of its foundation in November 1939, which was marked by the visit by Lieutenant Apfelbaum[3] and his colleagues, until the end of the ghetto uprising in June 1943. As a result of this military subordination, as well as the social origins of its founders (right-leaning Polish-acculturated men of the bourgeoisie), the ZZW's political program was restricted to armed struggle, in sharp contrast to the leftist and Marxist politics predominant among the Jewish population. Another consequence was an obsession with secrecy – the ZZW released no publications, held no public meetings, and issued only one leaflet during its three and a half years of active existence. This secrecy is one of the main reasons for the extraordinary silence surrounding the ZZW after the war and to this day.

THE ZZW'S EARLY ORGANIZATIONAL STRUCTURE

To get back to the ZZW's foundation: Following the model of the

3. Mieczyslaw (also known as Maurice, Moryc and Morycy) Dawid Apfelbaum was then 38 years old. The son of a well-off family, he was a lieutenant during the war and served valiantly during the siege of Warsaw.

OW, and working closely with that Polish organization, recruitment was to be very selective and elitist, restricted to trustworthy friends, all at least middle-class, who had fulfilled their military service. Recruits were organized into circles or sub-circles, according to their profession.

Two months later, at the end of December, the ZZW held a formal meeting presided over by Apfelbaum. Iwanski also took part, along with 39 members and a rabbi. Candles were lit and each man individually took an oath. Previously, in November and December 1939, the organization had been known as Swit (The Dawn); now the name ZZW was definitively adopted. During this meeting, Iwanski promised more weapons. Soon he was to deliver 29 Vis pistols and ammunition for them.

During the same period of November–December 1939, another embryonic armed Jewish resistance organization was also formed as part of the OW-KB. Its founding members included Tadeusz Makower, Frank Berenbaum and Mieczyslaw Ettinger, with Tadeusz Bednarczyk as their contact in the OW-KB, to which he and Iwanski belonged. They, too, followed the model of the mother organization and formed professional circles. The two groups headed by Apfelbaum and Bednarczyk respectively merged at the end of March or early April 1940. Here is an account given by Mendelson, the sole surviving ZZW officer:

> The ZZW was founded, in embryonic form, in November 1939. Although Professor Mark, C. Lazar [two Jewish historians], Zajdler-Zarski and especially Bednarczyk [two Polish officers very active in the fighting carried out by the ZZW] have written about it previously, they were off the mark on a number of points because they were not ZZW members and relied mainly on interviews with ZZW veterans. Thus as deputy commander and the last surviving ZZW officer, and now that I am retired, I am hereby making a statement to clarify some details.
>
> It is unfortunate that the book written by Tadeusz Bednarczyk, alias "Bednarz," alias "Tadeusz," has not yet been published. Out of

everything published on the subject so far, that book contains the best and most exhaustive description of the zzw's work, its collaboration with Polish organizations and the whole history of the enormous aid Poles gave the ghetto, including the little-known aspect of economic aid. But in regard to the founding of a zzw unit, the "w" unit at the Saint Stanislas hospital for infectious illnesses located on Wolska Street where it carried out its work [this is a reference to Apfelbaum's group which was to merge with Bednarczyk's], Bednarczyk made significant errors in his articles and his book *Walka i Pomoc* [*Struggle and Aid*] published by Iskry in 1968. These mistakes are the result of erroneous eyewitness accounts and a certain personal bias that led him to leave out any mention of [...] the deceased "forgotten" fighters whose actions were later claimed by others who were actually less involved and active at that time. [This obscure phrase has to do with survivors of that period and what seem to be petty quarrels among aging heroes.] For the sake of historical accuracy, it is essential to show the real dimensions of what these "forgotten" fighters did.

In November 1939, among a Jewish population terrorized by the repression, the need to fight the Nazis was recognized only by a handful of "September" veterans, Polish Army officers and noncommissioned officers. But since these Jews did not have the means or any real desire to form their own organization, various small groups of them joined existing Polish military units through their connections with former friends or relations. This was the origin of the first two groups of fighters, first Tadeusz Bednarczyk's unit in Srodmiescie and then the "w" unit in Wola, both part of the OW-KB. Bednarczyk has furnished a precise and accurate description of the Jewish group's initial collaboration with his unit and his own role in founding and expanding the zzw, for which he personally worked inside the ghetto every day.

But on the other hand, he could not be equally familiar with the activity, collaboration and aid of other OW-KB units exactly because they were clandestine, even though he himself may have coordinated or supervised this work. Further, after so many years, failing memory may be the explanation for certain mistakes. Here I am especially referring to the second Jewish group, linked to the "w" [Apfelbaum] unit formed among employees, doctors and others who originally worked at the hospital for infectious illness at 37 Wolska Street where its work was generally centered. Its commander, Zdzislaw Nosarzewski, alias "Nosek," was head of the administrative service, and his deputy, Jan Skoczek, alias "Wasik," was in charge of the finance and payroll department.

There was no other underground unit at the hospital during the first two years of the Occupation. Thus there was never any change of commander or deputy commander in the "w" unit. Actually, Nosarzewski and "Wasik" did not leave the hospital until February 1944, when the latter was arrested by the Gestapo. Later, I frequently discussed the subject with Lieutenant Jozef Niemirski [J. Celmajster's nom de guerre] and Wanda Skoczek, alias "Baska," married to the murdered Jan "Wasik." They both repeatedly confirmed these memories. In his book *Memoirs of Auschwitz*, Edward Ciesielski, who worked in the hospital administration for more than a year until the arrest of "Wasik," treated all this extensively. Henryk Iwanski, alias "Bystry," took charge of the "w" unit in February 1944.[4]

The first group, made up of a few Jewish officers headed by Apfelbaum and Niemirski, made contact with the "w" unit through Skoczek. Skoczek had previously worked and lived at the Jewish hospital in Czyste, where he held the same job as on Wolska Street, head of finance and payroll. Thus many Jews knew him well, and it was natural to go to him for advice and aid. Doctor Jozef Niemirski, who worked in Czyste, had a great deal of confidence in him. This feeling was shared by the whole group and it was to be constantly reinforced by the cooperation and support provided by the "w" unit and the OW-KB as a whole. From the beginning, I was very close to

4. Nevertheless, other sources indicate that he had been in charge since 1940, which was attested to by Mendelson himself in 1959 – see appendix 1. At any rate, the only difference between these two firsthand accounts is a detail, the name of the first commander of the "w" unit. But as a matter of principle, in my citations I am including and commenting on any inconsistencies, no matter how slight, regardless of the danger of repetition.

this group that worked with the "w" unit. We began by all joining the "w" unit, which in turn delegated us to form Jewish resistance cells in the Jewish quarter that became a walled ghetto. Skoczek was the main one behind this. In order to emphasize the seriousness of the newly-born Jewish organization, and for the protection of the resistance fighters, he gave them some of the large stock of weapons he and Nosarzewski had stored inside the hospital in September 1939. Thus, under the aegis of the "w" unit, at the end of November and in December 1939, the first four cells were formed, including the one I belonged to, named Swit, headed by Lipszyc-Lipinski. By early 1940, these cells had more members than is usual in a military group. Swit was one of the most developed of them. Furthermore, it had made a name for itself in the ghetto [actually, the ghetto did not come into existence until October 1940, although the quarter was de facto Jewish then – see the next chapter]. At that time it specialized in monitoring radio broadcasts and put out *Swit*, the typed (and later mimeographed) news bulletin it was named after. It involved a few journalists, including myself.

That was how things stood until February 1940, in other words, until the reorganization and activation of the zzw. At a preparatory meeting held in the end of February 1940 [...], Nosarzewski and Skoczek informed the heads of the four cells attending this gathering that as of March, these units would be elevated to the status of squads and their heads were named squad leaders. They were to reorganize these units along military lines, bring themselves up to fighting strength by recruiting trained reservists, and organize training activities. Each squad was given a small quantity of weapons for this purpose. At that time we were also informed of the existence of other groups that would join with us to form the zzw, defined as an autonomous Jewish resistance organization linked to the Polish resistance currently rallying around General Sikorski and his politics. This grouping was to provide the zzw with constant material and organizational support.

Nevertheless, the plans sketched out at this meeting proved difficult to put into practice at that time. German persecution of the

Jews made them increasingly unwilling to risk further punishment by actively opposing German orders. It was impossible to expand the Jewish resistance movement under such conditions. In June 1940, after the capitulation of France, and affected by the general mood of discouragement, many people left the ZZW. There were too few fighters to transform these groups into squads in practical terms, even though up until that point they had been growing slightly. Because of this growth, the Swit group was split up. I left with a few other men and started a new circle at 5 Karmelicka Street. The other four circles were headed by Mieczyslaw Apfelbaum, Henryk Lipszyc-Lipinski, Leon Rodal and Szymon Bialoskora.

After the founding of the new circle, I found myself working in an action area under the responsibility of another Jewish group linked to the ZZW. It was near mine, at 12 Leszno Street, and its leader was Tadeusz Bednarczyk, our Polish "protector," who at that time was an employee of the Treasury office on Leszno Street.[5] Now I had new contacts with whom I was to work until the ghetto was destroyed. At that time, Bednarczyk was carrying out a tax audit in an area centered on Leszno Street. It ran from Tlomackie Street to Solna Street, and included the cross streets Elektoralna, Nowolipie, Nowolipki, Orla, Przejazd and a part of Karmelicka Street. Because my circle was located so close to Bednarczyk's workplace, I met with him frequently. His official capacity made this easier. Bednarczyk gave the ZZW various publications, including the *Information Bulletin* [official organ of the AK]. Through him, I met his friend Tadeusz Makower, head of the Grzybowska Street underground cell; Mieczyslaw Ettinger, also a resistance member; Colonel Szopinski, head of the second section of the OW-KB general staff; Colonel Janiszek, deputy commander; and Colonel "Tarnawa"-Petrykowski, in charge of helping the Jews. On that occasion I learned that the first organization to take action in support of the Jews in general, and the ghetto in particular, and the only one to do so for a long

5. The Polish Resistance had appointed Bednarcyzk as coordinator of aid to the Jews when the ghetto was first created. See appendix 2.

> time, was called the *Organizacja Wojskowa* – OW (later called *Kadra Bezpieczenstwa* – KB [Security Cadres] and *Korpus Bezpieczenstwa* [Security Corps]). I also learned that many other organizations were taking part in this activity, working closely with the OW as part of the movement around General Sikorski led by General Sikorski's Political Bureau.
>
> Among these organizations was the ZPN [*Zwiazek Polski Niepodleglej*, Committee for Independent Poland], an organization that included veterans of the Silesia uprising, and former volunteer and professional firemen; the *Zbrojne Wyzwolenie* [ZW – Liberation Army]; and others. I learned that following an agreement between these organizations, the Political Bureau and the OW had delegated the responsibility for taking action in support of the Jews to the Zbrojne Wyzwolen. "Tarnawa"-Petrykowski, general commander of the ZW, was in charge of this work. Bednarczyk was his deputy and acted in his name. Working closely with "Tarnawa," he coordinated this aid with other organizations that all subsequently joined the KB. Bednarczyk was also the official representative of the OW general command in charge of Warsaw ghetto affairs. Since at that time Warsaw was the only site of Jewish resistance in Poland, that was where the support work was most concentrated and consistent.[6]

In another article, the same source describes the numerous organized ties between the ZZW and a variety of Polish clandestine organizations.[7]

---

6. Kalmen Mendelson, "*Historia powstania* ZZW," *Kronika*, no. 18 (May 2, 1970).
7. "[...] The same was true of the military aid provided to the ghetto. The ZZW – *Zydowski Zwiazek Wojskowy* – was founded in November 1939, while the ZOB did not really come into existence until December 1942. As the last living ZZW soldier in Warsaw, and in my capacity as deputy commander, in charge of evacuating the Jewish population of the ghetto, I am familiar with the situation and the people who helped us at that time. On the occasion of the fortieth anniversary of the ghetto uprising, I would like to say a few words about it. The initiative for organizing Jewish resistance came from two sources. The first was Lieutenant 'Bednarz' (Commander Tadeusz Bednarczyk), a member of the general staff of the OW-*Organizacja Wojskowa*, later called the KB – *Kadra Bezpieczenstwa* – and the 'W' (Wola) unit commanded by Nosarzewski and Skoczek, which was part of the *Zbrojne Wyzwolenie* led by commander 'Tarnawa'-A. Petrykowski. In November 1939, Lieutenant 'Bednarz,' in his capacity as head of the unit in charge of the security of the offices of the OW-KB and

THE POSITION OF JUDENRAT CHAIRMAN CZERNIAKOW

A meeting that took place at the urging of the OW-KB on January 10, 1940, was to have decisive and far-reaching political consequences. Participating on behalf of the OW-KB was Zofia Sikorska-Lesniowska, General Sikorski's daughter, who was to join her father in France a few weeks later, and high-ranking officers and political leaders. The main guest was Adam Czerniakow, chairman of the Warsaw Judenrat. He took a firm and explicit position with regard to the ZZW, which he was to maintain unwaveringly until the end.

He believed that the war would last many years and that the organization of a large-scale Jewish resistance movement was bound to be discovered, thus furnishing the Nazis with a pretext for ferocious reprisals. Consequently, the Jews had to appear to be very obedient to German orders. Czerniakow recognized the need

---

the CKO – *Centralny Komitet Organizacji Niepodleglosciowych* (the latter was the highest political body representing General Sikorski inside Poland), named a number of Jewish comrades from his unit (Tadeusz Makower and his brother, Frank Berenbaum, the lawyer Mieczyslaw Ettinger and others) to set up military resistance circles among Jews with previous military training. The second initiative was by Mieczyslaw Apfelbaum, the future commander, Leon Rodal, Henryk Lipszyc-Lipinski and Jozef Celmajster (Niemirski). The four of them sought out an acquaintance, Jan Skoczek, alias 'Wasik,' head of payroll and finances at the hospital for infectious diseases at 37 Wolska Street, to ask for his advice and aid. This took place at the end of November or early December 1939. Through Skoczek, they became resistance members and were given responsibility for organizing military circles in the Jewish quarter of the city. On January 20, 1940, there was a meeting of representatives of the CKON, the OW-KB, the Skala Firemen's Association, the *Zbrojne Wyzwolenie* and the ZPN [...], an organization of veterans of the Silesia insurrection, with the engineer Czerniakow, chairman of the Judenrat, in attendance. Lieutenant 'Bednarz' was named representative of the general staff of the OW-KB and its organizations, in charge of aid to the Jews and ghetto affairs. Henceforth all aid to the ZZW was to pass through him. At the same time, these organizations put the ZW commander 'Tarnawa;-Petrykowski in charge of aiding the Jewish population throughout Poland, with special attention to the support for the ZZW in Warsaw to be provided by the unit he headed, namely the 'W' squad. Thus aid was to be supplied to the ZZW through two channels: the unit headed by 'Bednarz' and the 'W' unit. But the aid that went through the former was not from the OW-KB alone. Much of it also came from the Skala, the ZPN and other organizations, and Lieutenant 'Bednarz' was given the task of coordinating this support [...]." From Kalmen Mendelson, "*Oni byli z nami*," *Rzeczywistosc* 3, no. 14 (April 3, 1983): 76.

for a Jewish resistance organization and agreed to be a part of it, but he imposed restrictions that ran counter to the initial plans of the OW-KB and the ZZW. He wanted the organization to be exclusively local, confined to Warsaw alone, and recommended extreme prudence with regard to both recruitment and action. In effect, it was to be a cadre organization with no troops, no publications, no public meetings, and, above all, no attacks against the Germans.[8] Czerniakow said he was convinced that some Judenrat leaders were in direct contact with the Gestapo or Gestapo members, making the strictest clandestinity even more crucial.

Czerniakow's demands were accepted and scrupulously followed for the next two and a half years. Bednarczyk, the representative of the Polish Resistance Military Organization, describes his meeting with Czerniakow:

> I met Engineer Adam Czerniakow in early January 1940 at a meeting in the courthouse on Leszno Street, and worked with him for two and a half years, until his suicide in July 1942. During this period marked by German orders and actions to exterminate the Jews, I came to appreciate the greatness of his spirit, his courage and his extraordinarily selfless devotion to the cause of saving his people. I also came to consider him the greatest patriot and hero of the Jewish people in Poland, a courageous soldier, even if he did not resort to arms in his struggle against the Germans.
>
> In December 1939 the Germans issued an order requiring the Warsaw Jews to wear an armband with the Star of David. By then,

8. Bednarczyk's description (see following note) has been confirmed by Czerniakow's secretary, L. Tyszka: "By the spring of 1942 [...] the Chairman [Czerniakow] saw no possibility of salvation. He believed that there could be no question of armed struggle. The Germans were at the height of their power and glory. The hungry and downtrodden inhabitants of the ghetto were sick more often than not. They had practically nothing. They had neither arms nor money to buy them. Any action, no matter what, would have only historical implications, but it was too soon for that, certainly too soon. It was necessary to wait until the Germans weakened, which was inevitable as the war dragged on. Until then, the struggle should be prepared secretly, in coordination with the resistance organizations on the Aryan side. Under the current circumstances, an armed action would amount to an immediate sentence of death." Leon Tyszka, *Sukcesy i kleski jednego zycia* (London, 1984), p. 63.

OW-KB had acquired strength due to its systematic efforts to expand the resistance. Therefore it put the Jewish question in Poland on the order of the day, and made support for them and their enlistment in the resistance an immediate task for the organization. Although this activity was unfolding through the country, at that time it was concentrated in Warsaw because of the city's geographical, political and symbolic importance. Through the connections and ties of friendship its members had established, the OW-KB had been able to make contact with various Jewish personalities.

This made possible the foundation of the ZZW (*Zydowski Zwiazek Wojskowy*) under its auspices at the end of 1939–early 1940. From the beginning, the ZZW was made up of many groups and circles, a number of them grouped under the name Swit for the first three months of their existence until the name ZZW was given to the whole organization. At that point, Lieutenant-Colonel Andrzej Janiszek, a member of the general staff [of the Polish Resistance], made contact with Czerniakow through Professor Hirszfeld. During a preliminary conversation, they agreed to hold a bigger meeting in the first half of January 1940. In deciding to take part in the organization of the Jewish resistance, the OW-KB counted, to a large degree, on Czerniakow's charisma.

The probity and honesty of this senator of the Republic of Poland were well known. He was considered an eminent representative of the policy of assimilation and fraternal cooperation with the Poles for the sake of their common fatherland. His studies abroad, his familiarity with the Germans and his mastery of the German language made him the perfect leader for the Jews during the period of Nazi oppression. He was to become the spiritual head of that current in the Jewish resistance movement that identified with the social and political ideology of General Sikorski and united Jewish patriots of all political persuasions.

On January 10, 1940, in the office of Judge Karol Szwarc, alias "Kruk," on the fifth floor of the Courthouse on Leszno Street, there was a meeting between Czerniakow and representatives of the OW-KB general staff: Lieutenant-Colonel "Wilk"-Edward Biernacki;

Zofia Sikorska-Lesniowska, General Sikorski's daughter who was about to travel to France via Italy to join her father and report on the situation in Poland; General "Tarnawa"-Petrykowski, commander of the Zbrojne Wyzwolenie; Leon Lempke, senator of the Republic of Poland; professor Antoni Karczewski [...]; Lieutenant "Kruk"-Szwarc; and myself.

After being briefed in greater depth about the OW-KB's organizational plans, Czerniakow declared them inappropriate for the Jews. In fact, he believed that the Second World War would last many years and that the organization of large-scale Jewish resistance at the beginning of the war would lead to all kinds of mistakes that would in turn provoke the fury of the Gestapo. This might give rise to measures to exterminate the Jews. He held that precisely because the Jews were the most exposed to the risk of persecution, they had to remain passive and pretend to be docile for the sake of their own survival. He emphasized the possibility of corrupting Gestapo members who would spare the Jews out of their own financial self-interest, abiding by the saying, "You don't saw off the branch you're sitting on." But to succeed in this, the Jews had to obey all German orders.

Although Czerniakow disagreed with the idea of broadening the resistance, because he believed that no armed struggle could be successful, at least not at that point, he went along with the organization of a rank-and-file Jewish resistance organization tied to the OW-KB and General Sikorski. The subsequent expansion of such an organization would depend on the turn of events. When Czerniakow was told that such an organization, the ZZW, already existed, he said he was willing to join it, although he would not be able to provide much help because of his highly visible position in the Judenrat and because the Gestapo was keeping a close eye on him, including, he suspected, through informers within the Judenrat. It was decided that General "Tarnawa"-Petrykowski would be in charge of coordinating the Jewish resistance on a national level, which was confirmed by the representative of the Government in Exile. He was to keep Czerniakow apprised of developments and organizational and political needs, either personally or through myself in my capacity as a specialist and representative for Jewish and Warsaw ghetto affairs named by the general staff of the OW-KB.

During that meeting, the participants discussed the possibility that the Germans might increasingly intensify their anti-Jewish policies, going so far as to wall off the ghetto and exterminate large numbers of people, spurred on either by Nazi victories or by defeats. But Czerniakow was fairly confident and counted on the power of money over Gestapo members. He also insisted that General Sikorski be informed of the particularly discriminatory policy the Germans were carrying out against the Jews in Poland, including the confiscation of their property. He demanded that world public opinion be alerted, if necessary, to prevent the Nazis from intensifying their repression.

Consistent with this thinking, Czerniakow was absolutely opposed to the creation of a national organization of Jewish resistance, even on a piecemeal basis. Instead, he argued for the formation of small local groups, composed of only the most trustworthy people, so as to avoid traps and provocation by Jewish Gestapo collaborators.

After that memorable meeting, I met with Engineer Czerniakow on numerous occasions and discussed the most important events with him. General "Tarnawa"-Petrykowski and "Bystry"-Henryk Iwanski, the head of the ZZW Jewish resistance movement in Warsaw [here the accounts given by Bednarczyk and Mendelson are in accord] met with him many times. Commander "Bystry" was responsible for the ZZW's organizational affairs and military activity, and for its expansion, armament, training and preparation for combat. As the head of training and intelligence, I was to be second in command under "Bystry." Despite his heavy schedule, Czerniakow often attended meetings of the inner circles of the ZZW and OW-KB leadership along with commander "Bystry," ZZW commander Moryc Apfelbaum, Lieutenant Federbusz and sometimes me. These secret meetings took place in safe houses – in the apartment of Engineer X (who shared it with the dentist Finkensztajn) on the third floor at 42 Muranowska Street, in Urbach's flat on the second floor at the corner of Dzielna and Karmelicka Streets, or at the lawyer Kahane's place at 40 Ogrodowa Street.

During these meetings over the next two and a half years, Engineer Czerniakow and the others discussed, and brought each other up-to-date on, the following points:

1. The Gestapo's proposal that offices [of the Judenrat] be opened on the Aryan side. Czerniakow rejected this because he wanted to live with his people, to remain with "his children" like Doctor Korczak.
2. The repeated beating and humiliation of Czerniakow by the Gestapo, which he endured with dignity and a spirit of self-sacrifice so as to avoid irritating them and so as not to risk losing the close contacts he had managed to develop with some Gestapo members. He hoped that this stance would make them reluctant to carry out more severe measures, gain time and finally save his people from destruction. Even the men he was paying beat him. Later they explained that if they wanted to protect their secrets, and not expose themselves in the process, they had no choice but to beat him (I myself saw the marks of beatings on his face).
3. The beatings of Czerniakow were intended to force him to reveal the names of Polish and Jewish resistance members working in the ghetto. It was obvious that various resistance organizations had been set up there. In addition to the KB-ZZW groups, these included the ZWZ-AK and the GL-AL (for example, Kilianowicz – Korczynski's unit based in Czerwonka's apartment on 14 Twarda Street), even if they had not been able to set up a military Jewish resistance organization.
4. The fact that Czerniakow always carried poison with him so as to escape possible German torture. This was in 1942, when his brutal treatment at the hands of the Germans reached a high point and little by little, he began to lose all hope in the possibility of surviving or saving his people. I must add, however, that he never completely lost hope until the day of his suicide. In the

end, he was counting on an increasingly difficult and exhausting situation for Germany on the eastern front and the respite that would mean for the Jews.

5. The circulars and instructions he wrote in the name of the Judenrat. Aimed against the resistance movement to which he himself belonged, their purpose was to satisfy German exigencies and keep the Germans from suspecting him. As far as possible, these measures remained purely formal and were sabotaged.
6. The German selection of Jews to be sent to do forced labor. This was a source of conflict between Czerniakow and myself. In the end, the OW leadership and its representative accepted his arguments, which I will briefly summarize here: Any official refusal to carry out German orders would mean fighting them, which neither the Jews nor the Poles were in a position to do. A certain diminution of the number of Jews in the ghetto would improve conditions for those who remained, in terms of nutrition and sanitation. If Jews were taken to the German side, they could provide useful intelligence, since the Germans mistrusted Jews less than Poles. Furthermore, these Jews were skilled and talented craftsmen and workers, in addition to being completely terrorized, so that many Germans would become dependent on them in their daily lives. For the sake of their own comfort and profits, these Germans would "fight" to protect the health and lives of their Jewish workers. These arguments turned out to have some – and only some – truth to them, especially during the liquidation of the ghetto. In the fall of 1944, I myself saw a few Jews saved by Kriegsverbrecher W.C. Többens, in the Többens factory in Piotrkow Trybunalski, not to mention the labor camps in Czestochowa and Walbrzych where thousands of Jews were saved.
7. The walling-off of the ghetto, which Czerniakow never wanted to believe possible. Even after the ghetto was enclosed, he continued to think that the walls could be brought down in exchange for a large sum of money. At the same time I also brought up the question of the Judenrat's aid to the development of economic

exchanges with the Aryan zone, productivity problems, and the need for aid to the Jewish workshops engaged in clandestine production of goods to be sold on the Aryan side.

8. Material aid for the poor through, among other organizations, the clandestine RGO (for example, the soup kitchen on Dluga Street) and later Zegota [this chronology is obviously wrong with regard to Zegota, which was not founded until the end of 1942, or in other words, not until after Czerniakow's suicide]. At Czerniakow's insistence, General "Tarnawa" took up this problem and that of medical help with the in-country representative of the Government in Exile.
9. General Sikorski's position and his instructions in 1940–42, in which he recommended helping the Jews, broadening this support among the Polish population and bringing in organizations such as *Pobudka* (*Oboz Narodowy*) [National Camp, a rightist group], headed by the lawyer Rosciszewski and clergymen following the example of Father Godlewsk i, prelate of the W szystkich Swietych [All Saints] church. Sikorski's action did in fact give a considerable morale boost to the Jewish population.

It is important that historians of World War II note that the close relations between General Sikorski and the OW-KB were confirmed by Doctor Lados, a minister of General Sikorski's government in France, during a conference held on September 6, 1961, at the Institute of Contemporary History of the PAN [Polish Academy of Sciences], which corroborates the neutral and objective character of my account of these events here. This relationship is also confirmed by the fact that the general's wife and their daughter took part in the resistance as members of the OW, and, furthermore, by the special character of his military, political and financial instructions concerning the OW (sums of money meant for aid to the ghetto) issued by the general and his political bureau, the CKON, set up by his friend, General Ryszard Swietochowski , also a co-founder of the OW. Minister Lados was very familiar with all this, thanks to his personal contacts with the general. In his speech, Minister Lados mentioned the steps taken by the general to save the Jews in Poland. He also emphasized the existence within the government of a National Minorities Committee and the general's strong relationship with the Jews, which explains, and to some degree confirms, the instructions and special dispositions concerning aid to the Jews he issued to the OW-KB, which faithfully carried them out throughout the war and throughout the national territory.

10. The situation in other ghettos and the aid given to them by the KB, for example in Lublin (Lieutenant-Colonel Janiszek) and Lwow (Captain Zarski-Zajdler); the question of the liquidation of the small ghettos in the area around Warsaw and the transfer of their population to the capital, and the problem of finding lodging and work for them.
11. The rescue and evacuation from the ghetto of scientists and member of the Jewish intelligentsia. This subject of arguments with Czerniakow should be gone into more deeply since the Representative of the Government [the representative of the Polish government in exile in France during the occupation] gave it particular importance.

The OW-KB's support and aid to the Jews based on the instructions of the government's representative and the most outstanding points related to this matter were discussed in detail with him. As head of SOS Section II, General "Tarnawa"-Petrykowski [...] had a special relationship with the government representative. Thus he had occasion to discuss the problems of the ghetto and, among other matters, the question of rescuing the most prominent members of the intelligentsia and representatives of science not only with C. Ratajski, the government representative, but also, during 1942–43, Professor Piekalkiewicz, Director Miklaszewski, Krahelska and Colonel "Edyta"-Kazimierz Gasiorowski. On the recommendation of the government representative and Miklaszewski, during a meeting in the Courthouse in the spring of 1941, General "Tarnawa" ordered Czerniakow to gather together an initial group of scientists. They were to be taken to the contact point (Sawa-Wrzesinski's contact) at the Jewish hardware store on Dluga Street, near Miodowa Street, or to the electrical goods shop at 16 Bielanska Street next door to the shoemaker Marek (Captain Ostoja-Markowski's contact), where they would receive papers and food and could be assured refuge and transportation. But Czerniakow categorically refused, explaining that it was much too soon, that the moment had not yet come. He saw no dark clouds on the horizon. The flight of well-known figures, he held, would demoralize the Jewish population. Czerniakow added that as much as he might want to follow the recommendations of the government representative, he could not – they contradicted the specific policy toward the Germans being carried out in the ghetto, which was very different. He alone was responsible for that policy and he understood it better than anyone else. He hoped to continue carrying it out as well as possible without endangering any lives until the ghetto was finally abolished. This evacuation proved impossible to effectuate at that moment, but the OW-KB did do so during the later half of 1941 and 1942, this time without consulting Czerniakow. In fact, despite the failure of his "game" to bring about the end of the ghetto or other results, he had not changed his mind on this. Still, when Czerniakow was informed about the step-by-step and non-violent evacuation of ghetto people, he did nothing to stop it. He saw that the situation in the ghetto was deteriorating. In mid-1942, he even asked me to help him get out a group of some 15 people. As usual, Commander "Bystry" took care of it.

12. [PARAGRAPH CROSSED OUT IN THE POLISH ORIGINAL]
13. Commander "Bystry"-Iwanski often discussed the work, expansion and needs of the ZZW with Czerniakow in the presence of Apfelbaum, Lieutenant Federbusz and sometimes myself. On that occasion, he also referred to the activities of the Jewish collaborationist organization Zagiew, which was twice eliminated and twice reactivated between late 1940 and 1944. [In another text, Bednarczyk speaks of it being eliminated three times.] He

cautioned Czerniakow about certain already-known traitors who had infiltrated his entourage.

14. Acting on orders from the government representative and General "Tarnawa," Commander "Bystry"-Iwanski warned Czerniakow about the measures taken by the Germans in preparation for the liquidation of the ghetto. This liquidation took place in July–August 1942.

On the recommendation of Commander "Bystry," I personally discussed this with Czerniakow, but he refused to believe it. As if hypnotized, he continued to trust in the corrupting power of money. In early July 1942, while giving his official assent for evacuating members of the intelligentsia – which in fact the OW-KB had already been doing for a year on the orders of the government representative, making it possible to get about 3,000 people out of the ghetto – and while furnishing me with a list of names of people to be evacuated, he reiterated his unshakable determination to stay at his post, along with his family, and share the destiny ("*moira*") of the Jewish people. He continued to sincerely believe that such a thing would never be implemented, noting that rumors of this kind had circulated before without being realized. Since he wanted to avoid provoking the Germans, he was loath to inform the population that an extermination might be carried out. He emphasized that it was impossible to save all the Jews. Only a few thousand members of the intelligentsia could be rescued at most. These people would somehow manage to get out of the ghetto in any case because they were in the best position to find hiding places and protectors willing to risk their lives to save them. It was his duty to do his best to save everyone. He pointed out the injustice afflicting the poorest layer of people in the ghetto, the simple people suffering hunger and misfortune, while the rich intelligentsia often – although not always – had a better chance to survive, and, at this particular moment, to save their necks by escaping. The educated classes, and especially the merchants, some of them speculators, would not err on the side of solidarity with the people. Often they were ashamed of their poverty and their Hasidic attire. In these difficult times, everyone was looking out for him or herself and was happy when instead of being sent to do forced labor, someone else – poorer and homeless – was chosen in their place. Under these conditions, as chairman of the Judenrat, he had to show by his attitude that God loves all Jews, rich or poor, just the same, and that they all had an equal right to be saved. At that point, he told me that if he ever lost hope in the salvation of his people, in one way or another he would make this known to the whole Jewish population. This is in fact what he did by committing suicide on the eve of the mass extermination of July 1942.

This was a dramatic and heroic act of protest thrown in the face of the whole world, similar to that of Deputy Zygelbojm, a member of the Rada Narodowa [National Council] in London after the ghetto uprising broke out in 1943.

15. In mid-1942, on orders from Commander "Bystry," I held a discussion with Chairman Czerniakow about the zzw's firepower and the chances of success if an armed struggle were launched. In that period, the zzw changed its name to *Zydowski Zwiazek Walki* [Jewish Combat Union, with the same initials, zzw].

At the same time, following orders from General "Tarnawa," I demanded that the Judenrat provide the financing for setting up Jewish units in the forests (headed by Commander Apfelbaum) and for the purchasing of German and Hungarian weapons for these units, and that it send Jewish youth to the woods so that they could carry out an armed struggle outside the ghetto. Because of the unpredictable consequences of an armed struggle within the ghetto, at that point the ow-kb was not counting on the possibility of armed resistance, which was not to be concretized until 1943. The zzw was not yet sufficiently prepared for such a fight; its arms and forces were too few and since it did not foresee any big expansion it limited its activity […] to evacuating the population and concerning itself with the morale and ideological conditions of the Jewish population. In fact, it was the zzw that liquidated the *Zagiew* [a group of Jewish provocateurs organized by the Gestapo – see the following chapter] and other collaborators.

[Readers will have difficulty understanding the following paragraph, since the narrator gets ahead of himself, but I have included it here to preserve the integrity of his description of Czerniakow.]

Furthermore, what could be done against such a powerful enemy by the ZZW's handful of fighters? These 300 men were armed, of course, but without bases anywhere in the country or help from abroad, and surrounded by a mob of half-a-million defenseless, starving and terrorized people. At that time, neither the AK, nor the OW-KB nor the GL could come to its aid. The second Jewish resistance organization, the ZOB, was then just getting organized and had no real military strength. All that made it particularly urgent to evacuate the Jewish youth fit for combat to the partisan groups in the forests. Given the massive scale of the course of action proposed by the KB, its breadth and its success depended on the amount of financial support the Judenrat could provide for Commander Apfelbaum's organization. In the course of another discussion touching on this subject, I had learned that this was unlikely to happen at that point. In fact, Chairman Czerniakow added, with a touch of sarcasm, had it been a matter of evacuating the notables of the Judenrat and their families, they would surely have found the necessary money, but since it was for youth they didn't even know, that was not likely. He was powerless for the moment because he could not use Judenrat funds on his own authority. When the subject of armed struggle came up, Chairman Czerniakow emphasized that it was necessary as the only way to preserve the honor of the Jews and cleanse it of the stain of inertia, although the ZZW's small number of forces and insufficient armament (he himself had previously opposed expanding the organization) meant that any armed struggle within the ghetto would be ineffective. He thought that a military uprising and the large number of victims that would result might goad the West into action, obliging it to step up its aid to the ghetto and intervene diplomatically to put an end to the Germans' bestial and unprecedented genocide of the Jews. As on other occasions, these were the words of an honest and just man and a great patriot and romantic. We planned to discuss the matter further, but this was prevented by his death and the massive liquidation of the ghetto that began on July 22, 1942.

16. During this whole period of cooperation with Engineer Czerniakow, Commander "Bystry"-Iwanski repeatedly discussed with him the details of how to place ZZW soldiers among the employees, who in one way or another worked for the Judenrat. The idea was to enable the ideologically strong ZZW fighters to influence the broader population, and also seek out and suppress collaborators, or at least carry out educational and punitive measures against them (following the example of the anti-*Zagiew* action at 13–14 Leszno Street) or the establishments where stupid and servile people worked to economically destroy their fellow citizens (for example, director Wajnberg at the Fryc Szulc company, whom I myself summoned and warned twice).
17. Since I worked [...] for the intelligence service, I myself repeatedly asked Czerniakow for special help from the Judenrat in finding trustworthy people suitable to send into German offices and companies, or in other words, the circles closest to the Germans, at the same time as the Germans were setting up shops and carrying out espionage in the ghetto [...].

All these contacts with Chairman Adam Czerniakow took place in the courthouse or the ZZW safe houses mentioned above, or in his apartment on the first floor of 11 Elektoralna Street (the Piekarski building).

For me, his noble and dramatic silhouette will always symbolize his love and fraternal sacrifice for his people, and I will always hold him in respect and esteem. Any other opinion of this exceptional man and patriot is unjust, dishonest and harmful to his memory. All the more so because he is no longer here to defend his honor and justice. May my account of this matter do so for him.

> While it is right to criticize his position, to reproach him for a lack of clear-sightedness and for seeking martyrdom in the style of Konrad [the mythical Polish hero], an act of little use to the population as a whole, it must be acknowledged that he did so with the honesty, honor and conviction that characterized him when he saw no other solution. No man was wiser than he.[9]

THE ZZW'S ARMAMENT AND RECRUITMENT

Thus Colonel (later General) Petrykowski,[10] alias "Tarnawa," was put in charge of coordination with the ZZW and contact with Czerniakow. In early February 1940, he created a military unit, the "W," that would have special responsibility for helping the Jews in close cooperation with the ZZW. At the time, this mainly entailed setting up escape routes for Jews to the central region of Poland occupied by the Soviet Union (this underground railway worked in both directions, although the westbound traffic was lighter).

The quantity of arms delivered, at first light arms (pistols and grenades), was proportional to the ZZW's strength. Thus it was not a limiting factor (nor would it become one, as will be seen later on). The very slow buildup of forces was in accordance with the plan agreed upon in January 1940 by the KB and the Judenrat chairman. In November 1940, when the ghetto was walled off, the ZZW had no more than three hundred members. Obviously the fall of France in 1940 made an Allied victory seem uncertain to say the least, and far off at best. This had a devastating effect on the organization's morale, its recruitment and activities, both in the highly developed Polish branch, and in the deliberately more limited Jewish one.

All ZZW members were military veterans, most of them offi-

---

9. Tadeusz Bednarczyk, "*Getto warszawskie i ludzie – jakimi ich znalem: Wspomnienia 1939–1945, Wybitniejsze jednostki Getta – Inzynier Adam Czerniakow-przewodniczacy Gminy Wyznaniowej Zydowskiej w Warszawie*," ZIH Archives, no. 5809.
10. Petrykowski, the grandson of a famous rabbi, was a career officer who converted to Catholicism.

cers or non-commissioned officers, making military training less urgent.

The outcome of this recruitment policy was an organization drawn from the social elite. It was almost exclusively bourgeois and in fact strongly weighted toward those better-off Jews who were most integrated into Polish culture and society (see chapter 3). As we will see, this situation was to change during the period of heavy recruitment after the deportation and extermination of the ghetto population began in 1942; there would no longer be any social or political exclusivity, even toward Communists.

The organization itself was apolitical. A great part of its members were Revisionist Zionists and the others had not belonged to any political organization before the war.

CHAPTER 3

IN THE GHETTO

LIFE IN THE GHETTO

On November 4, 1939, the Gestapo ordered the Judenrat to set up a ghetto and have all the Jews in Warsaw move there within three days. During this meeting, half the Council members were arrested. It was announced that they would be executed if these orders were not implemented on time. Czerniakow responded by saying that it would be impossible to comply within that timeframe, so he was granted an extension. (This sole and unique victory was apparently a German maneuver designed to give the newly established Judenrat credibility in the eyes of the Jewish population.)

In actual fact, the massive population transfer – 100,000 Poles moved out, 180,000 Jews moved in – did not take place until a year later, in October 1940. An epidemic of infectious diseases was the pretext the Germans used to justify the establishment of the ghetto. In fact, an epidemic of exanthematic typhus broke out in December 1939. It was to last until the spring of 1942.[1]

1. The Statistical Department of the Judenrat did not record a single case in September, October and November 1939. In December, there were 88 cases among Jews and 5 among non-Jews; in January 1940, 101 and 5 cases, respectively; in February, 214 and 5; in March, 398 and 15; in April, 407 and 28. Thus, in a city where there was a Jewish quarter but not yet a walled-in ghetto, there was in fact an epidemic among the Jewish population. In the same internal report the Statistical Department noted that until the war, the overall health situation of Warsaw's Jews had been better than that of the non-Jewish population. The explanation for this epidemic was the more rapid pauperization among the Jews. "The average

On November 16, 1940, without warning, the gates in the walls that had just been built were closed to Jews. Only the very few who possessed a pass were allowed to go through. (On November 30, this prohibition was extended to Poles as well.) A year later, on October 15, 1941, leaving the ghetto or giving aid or refuge to Jews became a crime that was punishable by death.

The January 1941 census counted 390,000 Jewish inhabitants – 40% of the city's total population – huddled in 8% of the city's total area. Map no. 1 shows the ghetto borders as of November 1940, indicated with a solid line.

The boundaries of the ghetto were repeatedly altered during the course of 1941. Some parts were cut off, others added. "The ghetto's area and number of inhabitants changed ceaselessly throughout its existence. Whole blocks were separated off. Usually these were areas where the buildings were in better condition and the apartments more spacious."[2]

---

life expectancy of a newborn child, the most widely used indicator of life expectancy in statistical tables, was 52.6 years among Jewish men (which meant that theoretically a newborn Jewish boy could be expected to live until the age of 52.6), almost 7.5 years longer than for non-Jewish men. Jewish women had an average life expectancy almost 4 years longer (59.1 years) than non-Jewish women." From *Biuletyn ZIH*, no. 74 (April–June 1970): 106.

Another account states: "The German pillage of the ghetto ceased with the spread of this terrible typhus epidemic that had broken out within the first few months of the occupation of Warsaw. The reasons for the ravages of this disease were simple. Hunger and poverty were growing day by day. Food rations were particularly meager. In fact, people received practically nothing aside from irregularly-distributed black bread and some vegetables. Meat or fat was completely out of the question. Undernourished and suffering from nervous exhaustion, people gave up resisting the filth that increasingly invaded their apartments. Since there was no money even to buy a crust of bread for their children, where were they going to find enough to buy soap? I know this side of ghetto life intimately because for a long time I worked for the committee of the building on Ogrodowa Street. In the building where I lived, there were some 30 families (about 150 people in all) staying in an annex at the back of the building who were in dire need. They had no electricity, gas or running water. Living in this wooden outbuilding were a coachman whose horse had been requisitioned by the Germans, a corset-maker and her two children, the widow of a provincial teacher who had been killed, a bakery worker with ten mouths to feed, and others. About 15 people crowded into each apartment – elderly parents, infants, young people driven from their jobs who had turned to street peddling in an effort to earn a little money to buy bread […]." Michal Grynberg, ed., *Pamietniki z getta warszawskiego* (Warsaw: Panstwowe Wydawnictwo Naukowe, 1993), pp. 41, 43–44.

2. Israel Gutman, *Zydzi warszawscy 1939–1943* [*The Jews of Warsaw, 1939–1943*], (Warsaw: Rytm, 1993), pp. 62–63.

The ghetto was divided into two parts and the Jews could travel between them only by permission and in convoys. The "big" ghetto comprised 77% of the total area; later, a wooden footbridge was to cross over Chlodna Street, henceforth exclusively reserved for "Aryan" traffic. Map no. 1 shows the configuration of the ghetto just before the summer of 1942, indicated with a dashed line.

A great deal of autonomy was allowed inside the ghetto. The Judenrat was given extensive responsibility in all fields. Its administrative services employed 2,000 people. It also had about the same number of policemen (divided into six district police stations) and a jail. The Germans exercised their powers directly by starving the inhabitants. During the first year of life in the ghetto, in 1941, 43,258 deaths by starvation or diseases linked to malnutrition were recorded, out of a total population that theoretically numbered 540,000 (150,000 Jews from small towns and from Germany had been sent to join the original inhabitants). But apart from that, the Germans worked through the intermediary of the Judenrat. The Gestapo had its own branch office in the ghetto, nicknamed "Thirteen" because it was situated at 13 Leszno Street; they had another office at number 14. We will come back to this point shortly.

People were dying of famine:

> There were so-called special houses for the poorest. For example, at 46 Mila Street, out of the 500 inhabitants, 233 died. Out of the 794 people who lived in the building at 63 Pawia Street, there were 400 deaths, 200 of these during the last three months [this information is dated April, 1942]. The record among these tragic statistics was held by the house at 21 Krochmalna Street, where all of the 400 occupants died. Frequently whole families died in these special buildings [...].
>
> Few homes had any heat at all. In the 17 special buildings, out of the total of 780 apartments, 718 never once had a fire in their kitchen all last winter [...]. Right now [...], people are sleeping on the ground, covering themselves with rags and eating raw garbage.[3]

---

3. *Biuletyn Informacyjny*, April 30, 1942; cited also in Wladyslaw Bartoszewski, *Warszawski*

In counterpoint to the famine, the corpses in the street and all the other signs of suffering that marked daily existence in the ghetto, there was a highly-developed social, cultural and artistic life. Many writers have chronicled the almost caricatural contrast between the poor and the nouveaux riches who profited from contacts with the Gestapo, smuggling and Judenrat corruption. Here is an account published in 1946 by a surviving eyewitness who had been well known as a pianist before the war:

> The best time for smuggling was the afternoon, when the soldiers, worn out by their morning labors and feeling self-satisfied with their business dealings, were less vigilant [...]. Nervous silhouettes would appear at windows and in the doorways of houses next to the wall and then disappear again. Hidden men impatiently strained their ears to hear the approach of a carriage on the other side. Suddenly a horse would be heard approaching at a trot, and when the wagon was close enough, whistled signals would be exchanged and packages flew over the wall. People ran out of the doorways, caught the packages and slipped back into hiding. For a few minutes the street would be filled with a tense silence as they waited. Sometimes, when the police were doing their job more conscientiously, shots would ring out above the sound of running hoofs, and instead of packages, hand grenades would fly over the wall and loudly explode, causing serious damage.
>
> The ghetto wall was set back from the street along almost all of its length. At the bottom, at regular intervals there were long holes just above street level so that water could run from the Aryan side to the sewers situated alongside the sidewalks in the ghetto. Children used these openings for smuggling small items. On both sides you could see them running toward these slits on matchstick legs, their terrified eyes sweeping left and right. Then they would pull through a package that was often bigger than themselves.

---

pierscien smierci 1939–1944: Wydanie drugie rozszerzone (Warsaw: Wydawnictwo Interpress, 1970), p. 180.

Once the packages were through, the little smugglers would slip them onto their shoulders. Bent and stumbling under their weight, the veins in their heads bright blue and gasping for air with their mouths wide open, they would scatter in all directions like frightened rats.

Their work was dangerous; they ran the same risks as adult smugglers. One day, as I was walking along the wall, I saw an operation that seemed about to be successful. A Jewish child still on the other side of the wall was following his package through an opening. Just as his bony face came into view, he suddenly began to scream. At the same instant, I heard a German yelling brutally on the other side. I ran toward the boy to help him get through as quickly as possible, but despite our efforts his hips were stuck in the hole. I pulled his little arms as hard as I could. His cries grew increasingly desperate and I could hear the sound of studded police boots kicking him on the other side of the wall. When I was finally able to pull him out, he was dead. His backbone was broken.

Most of the bags and packages that came through the wall were gifts from Poles meant for the poorest Jews. The bulk of the ghetto's supplies came from the organized smuggling rings run by kingpins such as Kohn and Heller [agents for the Gestapo, murdered by the Germans at the end of the summer 1942 "transfer" to the Umschlagplatz, where the Jews were loaded onto trains]. They carried out their operations without the slightest hindrance and in complete safety. The guards were bribed and simply looked the other way at an opportune moment as whole columns of cars passed through carrying expensive liquor, luxury food items, tobacco from Greece and French cosmetics and clothing.

Every day I would admire these products at the Nowoczesna café, a hangout for the rich who would come dripping with gold jewelry and diamonds. These war profiteers sat at groaning tables as the sound of popping Champagne corks filled the air. It was there that I lost two of my cherished illusions: my belief that Jews would take care of each other and my belief that they loved music.

Beggars were not allowed to stand in front of the café. Fat

> bouncers would rain blows on them with sticks and run them off. [...] Men and women sprawling in rickshaws wore luxurious woolen garments in winter and French silk hats and dresses in summer. In order to reach the security zone protected by the club-wielding guards, they had to use their canes to clear the way through the crowd of beggars. Their faces were distorted by hatred. They never gave alms. They claimed that charity would demoralize people. Everyone should work and earn money as they did. Anyone could do it, and if you didn't know how to get along in life that was really your own fault. [...]
>
> At the Nowoczesna, no one paid any attention to my music. The louder I played, the louder the customers talked, and every day there was a contest between me and my audience [...]. One day, a customer even sent a waiter to tell me to stop playing for a minute because the music was keeping him from hearing the sound as he tried to test the purity of the 20-dollar gold pieces he had just bought from his neighbor.[4]

Here is another firsthand account by one of the very few Poles who entered the ghetto every day because of his profession. He too underlines the co-existence of extreme poverty and luxury:

> A lively café and restaurant scene arose in the ghetto, particularly in the spring of 1942. In addition to well-established and well-known restaurants [...] many modern and elegant establishments also sprang up [...] offering trout and French spirits [...]. Next to the Wall and the Dance Palace, with excellent orchestras [...] Bogucki sang and Trzonka played the trumpet, despite the wall they had crossed over illegally [...].[5] [After November 30, 1940, Poles caught on the "wrong" side of the wall without authorization were subject to the death penalty.]

---

4. Wladyslaw Szpilman, *The Pianist–The Extraordinary Story of one Man's Survival in Warsaw, 1939–1945* (London: Picador, 1999), pp. 11–14 (adapted from the Polish book *Smierc miasta* [*Death of a City*] published in Warsaw in 1946).
5. Bednarczyk, *Zycie codzienne warszawskiego getta*, pp. 53–54.

The theater also blossomed:

> For a whole year, in other words, until the deportations of July 1942, three theaters operated in the ghetto: a small one on Leszno Street [in Polish] and two Yiddish theaters […]. The Femina Theater put on several reviews […], three operettas and a number of musical comedies […]. Czerniakow […] hoped to establish an opera house. The Theater Council repeatedly discussed the matter, but Czerniakow was unsuccessful.[6]

Thus, in this more or less autonomous world where the Germans ventured only occasionally, the only – but terrible – danger was poverty and its consequences, death by starvation, illness and freezing.

GROWTH OF THE ZZW

Among the many parties and organizations that existed before the summer of 1942, the ZZW was the only one to advocate resistance and prepare for it. It expanded, reorganized and, theoretically, carried out resistance work, but with moderation and discretion, in conformity with the agreement between the OW-KB and Czerniakow. The ZZW's numerical growth was remarkable. From 100 members at the time the ghetto was established, its ranks swelled to 250 during the first three months of 1941 and to almost 300 by the first half of 1942. Mendelson, the sole ZZW officer to survive, recalls:

> During the latter half of 1940, up until November when the ghetto was sealed off, the ZZW did not grow significantly. All in all, its forces numbered slightly more than 100 people. The October German decision to erect a wall around the ghetto began to change

6. Michel Borwicz, *Ecrits des condamnés à mort sous l'occupation Nazie (1939–1945)* (Paris: Gallimard, 1973), p. 35.

this situation. As the inhabitants saw the barriers going up around them, they found their daily lives becoming more difficult. They began to try to contact and join the ZZW, to some extent because they hoped...that it could help them, but above all because they saw it as a way to fight the Nazi occupiers.

The OW-KB became aware of this influx of volunteers into the ZZW and wanted to take advantage of the as-yet relatively unhampered access to the ghetto. They sent the ZZW two combat rifles, two carbines, two machine guns, ten pistols and dozens of hand grenades.

It should be noted that in mid-1940, a command structure had begun to crystallize within the ZZW. The ZZW officers and the OW-KB leadership chose Moryc Dawid Apfelbaum as commander-in-chief [I have retained the various spellings of Apfelbaum's first name, Mieczyslaw, alias "Mietek," alias "Jablonski," alias "Kowal"]. At the end of the fall of 1940, Apfelbaum's circle was transformed into the ZZW general staff. Thus, the Jewish resistance movement was sufficiently prepared, in organizational terms, to face the difficult period to come with the sealing of the ghetto.

The ZZW's social composition is worth briefly reviewing. The fact that the bulk of its membership was from the Jewish intelligentsia explains the organization's somewhat elitist character. Most of its members were apolitical, but some, such as Jacob Hersz, belonged to the PPS (Polish Socialist Party), and others were Revisionist Zionists, including Leon Rodal, Pawel Frenkiel and the lawyer Dawid Szulman.

The ZZW experienced its greatest growth during the years 1941–42. All the officers (about 20 had joined up) lived in the ghetto. The ZZW general staff was enlarged, and two companies were formed. Their core, in terms of membership and leadership, came from the two original groups that had made up the ZZW. By mid-1942, the ZZW's forces numbered almost 300.[7]

---

7. Mendelson, "*Historia powstania ZZW*."

In addition to the Polish army officers and the intellectuals recruited during the initial period, all of them adults, now a numerous contingent of young people joined the ZZW's ranks. They had been given cursory military training in the countryside by Betar, a Revisionist Zionist youth organization.

> In April 1941, two Betar members, J. Brand and H. Bradwein, came to Warsaw from Hrubieszow full of hope. Farmhands were sorely lacking in that region [...]. Two months later, Brand wrote that everything had been arranged and that he was coming with work permits for 30 Betar members [...]. Both men wrote that the living conditions were comfortable [...] and that there wasn't a single German to be found in the region. The good news spread [...]. It was suggested that all the Betar members in the ghetto be sent [...], hundreds of Betarites signed up that summer. More than 600 of them [...] including all the active members and the leadership, left for Hrubieszow. The men lived and worked on different farms [...], Brand was also able to send a group of leftists, despite the attitude of their parties, at the request of Cywia Lubetkin [...] Perec Laskier came on an inspection tour [...] he visited the farms for two weeks [...]. He also went to the parades held by 11 Betar companies, well-disciplined and well-trained young people who were ready to overcome any obstacle. [...] All the company commanders and their deputy commanders [...met] for a day, and discussed military preparations and tactical problems [...]. In June, the Germans put up posters announcing that all the Jews in the region were to present themselves at the Hrubieszow train station to be sent to work camps [...]. It was decided that some of the groups would return to Warsaw and others would hide in the forests.
>
> The first group arrived in Warsaw without incident [...]. The other groups had no such luck [...]. The Betar members who stayed behind in the forests were in desperate straits [...]. The few who could escape went back to Warsaw [...] where they naturally joined Pawel Frankiel's group [...]. The volunteers had been carefully

> selected. Those who were chosen were informed of the strict discipline imposed by the Organization [the ZZW].[8]

The surviving Betarites, who returned to the ghetto at the beginning of the summer of 1942, gathered around Frenkiel and Rodal. They merged with the ZZW, which had been led by Apfelbaum. The Political Committee of the Revisionist Zionist Party, presided over by Wdowinski, played no role in the resulting expanded military organization, as he himself was forced to admit in his memoirs.[9] His role was limited to attending meetings of the political leadership, as ineffectual as they were frequent, as will become apparent in the two following chapters.

There is some uncertainty about the division of labor between Apfelbaum, Frenkiel and Rodal instituted in the summer of 1942. Mendelson, Iwanski and Bednarczyk reported that the commander was David Apfelbaum, who held the highest military rank among the three (lieutenant in 1939, then captain and subsequently major), and that Frenkiel and Rodal were his deputies; Wdowinski and Ketling (a leader of the Polish resistance organization PLAN) report that the military chief was Frenkiel, a student who held no military rank but was a Betar political activist, said by "others" to have headed a company. All agree that Rodal was in charge of the strongest unit, the first company.

In addition to the Betarites, the ZZW also accepted, without regard to their politics, a small number of young people who lacked military training but were highly motivated and in excellent physical condition. Nevertheless, this policy was not actively pursued until after the Great Deportation.

This numerical growth and more heterogeneous composition

8. Lazar Litai, *Muranowska 7*, 56–60, 89–90, 91, 93, 94–95.
9. "I was the head of the ZZW. We had a three-man Political Committee composed of Dr. Strykowski [...], Leon Rodal [...] and the chairman, me." Wdowinski, *And We Are Not Saved*, p. 79. Rodal, one of the ZZW leaders, was to die in combat during the second battle of Muranowski Square. In contrast, Chairman Wdowinski's role was purely formal. According to his own memoirs, he took part neither in combat nor in making military decisions.

necessitated structural changes. The reorganization was carried out in three stages. In 1940, following the model of the OW, the basic unit comprised eight members who knew each other well, came from the same social background, and often worked in the same profession.

Here Mendelson sheds light on the ZZW's expansion in the ghetto:

> The walling-off and isolation of the ghetto marked a turning point in the way Jews dealt with their situation and made them completely dependent on Polish good will and aid. The starvation conditions (average daily caloric intake fell from 500 calories at the beginning to 300 after that) and the lack of money in the sealed ghetto could be read as warning signs that the Germans were preparing to commit genocide. This was understood by Poles and Jews alike. Right away, Poles furnished regular food supplies, work and money. This is what allowed the ghetto population to survive for two years in complete isolation. [This oversimplification is not false, but obviously somewhat one-sidedly positive.] People of various social categories and walks of life tried to establish relations with their Polish counterparts on the other side of the wall and sought out aid from them, although in theory there was no political activity at that time. [This opinion, too, is a bit oversimplified: from July 1940 to April 1943, a total of more than 30 clandestine publications were released by political parties.[10]] Dozens of veterans who had fought in "September" [the defense of Warsaw in September 1939] sought precisely this kind of aid by enrolling in the ranks of the ZZW. As a result of this influx of new recruits, ZZW circles were reorganized according to the professions and residence of their members, and, further, at last the circles could be transformed into platoons, although they were not at full strength in the beginning. Each platoon was to comprise a minimum of 25 people. Structurally, they were subdivided

10. Henryk Piasecki, "*Ruch oporu i powstanie w getcie warszawskim w prasie podziemnej*," *Biuletyn ŻIH*, no. 2–3 (1973).

into groups [...]. At the beginning of 1941, the ZZW was composed of a general staff [Major Apfelbaum's former circle – at that time he was only a captain and would not become a major until later] and ten platoons made up of 25 fighters each. By the middle of that year, these platoons were grouped into two companies of four platoons each; a third, incomplete company made up of only one platoon; and a special, independent platoon under my leadership.

Rodal's first company had clandestine quarters at 27 Nalewki Street and 7 Muranowski Square. The second company was located at 20 Grzybowska Street and 7 Nowolipki Street, near Smocza. This company was headed by Henoch Federbusz, a porter by trade, assisted, in his organizational work, by Frenkiel, a member of the intelligentsia who was to command the future fourth company. The third company under Mojsze Weisstok was headquartered at 42 Muranowska Street. My platoon was still at 5 Karmelicka Street. Each platoon also had organizational offices. The long-term plan was to expand the companies to battalion size, but this proved impossible due to the grave lack of volunteers and weapons (almost nonexistent in the ghetto, and even the Poles had only a minimum of arms, as I was to witness later as a participant in the 1944 Warsaw Insurrection). The seriousness and efficacy of a military organization are always determined by its armament, its training, and the courage of its soldiers in combat.

The lack of guns was the ZZW's biggest problem, as it was for all the Polish organizations. Our difficulties were all the greater because the Poles were our only source of weapons. Both "Tarnawa"-Petrykowski [the commanding general of the OW-KB, see chapter 2, footnote 7] and Bednarczyk grasped this perfectly, and they did their best to obtain arms for the ghetto and get them to us. Actually, half of our soldiers – those in the first and third companies – were linked to the "W" unit and received arms from it. The other half, the second company and my platoon, were linked to Bednarczyk and his organizational views. Consequently we expected him to aid us both with material and in organizational matters, which he did.

The "W" unit, which belonged to the ZW [*Zbrojne Wyzwolenie*,

Liberation Army], transferred weapons from the mother organization as well as from its own stock. Among those who took part in this work were Jan Skoczek; his wife Wanda, alias "Baska"; and Marian Kowalski, alias "Sep." [Once again Mendelson fails to name Iwanski, which is all the more odd since it was certainly Iwanski who saved Mendelson and his family – see Mendelson's affidavit in appendix 1.] Bednarczyk organized arms shipments from the depots of the OW-KB general command and of other organizations, especially the ZPN organization of veterans of the Silesia uprising and the Skala firemen's organization. In this arms procurement, the most active role, apart from that of Bednarczyk himself, was played by the police superintendent Tadeusz Zmudzinski and Teodor Niewiadomski [see chapter 6], who at that time was working with the ZOM [Municipal Sanitation Department] and today is a journalist. I also recall the engineer Stanislaw Szopinski, a retired colonel who organized the aid given by the ZPN, and Lieutenant-Colonel Michal Pogorzelski, later deceased, who organized the aid that came through the safe house used for sending and receiving by the Mirow firemen's section.

It was extremely important to get a certain additional quantity of arms, not only for organizational and training purposes but also to fight the collaborators of all kinds whose numbers were constantly increasing. Through his direct contacts and administrative connections with Jews in the quarter, Bednarczyk uncovered the existence of an organization set up by the Gestapo called Zagiew, headquartered at 13 Leszno Street in the offices of the Jewish police. Abraham Gancwajch, a notorious Gestapo agent, was its head. Bednarczyk also discovered a Jewish Gestapo-run cell on 14 Leszno Street (Kohn and Heller). When he realized the danger their work represented, he passed the information to the ZZW command and ordered them to fight these collaborators. To this end, Bednarczyk established intelligence cells in his tax sector and sent these men to work in various places such as stores and especially the cafés and restaurants where the Zagiew Gestapo agents met. He had a number of soldiers from his intelligence cells become waiters. Thus the

ZZW was able to figure out the organizational structure of the Gestapo-run Jewish cells on 13 and 14 Leszno Street and that of the Zagiew, whose objective was to infiltrate and liquidate the Polish units helping the Jews.

In this way Bednarczyk's work helped protect both the Polish and the Jewish resistance. It made it possible to smash the Zagiew, which sprang up again and again; but it also enabled us Jews to settle accounts with our own Gestapo scum and save our national honor through our own counter-action. The fight against the Zagiew continued even after the ghetto was destroyed because its agents sought to catch the Jews hiding out on the Aryan side and blackmail the richest among them.

During the period of the struggle against collaborators, which was both an opportunity for training and a chance to demonstrate the existence of an armed Jewish organization to the Jews as a whole, conditions were created that facilitated the ZZW general staff in exercising its command and surveillance functions throughout the Jewish quarter in Warsaw. In the fall of 1941, after consultations between "Tarnawa"-Petrykowski, Szopinski and Bednarczyk, the general staff was enlarged. The ZZW carried out these consultations in two places provided by Bednarczyk, the Courthouse on Leszno Street and the firehouse on Chlodna Street. At this point, before the publication of Bednarczyk's book, which will explain this whole issue in detail [see appendix 2], I would like to give a succinct description of the organizational structure of our general staff.

Apfelbaum was the overall commanding officer, Leon Rodal (head of the first company) his deputy for military affairs, Mojsze Weisstok (head of the third company) his second deputy and chief of staff, Pawel Frenkiel his third deputy, and Henoch Federbusz his deputy in charge of the evacuation of the ghetto's population to hideouts situated on the Aryan side. The following sections, groups and services were created as part of the general staff: first, organization and recruitment; second, actions and training; third, radio monitoring and press propaganda; fourth, intelligence and investigations. The latter was headed by Kuperman, alias "Kuperski," a specialist and officer in the OKII [Intelligence Service]. His deputy for the main ghetto was Zelwanski and Makower for the small ghetto (Makower directed the principal efforts against the collaborators, backed up by my platoon, which was the nearest unit in the area). The other sections were the following: fifth, technical (construction of fortifications, bunkers, tunnels and the manholes mentioned by General Stroop); sixth, evacuation of civilians and liaison (the application of the decree of the Government in Exile representative regarding the rescue of scientists and intellectuals from the ghetto); seventh, transport and armament (receiving arms, medical supplies and provisions sent by the OW-KB); eighth, quartermaster and service corps (arms and provisions depots, manufacture of grenades and arms, maintenance of underground shooting galleries); ninth, medical; tenth, chaplainship; eleventh, judicial and investigations. The heads of these bureaus were, respectively, Mojsze Weisstok, Leon Rodal, Henryk Lipszyc-Lipinski, Alojzy Kuperman, the engineer Leonard Pisz, Kalmen Mendelson, Henoch Federbusz, Pawel Frenkiel, Roman Leon Weinsztok, Dr. Celmajster-Niemirski, Rabbi Feldszur and Judge "Balbina." In addition to the ZZW leadership, officers, platoon leaders and their deputies to whom we have already referred, mention should also be made of Bialoskora, Goldberg, Praszkiera, Dermatolski, Dr. Dawid Wdowinski, Blum-Binsztok alias "Rudy," Samuel Luft, Natan Szulc, "Ryba"-Staniewicz, Urbach, Eryk Zlotogora, Dawid Szulman, Janek Pika, Eliasz Alberstein, Winogron, the Lopata brothers and Dr. Ryszard Walewski (who joined in 1943).[11] [The latter's eyewitness account is given in chapters 7 and 8.]

---

11. Kalmen Mendelson, "*Rozwoj i dzialalnosc ZZW*," *Kronika*, no. 19 (May 9, 1970). The author of this article ends by saying, "Among all of these figures, only a few are still alive today: Dr. Wdowinski in the U.S. [...], Dr. Walewski in Israel, Lopata in Switzerland, the author of this article and a few soldiers." Following is a more complete list of survivors drawn up in 1993 by Chaya Lazar: "Dr. Jozef Celmajster died in Warsaw during the 1980s; Juta Hartman-Rotenberg now lives in Holon; Simcha Korengold presently lives in Haifa; Emilka Kosover-Rozenzweig currently lives in Tel Aviv; Kalmen Mendelson died in Warsaw during the 1980s; Yehoshua Prechner died in Haifa in 1985; Fela Szabszik-Finkelstein currently lives in Nordiya; Dr. Ryszard Walewski died in Tel Aviv during the 1970s; Dr. David Wdowinski died in Tel Aviv on Holocaust Day in 1970." See Lazar, "The Jewish Military Organization," p. 62.

Thus, according to Mendelson and Bednarczyk, each circle was made up of three groups of about eight people and at the time of the walling of the ghetto there were seven circles led by

- Apfelbaum, 10 Mila Street;
- Rodal, 27 Nalewki Street;
- Bialoskora, 40 Ogrodowa Street;
- Urbach, on Dzielna Street, at the corner of Karmelicka;
- Weinsztok, 42 Muranowska Street (which was to soon split up into two);
- Lipszyc, specializing in monitoring the radio, press and propaganda;
- Makower, 44 Zelazna Street.

During late 1940 and early 1941, four new circles were organized, each a mixture of "veterans" and new recruits: one led by Mendelson (5 Karmelicka Street) made up of intellectuals, like the previous circles, and three more socially diverse groups, two of them made up of tradesmen and led respectively by the tailor Kirszenbaum (27 Leszno Street) and the glove-maker Jacobson (6 Prawa Street), and the third a circle of porters led by Federbusz, himself a porter, Polish army sergeant and future ZZW second lieutenant (promoted by the OW-KB).

Subsequently the OW-KB gave orders that ZZW be reorganized following the model of the mother organization itself. These ten circles were transformed into platoons of 25 soldiers each, totaling 250 fighters in all, and a medical corps. During 1941 the first platoon, led by Apfelbaum, became the general staff.

In the summer of 1941, the OW called for a second reorganization of the ZZW. Three companies were formed. The first, commanded by Lieutenant Rodal, composed of four platoons, headquartered on 27 Nalewki Street and 7 Muranowski Square; the second, also four platoons, led by Federbusz and his deputy Frenkiel, on 20 Grzybowska Street; the third, initially composed of a single platoon, commanded by Weisstok, on 42 Muranowska Street;

and a separate platoon for special missions under Mendelson, on Karmelicka Street. Later the third company was to be brought up to strength and a fourth created under the command of Pawel Frenkiel; platoons were exchanged between companies to strengthen the leadership of those that lacked experienced officers and noncoms.

In the fall of 1941, the general staff and its sections were expanded to include an intelligence and investigations section and a legal section authorized to pronounce judgments.

Preparation for combat was the main activity. Constant training took place at the platoon level, with instruction provided by ZZW officers, while the latter were taught by instructors from the "Aryan sector." There were two underground shooting galleries, one in a basement on 29 Nalewki Street and the other on 12 Franciszkanska Street. Both locations included a gunsmith shop and grenade manufacture facilities.

Intelligence work constituted another major activity. It was directed by Lieutenant Kuperman, a veteran member of the Polish Second Bureau. Czerniakow had placed a half-dozen ZZW members in various Judenrat services, under the responsibility of Stanislaw Rozewicz. This section worked closely with Polish forces, particularly Captain Bednarczyk, who, as a representative of the Polish Treasury Department, maintained his office in the ghetto from the beginning until April 1943, and Lieutenant Radwanski, in charge of intelligence for the OW-KB.

The main target of the intelligence and investigations service was the Gestapo unit (the "Thirteen") active in the ghetto. It had set up Zagiew, a phony resistance organization which after recruiting people terrorized them into becoming informers. In May 1942, a group of 11 Gestapo stooges was surrounded, disarmed, and taken by rickshaw to a basement on 10 Karmelicka Street, where they were condemned (they all carried Gestapo credentials and service weapons), executed and buried on the spot. (The orders to hold back issued by the chairman of the Judenrat only concerned Germans; the occupiers were hardly concerned by conflicts among

Jews.) Three times Zagiew was smashed by the ZZW and reconstituted by the Gestapo. Other Gestapo stooges were executed in the street, including Blumberg, Branstein, Blum, Cementowicz, Erlich and some whose names have been forgotten.

TUNNELS

The technical section began to build fortifications. The most notable were those in Muranowski Square, which were to play a major role. They also included the first two tunnels leading out of the ghetto (one between Gesia Street and the Jewish cemetery,[12] and another under the Church of the Blessed Virgin[13] and Leszno Street); a system of interconnections between cellars; and camouflaged manholes meant to facilitate rapid "disappearances." The ZZW's tunnel system was to be used occasionally by other organizations as well. Following are some details concerning tunnels:

> The Church of the Blessed Virgin, located within the confines of the ghetto, was open to "Catholic Jews..." not recognized as "Aryan" by the Nuremberg laws. Unlike his congregation, the priest, Foder, a converted Jew [a Jew who practiced Christianity], had fraternal feelings toward the ghetto and understood...that he had a duty to aid his brothers in distress. He was friendly with Dr. Godlewski, a leader of the Catholic Church in Poland, who was known for his hatred toward the Jews before the war but considered the converted

12. "During this period the ZZW dug two underground tunnels. The first was built at the end of 1941. The entrance was on the corner of Gesia and Okopowa Streets, in the ruins of a burned-out house, about 15 meters from the street gates. It ran under the pavement of Ogrodowa Street toward the Jewish cemetery. The exit was under the morgue. This passageway was in use until early August 1942 when some traitors betrayed it to the Germans, who damaged it by blowing up the entrance. [...] All [the traitors] were killed by order of the ZZW." Bednarczyk, *Zycie codzienne warszawskiego getta*, p. 67.
13. "Another passageway was dug in July 1942. It started out under the Church of the Blessed Virgin and the convent (a basement was enlarged and a manhole built for this purpose), ran under Leszno Street and ended in a building on the other side, the Aryan side. The last part of this passage could also lead through the sewers. [...]." Bednarczyk, *Zycie codzienne warszawskiego getta*, p. 67.

> "saints who had purified their souls." Godlewski was an ardent Polish patriot...and his hatred for the Germans counterbalanced his hatred of Jews, so much so that he was willing to take action to save them. Through the Polish resistance Father Foder had met Lopata, a ZZW officer, who presented him with diagrams for a tunnel under the church with an exit on the "Aryan" side of Leszno Street. Godlewski agreed to this. [...] The entrance was excavated in a house standing next to the church and a broad bunker was built under the church floor. The tunnel led from this bunker to the "Aryan" side and included a number of escape hatches. The engineers created one opening in the platform on which the statue of the Virgin Mary stood and built a shaft so the tunnel could be entered through the church by pushing aside the platform and sliding down a three-meter-long slope leading directly into the bunker, which was fitted out with electricity, ventilation, alarms and sanitation facilities.
>
> The second tunnel, also designed and organized by the ZZW technical department, was dug under Okopowa Street and led to the Jewish cemetery on Gesia Street. The two tunnels worked perfectly during the German Grossaktion [Grand Operation, the final Nazi incursion into the ghetto], and it was thanks to them that the ZZW could preserve its troops and weapons.[14]

Between 1941 and April 1943, Mendelson's platoon got 4,000 people out of the ghetto.[15] This service was also responsible for

14. Lazar, "The Jewish Military Organization," 25–26.
15. "The ZZW took part in the evacuation of the Warsaw ghetto and with the aid of the OW-KB helped hide about 4,000 people without counting the many thousands sent to the USSR along this underground railway up to the spring of 1941 [...]. 'Tarnawa'-Petrykowski and Bednarczyk organized numerous safe houses in the area around the walls of the ghetto where the evacuees could stay until they could be more safely moved further on. I visited many of Bednarczyk's safe houses, such as the pastry shop on Dluga Street, the photography studio on Bielanska near Tlomackie Street, Woszczyk the tailor's place at 2a Nalewki Street (the Simons arcade) where Bednarczyk's section kept its weapons, and Morawski the carpenter's on Marszalkowska Street, near Krolewska. It was even harder to find more long-term hiding places, especially since they were often compromised during the constant raids carried out in the Aryan quarter of Warsaw and the evacuees had to be moved elsewhere." Mendelson, "*Rozwoj i dzialalnosc* ZZW."

transporting arms, munitions, food and construction material, as well as providing support for the intelligence service.

THE ZZW AND THE ANTI-FASCIST BLOC

In the beginning stages of the organization, the structure and even the name ZZW itself were all completely secret. Yet because of the execution of the Gestapo stooges, the people knew that there was an armed resistance movement.

On the eve of the mass deportation, the ZZW was the only existing military resistance organization, although of a size far disproportional to its tasks. Bednarczyk explained the situation as follows:

> In conclusion, regarding the organizational work during this period, it must be recognized that the ZZW was prepared for armed struggle. But due to the small number of its forces it could not harbor the slightest illusion that it could be successful in the open armed struggle it should have launched when the liquidation of the ghetto began in July 1942. At that time it would have been impossible to incite the Jewish population to make the leap to active resistance. The Jews did not want to take up armed struggle. Even the rich did not want to buy themselves guns, although they were not yet very expensive at that point. Although the ZZW was considering an armed Jewish insurrection, it could not be sure of the support of even its own members. What strength did this handful of people (about 300 soldiers) really represent in July 1942 in the face, on the one hand, of the violence of the Germans, and on the other, the total passivity of a half-million of their brothers and sisters who did not look favorably upon those who wanted to fight? Docile, obedient and all but on their knees, the population obeyed German orders and put up with humiliation as if it were decreed by fate.
>
> The only potential ally was the Anti-Fascist Bloc, with its as-yet embryonic fighting units, the Gwardia Ludowa [People's Guard]

> and the Organizacja Bojowa [Combat Organization]. But these units were just beginning to be organized. As yet, they had no weapons and thus were not in a position to fight. Furthermore, the liquidation of the ghetto had taken them by surprise, causing a certain dispersal of their forces and the loss of several leaders (including Lewartowski), which meant that they no longer could count on a unified command structure capable of mounting a riposte.[16]

In fact, the Anti-Fascist Bloc was formed late. Early 1942 had seen the founding of the PPR (Polish Workers Party), a reconstructed communist party (Stalin had dissolved the pre-war CP). The party included people from both sides of the wall but its membership was overwhelmingly on the ghetto side. In March, the PPR led in the founding of a Jewish Anti-Fascist Bloc including both Marxist and Zionist parties and organizations, with the aim of immediately launching a resistance movement that could aid the Soviet Union in its struggle. But in practice, military preparations had not even begun – no arms had been acquired before the deportations of the summer of 1942, during which many of the Bloc's main leaders were taken. Further, the Bloc itself was dissolved in late spring.

Cukierman, one of its leading members, describes the birth and brief existence of the Anti-Fascist Bloc, which disappeared before it even had the chance to act:

> An enlarged Anti-Fascist Bloc, now including the Hehaloutz, was organized during the second half of 1942. Under its aegis a special commission for the defense of the ghetto was set up, and Mordechaj Tenenbaum was put in charge.
>
> Sak, Lewartowski, Sagan, Tenenbaum and, I think, Breslaw were on the editorial board of *Der Ruf* [The Call, organ of the Anti-Fascist Bloc, which first came out on May 15, 1942. This information is from a footnote in Cukierman's book, and was originally

16. Bednarczyk, *Zycie codzienne warszawskiego getta*, pp. 67–68.

provided by Marian Turski]. Two issues were published, each with a different editor. I recall that Mordechaj Tenenbaum was to prepare the third.

The Anti-Fascist Bloc was short-lived. Its importance lay in the fact that for the first time an almost all-ghetto organization began to take shape. Only the Bund and the General Zionists [a politically centrist party] refused to join. [The Revisionist Zionists are not even referred to.] As I've already mentioned, the Bund was opposed to any Jewish action and the General Zionists considered our trends too revolutionary. Although not impossible, I don't think the communist participation in the Bloc was the reason for their refusal to join us. They abhorred the very idea of self-defense, of partisans and the creation of a Jewish combat organization (the ZOB had not yet even been conceived). Many cells – "groups of five" – were founded but their life span was only six weeks long. After that, a crisis exploded.

These "groups of five" were based on political parties because people who carry out clandestine actions have to know one another – they must be linked in some way. Thus the "groups of five" began to be organized. They had neither arms nor the time to get sufficiently organized. The crisis first broke out within the PPR. I think it had to do with Andrzej Szmidt, but I can't remember anymore. A typewriter or a mimeograph machine had to be brought over to the "Aryan" side of Warsaw. Somebody informed. Arrests began to take place on the "Aryan" side and ours as well. We were afraid these people would talk and bring about more arrests. The same people who took the initiative to create the Bloc now called for it to suspend its activity, which they effectively achieved. The third issue of *Der Ruf* never came out. Despite its rapid collapse, the very existence of the Bloc was a victory. To get back to the question of weapons, at least ten people claimed to have had a pistol in their hands but they were all talking about the same gun. A. speaks of it as though it were a cannon but it was just a handgun, the one and only weapon. Bernard Mark writes that Mordechaj Anielewicz organized a military group with Szmidt. That's a baseless statement.

And an underground resistance movement can't be brought into being with a single pistol.[17]

CZERNIAKOW'S SUICIDE

Further, within this context of extreme passivity, as the date for the mass deportation approached, the behavior of the Germans became relatively less harsh (we will come back to this point in the following chapter), as can be clearly seen in these extracts from Czerniakow's diary:

> 16 V 42. Spent the morning at the offices of Aureswald [general commissioner for Jewish affairs in Warsaw]. I informed him of the previous day's events. At the end, in passing, I brought up the question of the Order Police band, asking that they be allowed to play in the open air. The idea was that they would play for children in small parks…
>
> 24 V 42. The Community in the morning. At noon, concert by the Order Police band. They played and sang Jewish music [Jews were forbidden to perform "Aryan" pieces]. Kataszek was the conductor. Full house. Excellent performance….
>
> 2 VII 42. I received a note from the Religious Commission asking that during the following few weeks, which had always been considered a period of mourning, there be no holding of public festivities with music and singing. I answered […].
>
> 10 VII 42. […] I visited the miniparks on Nalewki and Nowolipki Streets. They'll be ready for Sunday. At 2 P.M., I inaugurated the advanced training course for teachers in the Community Hall. Speakers included […]. The room was full. […]

---

17. Yitzhak Zuckerman, *Nadmiar pamieci: Siedem OWych lat wspomnienia 1939–1946* (Warsaw: Wydawn. Nauk. PWN, 2000), pp. 137–38. *A Surplus of Memory: Chronicle of the Warsaw Ghetto Uprising*, trans. and ed. Barbara Harshav (Berkeley: University of California Press, 1993), pp. 183–84. Recorded in 1974, in accordance with the author's wishes, these memoirs were not published until after his death in 1990. (Translated from Hebrew: ed. Kibbutz Lohamei Hagettaot, 1991.)

12 VII 42. [...] At 9:30, inauguration of a playground for schoolchildren at the corners of [...] streets. A big crowd. In the street, on the roofs and on their balconies. Orchestra, chorus, ballet [...].[18] The children applauded me. At noon, inauguration of prison workshops. Speech. The first anniversary of the founding of the Jewish prison. [...]

22 VII 42 [...] The perimeter of the new ghetto encircled by a special unit, in addition to the usual [one].

At 10 o'clock, the arrival of General Höfle [the SS general in charge of "transfer affairs" and his staff came from Lublin, where the Jews had already been murdered] and fellow officers. We unplugged the telephones. The children were evacuated from the neighboring garden.

They told us that with a few exceptions, Jews of all ages and sexes were going to be transferred to the East. Today, before 4 P.M., 6,000 people are to be "furnished." And that a similar number (at least) will be required every day.

We were ordered to leave the house on 103 Zelazna Street and turn it over to the German functionaries in charge of the transshipment. They kept the furniture. Since Judenrat employees and their wives and children were exempt from being shipped out, I asked that this category also include the employees and families of the Joint Organization, the Craftsmen's Guild and the garbage men, etc. My request was accepted.

I asked that Gepner, Rozen, Sztolcman, Drybinski, Witner and Kobryner be exempted; this was granted. By 3:15 they were all back in the ghetto, except for Rozen.

Lejkin [deputy-chief of the Jewish police] sent word after lunch that glass had been thrown at the police car. They threatened to shoot

18. Here is what Zuckerman wrote about this: "I remember a spring day. I went out to buy newspapers and heard a band playing on Nalewki Street, perhaps in front of the building at no. 23, near the park. Adam Czerniakow was taking part in the festivities. The band played Hatikva ["Hope," a poem by Naphtali Herz Imber that was the Zionist anthem at that time and later became the Israeli national anthem]. I watched from afar, ashamed to see the Jewish 'governor' take part in this. Czerniakow came by car and the Jewish police stood at attention in his honor." Zuckerman, *A Surplus of Memory*, pp. 183–84.

the Jewish hostages if that ever happened again, even once. The most tragic problem is the children in the orphanages [...]. I mentioned it; perhaps it will be possible to do something about it.

At 5:30, one of Worthoff's functionaries came and demanded that Jozef Erlich replace Lejkin. He already has three stars.

Sturmbahnführer Höfle [...] asked me to step into his office. He told me that my wife would remain free for the moment, but if the transfer failed she would be the first to be shot as a hostage.

23 VII 42. The Council in the morning. Worthoff from the transfer service came; we discussed a number of things. He granted an exemption from the transfer for the students in the craft school, and the husbands of working women were also exempted. Regarding the orphans, he told me to take it up with Höfle. When I asked on which days of the week the transfer would take place, he answered all seven.

In town we have seen a growing pressure to open the "shops"...a sewing machine could save a life [...].

3 P.M. For the moment there are only 4,000 [people] for the transshipment. Our orders were that there be 9,000 by 4 o'clock.

Some officials came to the post office and ordered that all packages and letters be sent to Pawiak [German prison in the ghetto].[19]

Scarcely an hour after writing these entries, Czerniakow committed suicide in his office. He swallowed cyanide. The following note addressed to his wife was found: "They are demanding of me that I kill my people's children with my own hands. The only thing left for me to do is to die." Another note was addressed to the Judenrat Council:

Worthoff and several members [of the transfer bureau] came to see me and they ordered me to prepare a shipment of children for the

19. Raul Hilberg, Stanislaw Staron and Josef Kermisz (eds.), *The Warsaw Diary of Adam Czerniakow: Prelude to Doom* (New York: Stein and Day, 1979), pp. 354, 358, 373, 377–78, 379, 384–85.

following day. That was the drop that made the cup of bitterness overflow. I cannot possibly deliver up innocent children to their death. I decided to leave. Don't consider this as an act of flight or cowardice. I am powerless, my heart is bursting with pain and pity, and I can't stand it any longer. My gesture will let everyone know the truth and perhaps it will show them how to act appropriately. I am aware that I am leaving you an inheritance that will be difficult to bear.

CHAPTER 4

THE "TRANSFER" – SUMMER OF 1942

The "transfer," or in other words, the mass shipment of Jews from the ghetto to their deaths in the gas chambers of Treblinka, began on July 22. The meaning of this destination seems to have been understood from the very beginning – earlier survivors had reached Warsaw with the news of the gas chamber trucks and the mass murder of Jews in eastern Poland, the Baltic countries, Belorussia and the Ukraine. Bednarczyk[1] and Cukierman[2] say that the Judenrat actively participated in the construction of Treblinka by providing workers. Thus, in addition to the numerous indirect reports from Jews and Poles, this should have directly confirmed that these new installations were in fact death camps. Finally, the suicide of Czerniakow should have removed any remaining doubts. But as we will see, this was not the case at all.

1. Bednarczyk, *Zycie codzienne warszawskiego getta*, p. 70. See his account below.
2. "It is clear that the Jewish police took part in the building of Treblinka; there is documentary proof of that. I remember one night in the ghetto when the Germans ordered the Judenrat and the Jewish police to select a number of craftsmen from among the ghetto inhabitants – carpenters, ironmongers, masons, etc. They demanded that the Judenrat provide the barbed wire and the necessary construction materials. The Judenrat complied. It was all shipped by rail to Treblinka. This was during Pesach 1942." Zuckerman, *A Surplus of Memory*, p. 192.

JEWISH POLICE AND RABBIS

The first 100,000 people were picked up and deported by the Jewish police from July 22 through September 6, without the direct intervention of the Germans. Neither the ZOB nor the ZZW put up any resistance, although the Jewish police were armed only with rubber truncheons. Cukierman recounts:

> On the morning of the second or third day of the operation, we went to Dzielna Street. There were two couples, Cywia [Lubetkin] with Mordechaj Tenenbaum, and me and Frumka. Frumka and I got there first. All of a sudden, we realized that a round-up was underway. The Jewish police were doing it by themselves. A high-ranking Jewish police officer said something and stopped us. Frumka said something insulting to him. He reacted by cursing profusely and Frumka smacked him in the face. Everything was going fine until we got to the corner of Nalewki and Gesia Streets, where we were assailed by several dozen policemen. There were some horse-drawn carriages nearby and the police threw Frumka into one of them. They tried to do the same to me, but without success. I turned into a wild man and I think I hit them pretty hard. They hit me again and again but they couldn't get me into the vehicle. With my back up against the car I held on tight and kicked right and left. I remember seeing, from far away, a cop who belonged to Noar Hatzion [a Marxist Zionist organization] hiding behind a newsstand. Ashamed because he couldn't help us, he was trying to conceal himself so that he wouldn't have to play the "game." Suddenly I saw one of the comrades of our movement...who was shouting at them, "Bandits! Don't you know who you're dealing with? The head of the pioneers!" The situation became explosive. I could hear yelling and crying all around me. Hundreds of people were shouting and crying to high heaven. I felt strong enough to continue defending myself. Then a man I didn't know came up and said, "Stop fighting and get into the carriage. In a few minutes I'll set you free at my own risk." I didn't know him but I didn't hesitate for long. I got in and sat down next to

Frumka, who was bleeding from the nose. All of a sudden I realized that I was sitting in the carriage! And I knew very well what Treblinka was about! Here I was, being taken to Umschlagplatz. What I didn't know was at that very moment Mordechaj Tenenbaum, who had escaped from the round-up, was running toward Hashomer Hatzair on Nalewki street to get help.

Who was that man I'd trusted? That was the only time I ever saw him.... I don't know how long it all lasted because every minute seemed like hours, but finally Frumka and I were freed. A Jewish police officer stood in front of us. In one hand he held his gloves and in the other a rubber truncheon (nightsticks were the only arms they were given). He was a well-built man, perhaps a few years older than I (the majority of the officers in the Jewish police were members of the intelligentsia and mostly lawyers). He said to me, "They told me who you are but you act like a bandit." I didn't answer. If I said anything at all I'd find myself in the police car again. So instead I kept silent. And we were freed.

As I've already mentioned, I didn't know this man, but I was the one who acted like a "bandit." They weren't the bandits, I was, we were. Of course, there was always the danger that the Germans might appear at any moment but it was Jews, the Jewish police, who were doing the dirty work. Some people try to defend them and others denounce them. In my opinion, our worst mistake, or, I should say, my worst mistake, since most of my comrades are dead, was to have failed to wage war against the Jewish police from the start! Would this have made it possible for us to save people? No, absolutely not. But it is indisputable that the Germans could not have carried out their work so easily and so quickly if they hadn't been helped by the Jewish police. Undoubtedly the Jews would have run away and hid when confronted by the Germans. But when they saw a Jewish policeman, they never even dreamed that it meant death. And the Jewish police knew what this was about. Just as I knew all about Treblinka, the Jewish police knew too because they were the ones who brought the news of the massacre that had already begun there...

We failed to do what we could have done. The Jewish police

were armed with rubber nightsticks and knives. They had no firearms. We should have just killed them. […] And that's what I demanded that we do at the meeting held on July 22 [This meeting was attended by representatives of all the clandestine movements, including Cukierman for Hehalutz, and Adolf Berman; the ZZW does not seem to have been invited.[3]] […] We started by asking ourselves what we could do. Defend ourselves? Such an approach would require taking a stand. Schipper, for example, said that it was clear that only (!) 80,000 Jews would be deported. He spoke of the historic responsibility of the Jews. It's true, he said, that these people might be killed, but why should the lives of all the other Jews be put at risk? Schipper was a good speaker. He added that during the history of the Jews there were some times when they had to accept the situation and others when they had to fight for their lives. He claimed that this was not a time for self-defense. We were weak and had to resign ourselves.

What did I call for in that meeting? Above all that we had to take a stand against the deportations. What did I suggest? I couldn't think of much. I said that everyone at the meeting and the members of their organizations (we were in a position to rally a few hundred Jews) should march down the street chanting "Treblinka Is Death!" Let the Germans come and kill us. I wanted the Jews to see blood running in the streets of Warsaw and not just in Treblinka. Because very soon after the round-ups started – perhaps the first day – we knew that they were being sent to Treblinka and where it was. The police at Umschlagplatz saw the boxcars come back empty a few hours after they left. We figured out how far it was from Warsaw. Another thing: when they opened the doors of the boxcars to make people get in, there were bloodstains and even corpses. They hadn't even bothered to clean the cars properly. So people began to ask questions and the Polish driver told us that the train was going to Treblinka, near Malkinia. […] And so even before we knew exactly

3. "The only ones missing were the activists of the religious party Mizrahi and the Revisionists." Gutman, *Zydzi warszawscy*, p. 229.

where this place was located, we understood that it meant death. We already knew what had happened at Wilno, Chelmno, Lublin and Hrubieszow. That's how I argued at the meeting. I explained that we had no choice. The world doesn't hear us; it doesn't know what's going on. The Poles are not helping us. Even if we aren't able to save the Jews, at least they have to understand what's happening! So that they could hide, take refuge. I also said that we had to attack the Jewish police. If we had done that, maybe we could have slowed down the process, we could have made it more difficult for the Germans. Because in fact "getting rid" of 450,000 Jews would be harder than getting rid of 50,000 later. They would be forced to bring in major reinforcements to pick off the Jews day and night.

Aleksander Zysie Frydman from the group Agudat Israel responded to me with tears in his eyes. "What the Lord giveth, He taketh away." Since there was no hope, maybe that was the attitude we should all adopt, and then no one would care who died first. But we believed that it was possible to do something and to save something. We thought that if the Jews saw blood, if they understood that they were going to be sent to their death, they would not go quietly. But unfortunately we didn't do what we should have done at that point.[4]

I went home from that meeting aware that we were plunging into the abyss, but I also knew that there was a limit to how low we could go. I had already touched bottom months ago. I knew that they were going to take us all away, every last one. But I thought it

4. Here is Gutman's account of the results of the meeting described by Cukierman: "During the meeting a proposal was made that we fight, actively, in other words, with guns in hand. This was rejected by Zysie Frydman of Agudat Israel and Ignacy Schipper, a historian and well-known personality, two people with incontestable authority in the eyes of those attending the meeting. Frydman argued that it made no sense to put up opposition and that it would be better to put our trust in Providence and await a turn for the better. Schipper said we should draw the lessons from the Jewish past. Once before in their history, the Jewish people had been forced to resign themselves to seeing their blood shed in order to save the core of their nation and thus survive as a people. Active resistance was not a good solution because it might not only lead to tragedy on a bigger scale but make the end come even sooner. Frydman and Schipper's resolute declarations had a strong impact on the other participants at the meeting and prevented them from taking a decision to fight." Gutman, *Zydzi warszawscy*, p. 230.

would take months and months. We already knew all their tricks. They couldn't continue to fool us. We knew that the end was inevitable. But I thought that they would proceed in stages, as they had done in Wilno, where the deportations stretched out endlessly…

We called another meeting, the second meeting. The third one never took place. The representatives of the political parties didn't show up. […] We had to do something to save what remained of our Movement at least. We had hundreds of people who had to be saved from the deportations. They above all…

Czerniakow's suicide didn't have much effect on the Jews. Jewish families were preoccupied by daily survival and unable to feel anything but fear. They just wanted to protect their little Mojszele from German brutality. The average Jew wasn't thinking about Adam Czerniakow. […]

We sent a delegation to obtain arms. We didn't get any because they didn't have any confidence in us. They said, "The Jews won't defend themselves." These were Poles linked to the government in exile in London. They insulted us. "The Jews will go like sheep to the slaughter." The PPR sympathized with us, but they didn't have any guns.[5]

TWO VERY DIFFERENT WITNESSES CONCUR

In a long essay that he finished writing on January 17, 1943, just before the second round of deportations and the first revolt, the previously-mentioned Berman, at that time a Zionist representative to the Zegota and a member of its council, wrote:

> Why didn't the Jewish masses in Warsaw defend themselves at that point, in 1942? Why did even the socially-active segments of the population fail to oppose the Germans?[6] Some Polish underground

5. Zuckerman, *A Surplus of Memory*, pp. 190–198, 201.
6. Here the author, A. Berman, is referring to a mass opposition, since Jews had committed numerous individual acts of opposition during the first round of deportations in 1942.

publications raised this question forcefully. This amounted to subjecting the Jewish population to a crossfire by criticizing their passivity in the face of being wiped out [during the mass deportation of the summer of 1942 and until January 1943 – it should be recalled that this essay was written in January]. It is impossible for anyone who did not live among the Jewish masses throughout the whole "operation" and witness it from within to understand this at first apparently inexplicable attitude. The all but unbearable suffering that prevailed at that time cannot be fully grasped by anyone who did not experience it themselves. The following reflections are in no way written either to defend or to condemn the Jewish population. They are simply an attempt to explain its passivity at that time and to describe the political climate and public opinion concerning resistance.

1. THE POLITICAL CLIMATE AND PREPARATIONS BEFORE THE "OPERATION" IN WARSAW

By the end of 1941 and early 1942, as the news of the massacres of the Jewish population to the east and west began to reach Warsaw, and especially as word began to get out about the use of gas to carry out the mass extermination of Jews at the Chelmno death camp, there arose in the ghetto a sense of revolt and a still vaguely-defined desire to oppose the occupiers. Calls to struggle against the murders of the Jewish people and for armed self-defense appeared in all the underground Jewish publications (a dozen illegal newspapers came out in the first six months of 1942). With increasing frequency, articles on this subject would declare, "We can't let ourselves be led to the slaughterhouse like cattle," "We won't let ourselves be massacred like a flock of sheep," "If we must die, then let us die with honor!"

The as-yet unconfirmed reports of armed Jewish opposition at Nowogrodek [7] reached the Warsaw ghetto. It was said that a Jewish

7. There was a relatively strong underground Jewish resistance organization in Nowogrodek. A group of Jews who had managed to escape from the ghetto formed a partisan unit. In

self-defense organization led by the local schoolteacher resisted the massacre and killed several German gendarmes before they themselves were killed. This news spread like lightening and particularly affected the youth. It was the subject of numerous press articles and conversations and discussions in all sorts of social mileux. "Nowogrodek" became perhaps the best-known slogan among the youth organizations and the workers. Little by little, some organizations went from talking to action. Self-defense circles, although not yet very big, began to be set up by Zionist and socialist youth groups (the Hashomer Hatzair Scouts, which became radicalized, and Hehalutz, with Dror, its youth branch).

At about the same time, the far-left started to become more radical and more active. In March 1942, an agreement was reached between the PPR cell in the ghetto and the Jewish Workers' Party, the left Poale Zion. In conformity with the program of struggle against fascism and the Nazi occupiers, the two groups organized a united front, the Anti-Fascist Bloc. Hashomer Hatzair joined them. A joint political leadership was constituted and a joint combat organization began to be set up. Its aim was to carry out general political action and become the Jewish branch of the national movement of liberation fighters. If the ghetto were threatened with annihilation, it would be transformed into an organization for the self-defense of the Jewish masses.

Shortly after, Hehalutz, Dror and the right Poale Zion-CS, ideologically close to the first two organizations, also joined the Anti-Fascist Bloc. Thus the united front now included all of the workers' organizations except the Bund, which continued to carry out its own independent political action and propaganda and at that time showed no concrete interest in self-defense or combat.

Fairly quickly, the Anti-Fascist Bloc set up a combat organization, divided into groups of five people each, and began to train them systematically. The lack of arms and material was a real problem for

---

the area around that city, the three Bielski brothers organized a well-armed partisan unit as well as "family camps" that the partisans took care of.

the group, especially severe at the beginning but persisting throughout its existence. Nevertheless the organization began to work to expand. One of the events that had spurred this development was a night-time massacre during the month of April[8] – "explained" by the German authorities and the Judenrat as an act of reprisal against underground political activity in the ghetto and the circulation of the many illegal newspapers attacking the occupiers and those who carried out their orders. In May and June of 1942, the ranks of the Jewish anti-fascist combat organization grew to 500 people. A drop-off occurred in mid-June. On June 20, 1942, the Gestapo arrested the two main PPR leaders in the ghetto, who were also members of the combat organization's general staff. They were both murdered a few days later. In the wake of these arrests, the Anti-Fascist Bloc's apparatus had to be reorganized and new contacts established. This necessitated a temporary slowdown in the growth of the combat organization. [This "temporary slowdown" is an understatement. As cited in the preceding chapter, Cukierman speaks not of a slowdown but of the organization disbanding.]

It was not long – just prior to the beginning of the Nazi "removal operation" – before the organization once again became active, relying above all on the members of the youth organizations. The lack of arms continued to be its main concern. The atmosphere of terror and growing oppression made it practically impossible to obtain weapons in the ghetto, which was now almost hermetically sealed. Equally insufficient was the number of instructors qualified to teach the art of war. [The ZZW, for its part, included many trained regular army officers and non-coms.] The steadily worsening state of depression among the ghetto's population inevitably affected the morale of the combat organization's members as well, especially the least courageous among them. Further, there was a sorely-felt lack of practice and military training, even among the most enthusiastic

8. During the night of April 17 (between Monday night and Tuesday morning), the Gestapo murdered more than 50 people in the ghetto, among them many people who had been in hiding.

and devoted fighters. The combat organization was simply not up to tasks as enormous and difficult as those posed by the "removal operation." *There were no other combat groups.* [My emphasis – MA] Rumors circulated about a "Revisionist" group (a far-right Zionist organization founded by partisans of Jabotinsky), but its existence was never manifested by any activity. [Chronologically, this is the first "denial" text in regard to the ZZW.] The bourgeois parties were adrift and without organized cadres.

2. THE POPULATION'S REACTION IN THE FACE OF THE "REMOVAL OPERATION"

The Nazi "Grossaktion" in Warsaw, the "removal operation," began on July 22, 1942.

The population sensed the danger without realizing, for the moment, that "removal" meant death. [From my own childhood memories it seems that my family understood the significance of the removal, but that we thought it would not touch us.] A wave of panic shook the ghetto. People's first reaction was to try and save their lives by obtaining a job – any job – in a German company. There was a terrible rush to seek employment in the "shops." After a few days of all but universal panic, the representatives of all the political groups and other activists held a conference. They discussed the new situation. The members of the groups that made up the Anti-Fascist Bloc declared that this was "the beginning of the end," the beginning of the total annihilation of the Warsaw ghetto. They argued that under these conditions the ghetto's people had to be called to resist the occupiers. The Bund's representatives adopted a similar but slightly less radical position. Opposed were the leaders of the bourgeois groups and especially the leaders of Agudat (Orthodox Jews) and the "General" (bourgeois) Zionists. [This repetition of the attribution of blame to the bourgeoisie is not a translation error; it is clearly deliberate since Berman had plenty of time, between the writing of this essay in 1943 and its first publication in Israel in 1959, to reread and correct his work. In 1959, Berman was a politician in

Israel and the General Zionists were an important opposition party at that point.] The non-party activists also held that open opposition to the Germans would be premature. The conference went no further than deciding, first, to appoint a standing commission to closely follow the development of events and, when the time was right, possibly issue a call for active resistance and, second, to appeal to the Jewish population, through the intermediary of the organizations represented at the conference, for passive resistance to the Order Police [the Jewish police] who at the beginning were carrying out the "removal operation" by themselves. In fact, each of the organizations put out manifestos addressed to the people as a whole and appeals to the Jewish police to refuse to carry out German orders and take part in the murder of their brothers and sisters. But none of this had any effect whatsoever on the unfolding of events. Of course there were quite a few individual acts of passive resistance to the Jewish police. Usually these were spontaneous actions by people who had been arrested and the police tried to put an end to them quickly. Most people were not yet ready for active resistance during the first phase of the "operation," despite the agitation by the most active fighters and the stories brought back by refugees from various cities and areas who had learned through their own bitter experience what the "removal" was about (especially those removed from Lublin and the surrounding area).

What were the reasons for this attitude on the part of the majority? Here we will examine only the main ones.

1) The Tragedy of Illusions

Ceaseless and constantly renewed illusions were the main reason for the passivity of the masses at that time. Almost everyone continued to fool themselves throughout the deportations.

No one wanted to admit that the Nazis were out to annihilate all Jews as a people, or that Warsaw's Jews in particular faced complete physical destruction. They didn't want to believe that the Germans would dare to murder almost 400,000 people.

On the basis of a decree issued by the German authorities, at the beginning it was assumed that only those without jobs would be "removed." Since the number of employed people and their families was estimated to be about 200–250,000 people, it was thought that only 100–150,000 people were targeted for deportation. The ensuing work-certificate "psychosis" was a direct result of that illusion.

The second tragic illusion was about what would happen to the deportees. In general, everyone knew that children and old people were being sent to their death. But for a long time it was wrongly believed that working-age men and women would be shipped to the East to live in other ghettos or to work camps. It was not until a week after the beginning of the "operation" that disturbing news about the fate of the deportees began to filter back into the ghetto. Right away, the authorities had a poster put up on the ghetto walls to deny the "lies" circulating in the ghetto; they claimed that the Jews shipped out were all being sent to the East.

At that point postcards began to arrive, it was said, from Brzesc, Siedlce and Kozienice. Supposedly they were from deportees who wrote that they were "alive and working." No one actually saw these postcards, but this kind of rumor swept through the ghetto and set people's minds at ease. In short, people's survival instincts, their will to live, led them to constantly put a positive spin on facts that really did not warrant that interpretation. In the same way that often occurs with the terminally ill, many people entered a state of complete denial.

These incessant illusions also involved the so-called end of the "operation." Every few days a new rumor would claim that "the operation was coming to an end," that "tomorrow or the day after, the operation would be over." The slightest let-up in the pace of the deportations, a soothing word from an SS man or Gestapo agent or even some meaningless gesture was immediately taken as "proof" that the deportations were about to stop.

In addition to the Germans and their "removal general staff," who masterfully stage-managed this tragedy of illusions, the Judenrat and the Jewish police, the executive organs of the German "column of destruction," also played their role. From the beginning of the "operation" to the end, they confirmed these reassuring rumors and even fanned them. To a great extent the passivity of the Jewish population during this period can be considered a consequence of their attitude. The Judenrat officials and especially the top functionaries and the police believed that they were "untouchable" and did everything possible to oppose the propagation of the idea of resistance. Yet in the end most of the Judenrat functionaries and employees were "liquidated." During the last stage of the operation, in mid-September 1942, the Jewish police force was also decimated, its ranks reduced from 2,000 to about 240 officers. [See Bednarczyk, below.]

The illusions harbored by the laboring masses were a particularly tragic factor in holding back armed resistance. Indeed, during the first few weeks of the operation they were convinced that they, at least, were protected. After all, didn't German orders exempt employees of public agencies and private enterprises from involuntary deportation? Hadn't various top SS and Gestapo officers assured that those individuals engaged in productive activities would not be removed? As a result, the passive masses were quite understandably hostile to the idea of active resistance, and even the more militant masses were lukewarm on the subject of self-defense. If we take into consideration that the combat organization and the workers' groups of which it was constituted were counting on the support – the active support – of the working masses, it is easy to understand why this organization found itself in a very difficult position. It found itself way out on a limb at that point, socially speaking, unable to rely even on the moral support of the masses. It was a general staff without an army and without reserves.

Still, the illusions of the working masses were short-lived. Within a few weeks of the start of the "operation," the "column of destruction" began to clean out the factories and all the various workshops.

But some of those who worked in the shops continued to cling to their illusions. During the last stage of the "operation," since the "removal office" had decreed that all factories above a given size would retain a certain contingent of employees, many workers fooled themselves into thinking that if they numbered among them, their lives would be saved. Right up until the last day, this kind of false hope paralyzed the will to resist and fight.

During the last stage of the "operation," the grand "selection" among the surviving ghetto population began on September 6, 1942. At that point about 60–70,000 people were chosen to be deported, i.e., killed. Of the 105,000 inhabitants, only some 35,000 were left alive, most of them employed in shops or German subsidiaries. (To this should be added the approximately 10–15,000 people in hiding, the illegals called "cave people.") After the "operation," there were about 50,000 in all.[9]

The apparently incomprehensible fact that people reported for "removal" at Umschlagplatz willingly and en masse gives an idea of the tragic strength of these illusions. Some people were so desperate that they probably knew they were going to be killed but no longer cared. Starving, persecuted, homeless and propertyless, and, above all, without any surviving relatives since their families had been taken during previous round-ups, they gave themselves up out of sheer hopelessness. But the majority of these "volunteers," including an enormous number of healthy young people able to work, fooled themselves into thinking that they would be sent to work camps. The deadline for volunteering was put off twice. Even though by the second time the ration of bread and margarine was brought down to a kilo per person [other sources mention marmelade, not margerine], volunteers continued to pour in. Thus the ghetto police were able to send thousands of people to their death without the slightest effort.

2) A Climate of Terror

Continual illusions and the false hopes of being able to survive that lasted right up to the last moment were not the only obstacles

9. This figure is too low. At that time, about 70,000 inhabitants remained in the ghetto. See chapter 8, "The Uprising."

holding back the armed resistance. Equally important was the psychological state of the population as a result of the situation in which they had been forced to live since the creation of the ghetto, and especially the climate that prevailed since the beginning of the "removal operation" in 1942. What made these psychological conditions unprecedented in their experience was that the Nazis treated Jews like subhumans, "Untermenschen."

The Jews had been turned into outlaws. The only "law" that applied to them was that of absolute arbitrariness. It was quite usual for Germans to wander through the ghetto with a horsewhip or a pistol in their hand, hitting passersby in the face and on the body and often shooting at them as if they were rabbits. Any German could do whatever he wanted with the Jews in the ghetto. Germans driving through the ghetto streets in trucks had a special way of amusing themselves. They would beat pedestrians on the head with their rifle butts, clubs or canteens. The frequent round-ups in the street and the shipments to work camps, the torture chambers, constant shootings, numerous acts of humiliation by the guards at the checkpoints (people were ordered to take off their hats and anyone who responded too "slowly" was smacked in the face, etc.) [this happened in the ghetto streets as well – as a child I witnessed such scenes over and over again] and other similar techniques applied over a long period of time eventually created an atmosphere of ceaseless terror and panic. The ghetto's inhabitants ceased to react like people in normal society and became an enormous mass of prisoners in a kind of concentration camp sealed off from the world. Inevitably, this internment soon had a powerful psychological effect, distorting their emotional reactions. Their utter vulnerability to the continual attacks and humiliation unleashed by all-powerful and violent oppressors became a prime psychological factor in the sense of powerlessness and the passivity spreading among the ghetto masses.

The "removal operation" unleashed a climate of terror that grew stronger week by week and day by day as the "operation" intensified. When the ghetto police handed over the leadership of this process to the SS and their "ethnic" auxiliaries (Ukrainian, Latvian and Lithuanian fascists), the whole thing became the most frightful nightmare in history. [Does Berman really mean to say that the shipment of 6,000 people a day to their deaths by the Jewish police acting alone, without the participation of the Germans and their non-Jewish auxiliaries, was less of a nightmare?] Such a situation would have been difficult to stand even for a few days, and yet this nightmare was to last for many weeks, almost two months in total.

Every day, and, at the end, every night as well, the inhabitants were in an unbearable state of terror. Hundreds of thousands of people had become hunted animals surrounded by deathtraps on every side. Under these conditions, how could the ghetto's people organize mass resistance? How could they muster the necessary willpower and mental concentration? It is quite understandable that under these conditions the majority of people were in such a state that they had become walking balls of nerves.

It was not until August 28, five weeks after the "operation" began, when hundreds of thousands of people had already been deported, that a chronicler noted: "We pretty much know what happened to the deportees: Treblinka. This place is surrounded by a thick wall of silence but some news does reach us." Illusions, false hopes and the unbearable climate of terror were the main reasons for the passivity of the population at that time. Other obstacles – doubts and remorse – were holding back certain people active in community work.

3) Barriers and Doubts

At the previously-mentioned meeting, as well as in many heated conversations during the first stage of the "operation," certain community workers, and particularly those belonging to bourgeois circles [the bourgeois is repeatedly blamed here], put forward numerous doubts and constraints regarding the concept of waging armed struggle under the conditions prevailing in the ghetto. They often emphasized that they themselves were willing, that they personally wanted nothing more than revenge, to take up arms and fight, but that after coldly analyzing the situation, they had concluded that such a leap had to be prevented. The doubts most commonly used were the following:

a) Collective Responsibility

The Warsaw ghetto was a concentration camp and even though the German liquidation of the Jewish population was in full spate, any act of resistance whatsoever or any attempt to take revenge against the Germans would provoke the immediate extermination of the entire Jewish population trapped in the ghetto like a cage. Given the unfavorable balance of forces…between the Jews in the ghetto and the militarily powerful occupiers, the Germans would take the slightest act of resistance as a convenient and sufficient excuse to murder every single inhabitant…. Such an act would not be one of self-defense but of desperation, a collective suicide. Of course it might have an enormous moral impact, becoming an historical gesture full of tragic pathos. But who gave us the right to sacrifice tens and perhaps even hundreds of thousands of human lives for the sake of such a gesture? How could we take responsibility for the lives of others? Members of the combat organization often came up against this argument. The specter of collective responsibility continued to paralyze the masses. This argument was raised at a time when people still believed that after the operation was over, at least 100–150,000 would remain alive in the ghetto. Those opposed to resistance bolstered their arguments by pointing out that it would have little effect on the struggle against the occupier. They did not believe that such a "collective suicide" would have much of an effect, in the world or even in Poland; they didn't think it could spur further struggle.

Consequently, some of them questioned the social impact of the actions of teachers such as Janusz Korczak who had accompanied their children to their deaths, even though perhaps a few of them could have saved themselves. Certainly their actions were understandable from a psychological point of view and ethically very laudable. Since they felt as close to their pupils as members of their own families, these teachers refused to abandon them as they embarked on their last journey. But nevertheless, from the point of view of the interests of society, certain activists asked themselves, wouldn't it have been better if Korczak and dozens of other teachers had stayed alive so as to continue to serve society in the perhaps not-distant future? Didn't they sacrifice their lives in vain?

b) Social and Political Doubts

Similar discussions about whether or not resistance was worth it also took place among the workers during the first stage of the "operation." Although nearly all the workers' parties and all of their youth organizations had chosen the camp of active resistance and joined the Anti-Fascist Bloc's combat organization, some members of certain workers' groups opposed this policy. They also raised the specter of collective responsibility, but backed it up with social and political considerations. Their arguments were as follows: If there were any collective resistance in the ghetto, the Germans' first response would be to massacre the workers in the shops who had at least some chance of survival, however minimal. The occupiers would immediately suspect the workers of being behind such acts, and rightly so. No matter how small the chances for survival among the workers and young people employed in the shops, who had the right to cause the certain death of all the masses of proletarians and youth, so full of enthusiasm and ideologically committed and self-sacrificing, and thus capable of playing an important role not only in some "collective suicide" but also in the struggle against the occupiers and against fascism? Wouldn't it be better to do everything possible to spare the working class cadres and save them from immediate annihilation for the sake of a real struggle for liberation in the future?

It should be emphasized that while such discussions were taking place, the ghetto received word of the opening of the second front, the mobilization of the German forces in France, etc. It was a period of fairly optimistic predictions. The ghetto's workers thought that the chances for victory would soon shift in favor of the Soviet Union and the Allies. From this there arose an ardent desire to survive and live to see this victory. But these discussions in workers' circles soon ran out of steam. The march of events completely passed them by during the subsequent stages of the "operation" as certain illusions evaporated, especially those concerning the security and chances of survival of the workers in the shops and more generally everyone who worked in them. Little by little, the masses of workers became ready to act.

c) *The Lack of Arms and Material*

One of the main things that suppressed the idea of taking military action was the lack of arms and material. Despite the enormous efforts of the combat organization, it had not been possible to procure additional arms, mainly due to the almost airtight sealing-off of the ghetto and the halt of smuggling with the beginning of the "operation" (the checkpoints were closed and "ethnic" auxiliaries posted all along the wall). Even before the "operation," the combat organization had no more than a handful of revolvers meant to be used for training [as we have seen in chapter 2, Cukierman speaks of having only one gun]. During meetings and discussions, people were sharply critical of the Polish underground combat organizations for not having helped the Jewish fighters more by giving them guns.

Tragic illusions, the climate of terror, and objective as well as subjective obstacles, made any act of resistance impossible during the first stage of the "operation."

3. THE RESISTANCE DURING THE INTENSIFICATION OF THE "OPERATION"

After a few weeks, as the "operation" widened its target and became more bestial, the will to take up arms and resist began to crystallize, especially among the social workers.

At the insistence of the youth organizations, representatives of all the political groups and the social workers met once again. [See the remarks above concerning the previous general meeting.] This time, a number of activists present at the first meeting were missing –

for example, the head of the left Poale-Zion in the ghetto, Sz. Z. [Szachno Zagan (Sagan)], a leading member of the Anti-Fascist Bloc who had been caught in a round-up and sent to his death.

This meeting was marked by the tension between the "youth" and the "elders." The representatives of the youth organizations declared that they wouldn't wait any longer and had decided to take up arms. So as not to feel that they were acting all alone, they asked the representatives of the older people in society to give them their moral support. The delegates of the political groups and social workers conveyed their esteem for the young people's fighting spirit, and their sympathy, in advance, for the inevitable victims of any such combat. Yet in the speeches, particularly those of the bourgeois activists [once again!], the doubts and reservations just mentioned were expressed once again. When the meeting was over, neither the leftist parties nor the youth were satisfied.... In fact, the meeting failed to reach any concrete agreement. During that period, the youth groups were working out all sorts of plans, such as burning down their shops, opening breaches in the wall around the ghetto in order to flee, wiping out the checkpoints and attacking many of the SS teams taking part in the "operation," etc. But they did not have the necessary wherewithal to carry out such plans.

This was the period that saw the founding of the *Zydowska Organizacja Bojowa* [the ZOB, Jewish Combat organization], made up of the fighting groups of the Anti-Fascist Bloc.[10] The ZOB issued a call to the people to burn down the shops and fight back during the round-ups. This message was repeated in posters that supporters tried to put up on the walls. But the masses did not respond at that point. Certain shopowners were so maddened and fearful of the consequences that they tried to rip down these posters from the

10. As we have seen, this resistance organization made up of members of the Communist Party and leftist Zionist organizations had crumbled by July. The ZOB was founded on July 28, 1942, by a small number of people and was inactive after that time except for the attempt to kill the Jewish police chief, Szerynski; as we will see in the following chapter it was reconstituted at the end of 1942, at which point it would also include members of the left Zionist groups mentioned, the PPR and the Bund.

walls of their small factories. The youth organization leaders were dismayed. On the night of August 20, 1942, a month after the "operation" began, ZOB fighters committed the first acts of sabotage by burning down a number of shops. That was also the date on which the ZOB fired the first shot.[11] A fighter[12] seriously wounded Jozef Szerynski, head of the Jewish police.

As the "removal operation" intensified, and the ghetto population learned the hard way just what a traitorous and murderous role the Jewish police were playing in the ghetto, the ZOB decided to "take care" of those carrying out German orders, i.e., the Jewish police and their leadership. On the walls of the police stations appeared small posters with the slogans, "Death to the Jewish police who have helped the Germans murder 200,000 of their brothers and sisters! Let them be covered with ignominy!" The attack on the head of the Jewish police, "Colonel" Szerynski, a former Polish national police inspector for the Lublin district, had a huge impact on the ghetto. Szerynski (whose name was formerly Szynkman) was the very embodiment of the "virtues" of a police officer, an excessively zealous cop whose colleagues called him "the hammer." Although he had never before dealt with the Jewish population, he organized the ghetto "Order Police" in a professional and effective way, attracting a certain number of ex-officers and non-coms [from the army reserves] as well as a considerable number of people from the intelligentsia, especially lawyers.[13] For the most part, they were people with no moral or ideological fiber or any sense of honor at all. A number of criminals joined the police, along with individuals linked to the Gestapo. A bullet in the head was exactly what the

11. According to another, politically neutral source, it was the Revisionists who shot Szerynski, but the accounts of the ZOB members seem more reliable on this point. See Hillel Seidman, *The Warsaw Ghetto Diaries* (Southfield, MI: Targum Press, 1997), p. 188 (translated from Hebrew in 1946).
12. Izrael Kanal, also known as "Akiba"; the gun Kanal used to shoot at Szerynski was furnished to the ghetto resistance by the Warsaw section of the PPR.
13. "It is true that initially, there were some better and more honest people…[including] the lawyers Gombinski, Goldsztejn, Ettinger, Lewkowicz, Przeborskia and others." Seidman, *Warsaw Ghetto Diaries*, p. 154.

Jewish police chief Szerynski deserved. But the attack was not entirely successful. The bullets hit him in the neck and face, wounding his jaw and salivary glands without killing him. The only gain was that he was confined to bed for a long period. Leadership of the "operation" then passed into the hands of Lejkin.[14] Since the police were considered a disgrace, this attack was welcomed by the population. The Judenrat and police spread the rumor that the attempt had been made by a Polish socialist. It is worth noting that the Germans did not react to this event; the settling of accounts within the ghetto was not of any particular concern to them. Yet the fact that the Germans failed to carry out any reprisals against the population for this highly symbolic act concentrating the Jewish people's hatred of traitors and those who carried out Nazi orders could only encourage more of the same.

Around this time, the idea of sending some of the ghetto youth to join the partisan bands in the forests became very popular in ZOB circles and especially its left-wing (the PPR, the left Poale-Zion and Hashomer Hatzair). In the face of tremendous objective and subjective difficulties, there was a powerful attraction to the idea of sending some of the youth, the most "Aryan-looking" among them if possible, to fight against the enemy, not in a self-defense action inside the ghetto but as part of the war being waged outside its wall by the partisans. But this plan was very difficult to put into practice. There was not enough money to finance such a move, the wall would have to be crossed at the very height of the "operation" when surveillance around the wall was especially intense, and once beyond the wall these young people would need papers and temporary hideouts and would face other problems. All these factors meant that the idea of sending fighters to the woodlands could not be brought to fruition. Only a few dozen youth could be gotten out of the ghetto; and some of them died along the way, due, among other reasons, to badly organized transportation and poorly established contacts with the various partisan bands. Only a few were able

14. Jakub Lejkin was to be killed on October 29, 1942 (see following chapter).

to reach their destination and join up. As of this moment [it will be recalled that this was written in January 1943] we have had no news of them. Thus it is difficult to evaluate if and to what degree these efforts have been successful.

This was the culminating point of the "removal operation." The terror became completely unbearable. Now the streets were empty all day and all night as the Germans and their Ukrainian auxiliaries shot at anyone in their path as if they were small game.

The difficulty and sometimes complete impossibility of movement within the ghetto slowed down the expansion of the combat organization, which had already suffered major losses during the first "operation." For instance, on September 3, 1942, two ZOB members were killed. Both of them were Hashomer Hatzair leaders. The first, J.K. [Josef Kaplan], one of the eminent founders of that movement, was arrested by the Germans and murdered the next day. The second, Sz. B. [Szmuel Breslaw, called Bresler in some other documents], a well-known journalist whose stories appeared in *Jutrznia* and *Przedwiosnie*, two high-quality underground newspapers published by the movement, was stopped and searched on the street by the SS. They found a switchblade knife on him and shot him dead on the spot. There was another serious loss a few days later when a raid on a shop led to the capture of J.L. [Jozef Lewartowski], one of the main leaders of the PPR section in the ghetto, a veteran revolutionary worker activist loved and admired by all.

Despite these heavy losses, the ZOB continued to be the organization whose ranks included the most active and most courageous people in the ghetto.[15]

This firsthand account is consistent with the facts, except for the last paragraph. The ZOB did exist on January 17, 1943, the date on which the author wrote this text and described it to the Polish authorities, but it scarcely existed at all during the time of the

15. Adolf Berman, "*O ruchu oporu w getcie warszawkim: Refleksje*," *Biuletyn ZIH*, no. 29 (1959).

events described. The Anti-Fascist Bloc that had preceded it had accomplished nothing and quickly dissolved itself; the ZOB had at most a few handguns; only one according to Cukierman, its leader at that time.

Further, Berman claims that the ZZW was only a rumor and achieved nothing. Yet the ZZW did exist, as we have seen, and had been armed and carrying out training for more than two years. The ZZW was the only organization that was in a position to oppose the massacre. But, as Berman's silence truthfully implies, it, too, did nothing. Why? Berman points the blame at the bourgeois and religious forces.

Bednarczyk was a Polish nationalist, a practicing Catholic and politically on the right. He was a leading military figure in the Polish nationalist organization and the ZZW. The contrast between Bednarczyk and Berman – a Zionist, atheist Jew, Marxist and representative of the ZOB – could not be more dramatic. Yet the accounts given by the two men are astonishingly similar, except, of course, in regard to the roles they attribute to their respective resistance organizations. The two authors had nothing in common but their daily experience in the ghetto. Bednarczyk's account follows:

> In June 1942 the Polish resistance movement that worked with the ZZW – the only Jewish military organization in the ghetto at that time – informed the latter of a growing number of disquieting developments. The first transfers of Jews from small ghettos in the region to the Warsaw ghetto took place in the spring of 1942. The Germans greatly enlarged the camp at Treblinka, the camp nearest to Warsaw; the Judenrat constructed various installations and furnished workers for this project. The ranks of the SS and police in the district swelled ceaselessly and their commanding officer was replaced. High German officials constantly toured the ghetto, which the Jews themselves could not help but notice. Numerous German "entrepreneurs" appeared in the ghetto and set up workshops. They widely advertised that the employment they were providing would guarantee the security of the Jews. Some of the severe policies to which

the ghetto had been subjected were relaxed, and a certain increase in the number of children attending school was authorized. [This information is consistent with Czerniakow's diary cited above.] Reassuring denials were issued by Auerswald and Brandt. The leading Jewish Gestapo stooges, Kohn, Heller, Gancwajch, Sterfeld, Grajer, Erlich and Fürst, spread the rumor that there would be no further removals; supposedly this was confirmed by the exclusion of a few streets around the edge of the ghetto in June 1942. Finally, it was reported that 60 railway boxcars were being sent to Umschlagplatz. All these were disturbing signs that a major storm was brewing up. The OW-KB intelligence agents who worked in the German entourage confirmed this information.

In light of foreseeable future events, and aware of the dubious effect of any armed Jewish resistance [that this could be written by the man directly responsible for aid to the armed Jewish resistance by all the Polish resistance organizations is highly significant], the Polish resistance movement that took care of the ghetto and the ZZW insisted that the youth and whatever remained of the intelligentsia be evacuated from the ghetto as quickly as possible. On behalf of the OW-KW general staff, I discussed this with chairman Czerniakow many times. Unfortunately, nothing was done in this regard, mainly because of the position taken by the Judenrat. Even the announced liquidation of the Lublin district in April 1942 was not a sufficient argument.

My last conversation with Czerniakow took place on July 21, 1942, in the presence of the ZZW high command. Taking part in this meeting were a dozen members of the ZZW general staff, including its head, Captain Dawid Moryc Apfelbaum, the commanders of the two companies, Lieutenant Leon Rodal and Second Lieutenant Henoch Federbusz, and Mojsze Weisstok, commander of the freshly-expanded 3rd company. Also attending were January Dluzyk, Alojzy Junarski, Leonard Pisz, Henryk Lipszyc, Bialoskora, the lawyer Dawid Szulman, Kazimierz Mendelson-"Kalmyk," Roman Weinsztok, Maurycy Golfarb and others. Adam Czerniakow and two rabbis were invited to this meeting as representatives of the ghetto's civil society. The ZZW leadership and the very prudent Czerniakow agreed that if the rumors of the planned liquidation of the Jewish quarter proved correct, it would be time to take up arms to save the honor of the Jewish people and not let ourselves be massacred helplessly. At the same time, there was a general awareness that such a fight had no chance of success because the ZZW was not adequately prepared and lacked sufficient forces. That struggle was also meant to be an act of protest against the total failure of the Western powers to provide any support. But unfortunately, and against the will of the majority, the position of the two rabbis prevailed. They cited Job, Book V, verses 17–20, and succeeded in dragging the participants into religious mysticism, claiming that everyone had to die for the glory of God. Rabbi Nisenbaum opposed that approach. Despite the teachings of the Talmud, he called upon the Jews to fight to save their own lives.

This is why the insurrection did not break out in the ghetto in July 1942. The ZZW subordinated itself to the decision of the spiritual guides of the people. [It has been clearly and fully confirmed that the rabbis were rabidly opposed to armed resistance. But it does not follow from that that they alone bear the responsibility for our passivity, as Bednarczyk concludes far too eagerly, apparently out of solidarity with the ZZW.]

Furthermore, from the start of the liquidation operation, the ZZW was cut off from two main arms depots, the one ont 28 Smocza Street and the other in the Church of the Blessed Virgin, thus reducing its effective combat capacity. Also worth mentioning is the negative appraisal of the Jew's fighting spirit made by Marceli Nowotko (cf. *Nowe Drogi*, no. 4/61), first secretary of the Central Committee of the PPR [Communist Party]. [As we will see later, the commander-in-chief of the AK was in agreement with the first secretary on this point.]

On July 22, 1942, the Gestapo, with Höfle and Brandt at their head, threw a cordon around the ghetto manned by police, SS men, Latvians and Ukrainians. Then they marched into the Judenrat offices.

Aiming to frighten everyone and make them obey, they had arrested numerous Judenrat members on July 21, including Gepner, Jaszunski, Witner and some other well-known personalities. Many of them were killed right away. They avidly sought engineer Czerniakow's wife, but luckily failed.

On the afternoon of July 21, I was in the ghetto, not far from Grzybowska Street. I heard gunfire. It turned out that there had been shooting in the apartment of the antique dealer Abe Gutnajer.

Professor Raszeja and a ZZW member, Dr. Pollak, were killed that day. Pollak's wife, Babetta, later told me that Raszeja had a safe-conduct pass for the ghetto, but the outfit from Lublin who had come for the rich antiques dealer Gutnajer killed him anyway.

Höfle ordered the Judenrat and Czerniakow to put up posters that he himself had written with the orders to report for deportation. The first batch of people to be deported, some 6,000 were selected. To trick the ghetto's people and calm their fears, Höfle and his accomplices kept secret the dates and size of the deportations to follow. Thus they encouraged the daily rebirth of the false hope that what happened yesterday would not happen again and that those who remained would be spared.

Another perfidious psychological maneuver carried out by Höfle and his cronies was to start the first "removal operation" with the deportation of prisoners, poor people from the shelters[16] (who were mostly refugees from other ghettos, considered dead weight by most ghetto residents), the elderly and children, or in other words, people unfit for work. The lie that those unfit for labor would be brutally liquidated while the rest would be sent to work gave most of the population hope that indeed work camps would be their destination. In conformity with the posted notices, the Germans gave the able-bodied poor three kilos of bread and a kilo of marmalade (in the operations of July 29, 30 and 31, and August 1, 2 and 3, 1942). This was another psychological trick that unfortunately succeeded

16. This is a reference, mentioned previously, to the housing for the poor provided by the Judenrat.

in persuading people that they were really going to be shipped east to work. They told themselves, "The Germans are cold and brutal – why would they waste money on feeding people who were going to die?" The very poorest didn't care if this argument was true or not. As they were shipped out, most of them, for the first time during that year of 1942, could stuff themselves with bread.

At the beginning of the operation, the *Umsiedlungsamt* (removal office) and its chief, the Reichsamtsleiter Waldemar Schön, had the Jewish Order Police and Gestapo stooges spread the word that the removal would only apply to those without work, that it would be limited to 60,000 people and would last only until August 1, 1942. By encouraging a passive attitude among the majority of employed Jews in this way, the Germans succeeded in breaking the bonds of Jewish solidarity and preventing armed resistance. Particular mention should be made of the lawyer Jakub Lejkin, deputy-chief of the Jewish police (whom Höfle made chief-of-police in charge of the removal on July 22, 1942). He earned special "merit" due to his personal role in the destruction of the solidarity among Jews and their fighting spirit. Höfle had so much confidence in Lejkin that during the first week of the operation it was carried out by the Jewish police alone, without German help. The Jewish police worked hard and conscientiously to meet the daily quota of 6–7,000 people. Later, the Germans themselves could do no better.

The Germans were backed up by the Jewish police throughout the operation. The Jewish police commander "Colonel" Szerynski (Szynkman) showed a special zeal during that period. He had been in prison for smuggling. Brandt, the Gestapo officer in charge of the ghetto, had him released specially for this occasion. Szerynski was rigorously supported by the whole Judenrat council, chief among them the engineer Lichtenbaum.

Only Adam Czerniakow opposed the operation. He refused to sign Höfle's first deportation notice issued on July 22, 1942. This attitude earned him a beating. When Höfle ordered him to sign a request to the German authorities that Jews be deported because of overpopulation in the ghetto and the typhus epidemic, and fully aware that he could do nothing to stop the liquidation operation, Czerniakow committed suicide on July 23, 1942.

All the Jews and Jewish authorities refused to believe that the removal meant their final liquidation. One version of these events has it that even the leader of the Jewish communists, Icek Lewartowski, refused to believe it. People believed, or wanted to believe, in the authenticity of the letters from deported people, supposedly from "somewhere in the East," sent to their families still in Warsaw. But no one wanted to believe the stories told by people who had escaped from the trains bound for Treblinka, escapees who once back in Warsaw told the truth, like the words of Job, about the so-called "Eastern work camps." I heard this personally and talked about it with one of these escapees in Többens' shop on Prosta Street.

Czerniakow had reliable information about the results of these "removal operations" and finally he accepted the awful truth. By sacrificing his life he wanted to prove that despite the misery and humiliation to which they had been subjected…his beloved people had sons capable of heroism. In this way he hoped to cry out for the Jewish people's right to life. With his death, Czerniakow meant to tell the world (as he had previously promised to do) that there was no longer any hope.

The only way to survive in the ghetto at that point was to find a good hideout. They needed to wait for things to calm down and the German cordon to be removed – until some time in the future when it would become possible to flee the ghetto, at least for those few thousand fortunates whose lives could be saved.

After the first deportations of people from the refuges and orphans (we should recall the attitude of Dr. Janusz Goldszmit-Korczak who accompanied "his" beloved children into the box cars), Höfle gave orders that the inhabitants of entire neighborhoods should be taken by surprise and shipped out. Armed German units would encircle the designated areas and the Jewish police, accompanied by the Gestapo and the SS, would force people to come out of their homes, group them in columns and march them to the hospital emptied out for this purpose on Stawki Street at Umschalgplatz. There they would be loaded into boxcars. All this took place amid the cries of mothers separated from their children, the yelling and cursing of the Jewish police and the thuds of truncheons. The Germans often fired off a few shots. In fact, there was a lot of shooting because the Germans killed the aged and the sick on the spot. They also shot people they found hiding in apartments. Often, to save ammunition or for fun, they threw these people out of the window, and as they lay wounded and groaning stretched out on the sidewalk, they would kick them to death or smash in their heads with their heavy studded boots. The Germans or their auxiliaries, the Ukrainians, Latvians and Lithuanians, immediately separated mothers from their babies and killed them in front of them by smashing their heads against the wall of a house or by pulling their legs apart until it tore their bodies asunder.

The author of this account is conscious of the fact that today's readers will find it hard to believe this, and will have even greater difficulty believing that such inhuman acts occurred on a daily basis. Nevertheless, all of this really happened. I speak of it as someone who personally witnessed these scenes or heard the reports of other ZZW comrades.

Once the neighborhood was emptied, the columns of the unfortunate were marched off. Their clothing torn and in terror, people carried all sorts of odd objects, often whatever they happened to get their hands on. One might have a suitcase or a backpack readied in advance, another a cage with a canary inside, a violin or a cook pot, a fireplace poker or a chamber pot. The richest and most clever hid their fortune in these objects that seemed to be worthless and picked up at random. Sometimes the cook pot or poker was made of solid gold, merely covered with a layer of paint, meant to serve, if the owner successfully escaped, as the foundation stone of a new life. Of course, such successful flights were very rare.... The only real possibility was to try your chances before getting to Treblinka, but the route was bristling with Ukrainian and German guard posts. The Polish population along the railway were terrorized by the frequency and duration of these operations and could not risk providing significant help to any victims.

Some people would be "claimed" on the way to Umschlagplatz. Members of favored families, the families of policemen or Judenrat employees, would be taken out of the ranks of the less fortunate. In order to encourage loyal service, the Germans guaranteed such people immunity, at least for the first few weeks of the operation. The "claims" always proceeded in the same fashion. Some "privileged" person would station himself along the column's line of march in the company of a Jewish policeman or Stormtrooper, and in his presence they would yell out the name of the person he was looking for. For instance, a little man, the shame of Jewish lawyers, stands there while a cop shouts, "Mr. Lejkin's sister-in-law!" She hears and steps out of the ranks, while the others continue until they are loaded into the boxcars and sent to their death.

Atrocious scenes took place at Umschlagplatz where the unlucky destined for deportation were gathered. Szmerling, that foamy-mouthed Jewish police dog, was in charge of the square. On one side, the families and friends of the arrested would try to save their loved ones by offering sums of money amounting to thousands of marks, and on the other, the doomed themselves would try to save themselves by any means possible. No one who saw it will ever forget the violin concert given by a young musician who begged an SS man to take pity on him and his mother. The Stormtrooper was a music lover, and after being transported by the music and congratulating the young man for his skill and his knowledge of German composers, kicked him and locked him into a box car.... But the Jewish police, these zealous auxiliaries who were sometimes the worst of all during the "removal operation," finally got what was coming to them. Despite the enthusiasm with which, like all traitors and renegades, they served the Germans, the latter did not treat them very well. During the whole time of the operation, the streets of the ghetto and Umschlagplatz were littered with the corpses of dozens of policemen killed for not having come up with the required number of people to be deported.

After seven bloody weeks of operations, the Germans packed several hundred policemen and their families into the cattle cars and set them to Treblinka.[17] They walked to the trains without saying a word, submissive, their heads bent, without daring to look people around them in the eye – people lucky enough to be allowed a few more days of survival. Höfle ordered the killing of Kohn and Heller, the all-powerful trustees of the Gestapo in Warsaw. The Lublin outfit didn't have much love for these two because their interests clashed during the pillage. They were not able to come to an agreement with Grajer about how to share the booty and he squealed on them. A few diamonds found on them, meant for Brandt and not Höfle, brought their death.

With Höfle's agreement, Brandt and Hauptsturmführer Michalsen, the line officer in charge of the deportations on a daily basis, sent their Jewish auxiliaries to Treblinka. This was how orders were scrupulously and mercilessly carried out and the policy of genocide applied. It had all been worked out by the general staff with the creative inventiveness of Höfle. At first, there would be an appropriate co-existence between the Germans and the Jewish traitors of the police and the Judenrat, and then they would be sent to their death – this was the general rule throughout General Government territory…

Here a question comes to mind: what was the Polish resistance doing during the bloody days of the liquidation? Unfortunately, not much in comparison to what needed to be done. Because the Jewish quarter was sealed off tight at that time, the only access was through the underground passage leading from the convent of the Church of the Blessed Virgin on Leszno into the ghetto on the other side of the street. With the help of the ZZW, about 500 people were evacuated to the Aryan side via that route. A few dozen people were saved by Polish firemen (soldiers belonging to the Skala-KB). A further fifteen or so people who escaped from the Treblinka-bound trains were also rescued. A few of them were later brought back into the ghetto to alert the people about the real destination of the convoys.

---

17. Berman, who is quoted later on, gives the figure of 2,000 police, of whom 240 were spared.

It was also their job to tell people to hide. Within the limitations of our less than meager resources, we tried to do everything we possibly could under those conditions.[18]

THE VOICE OF A LEADING RELIGIOUS AUTHORITY

Cukierman, Berman and Bednarczyk all emphasize the responsibility of the religious representatives. Following are excerpts from the diary of H. Seidman, director of the Judenrat's department of religious affairs. His day-by-day description of events provides an insider's view of the attitude prevailing in religious circles:

Sunday, July 19 (1942). The news that a mass deportation may be coming is spreading rapidly.... A meeting of Jewish personalities and leaders has been called. [More than 20 people took part, a majority of them rabbis, along with representatives of all the political parties, including, this time, a Revisionist Zionist.] The first question on the table: Is it true? [...] The optimists say, there are so many of us and there is strength in numbers. A half-million people! They wouldn't dare. [...] There are some Christians and Germans who have a strong interest in the ghetto's continued existence. It's very profitable for them. [...] But above all, the ghetto produces a great deal. [...] The optimists put forward evidence to support their arguments: the opening of schools and kindergartens, the modification of "police hours," the authorization to start a teachers' training institute, the increase in food rations, etc. All of this indicates that the future holds more liberal policies. [...]

The pessimists respond, Of course they will dare. There is nothing the Nazis are not capable of. You can't believe anything they say. Furthermore, why would they make an exception of Warsaw? Won't the same thing happen in Warsaw as in Lublin, Tarnow and Cracow? [...] There's nothing stopping the Germans. We are faced

18. Bednarczyk, *Zycie codzienne warszawskiego getta*, pp. 70–76.

with an immense danger. We must figure out how to save ourselves. The pessimists win the day. You can see the anxiety written on everyone's face.

But how? What can we do to save ourselves?

All sorts of ideas and plans are sketched out. Gather large sums of money to bribe the Gestapo. Get such and such an amount of gold. Some people point out that the ranks of the Gestapo include special "extermination units." Others suggest sending a delegation to speak to the Governor of the Government, Frank, [...] in Cracow. It is proposed that shops be created on a grand scale so that Jews can be put to work; all those employed can be saved.

Shaking with nervousness, Joseph Kenigsberg, who has just come from Lublin where he had miraculously escaped deportation, recounts the horrifying details of the extermination perpetuated there. He insists that we must not let ourselves be numbed by illusions, that we have to do everything within our power to save the community from this threat. He and Zysie Frydman suggest that we secretly send an emissary to Switzerland, from where he could alert world public opinion. That England must give all Jews Palestinian citizenship, at least until the end of the war, the Americans must put us under their protection, Germans living abroad must be threatened with reprisals, a warning must be issued to the Nazis, the Pope must put out a special appeal, world public opinion must proclaim, must save, must, etc.

But how? We are locked in, imprisoned. How can we send an emissary to Switzerland when even crossing the street to the Aryan sector is forbidden and punishable by death? We are locked down, encircled by a terrible and merciless enemy. And even if we could get word to the outside world, would anyone listen? Would they react? Would our brothers and sisters abroad understand the danger this time, the danger of extermination? Could they stir the world's conscience? The world's conscience, that was it.

It becomes difficult to go on with these discussions. A sinister darkness falls over the narrow room. Black shadows spread across the walls and the faces and soon envelop the hearts of those gathered at this assembly of the representatives of the largest Jewish community in Europe. Slowly all our plans and all our impractical suggestions vanish into an unreal fog. Thus, gradually, we fall into utter despair.

We have been abandoned! This became more and more clear and obvious until finally it gave way to another sentiment: we are lost.

Slowly the meeting breaks up. People leave one by one so as not to attract attention. They leave through the back door and walk away furtively. I sneak down Krochmalna Street.... The street is lively, as always. Packed with people, their faces gaunt and their eyes dull. They hurry, some clearing their way through the crowd, running in search of a crust of bread. All they can think about is how to find what they need to stay alive. A hard-fought daily battle against starvation. It's all they can do to stay afloat, to keep from going under, to hold on. Will they be able to hold on? I feel as though I can see the shadow of the Angel of Death fall over these swarming masses. Will we be able to hold out? Will we survive?

I go home, feeling desperate, my heart closed tight against all hope.[19]

Note that in contrast to the accounts we have read of other meetings so far, all of which occurred within this same general timeframe and involved the same participants, or at least representatives of the same movements, there is no mention of any armed resistance and therefore no mention of the rabbis blocking it.

Seidman continues:

Tuesday, July 21...The streets are filled with hustle and bustle. No one is staying home. Everyone is hurrying somewhere. Where? Trying to find a position, a job. In the shops. The first thing people do is try to get hired at one of the German companies in the ghetto. For instance Schultz, Többens, Dhering, von Schöne...and so on. Any way they

19. Seidman, *Warsaw Ghetto Diaries*, pp. 44–48.

can. They use all sorts of connections [acquaintances and influence] and those that can proffer money. A job in a workshop costs a lot of money. The most energetic, those with the most initiative and a little money, start their own shop. Most of them are garment shops where they make apparel to be sold by German companies. They get some machines...Everybody roll up their sleeves and get to work! They can't do away with the workshops – that's one thing you can be sure of. But still everyone is very scared.

I walk back up Nowolipie Street. I go by the Schultz company located in the building owned by the Hassidic manufacturer Abraham Hendel.... People are crowded together in front of the two entrances to the factory at number 46. A lot of Orthodox Jews, in particular. Yeshiva students, rabbis, religious officials and ordinary Hassidic Jews. Thanks to Abraham Hendel, who runs the factory, it was easy for religious Jews to get hired there, whereas in other workshops it was difficult, if not impossible. That's why all the Orthodox Jews are running to Hendel's.

But it's hard to get through. The gates are closed. From time to time a door opens and a Jewish policeman lets in one or two waiting people, while outside thousands of people push and shove each other. The same scene is repeated in front of other shops....

In front of the W.B. Többens company on Leszno and Prosta streets, you can spot many leading members of the Zionist movement. Mendel Kirschenbaum...the Zionist notable, has influence there. In front of the Hoffmann company...on Nowolipki Street, I notice numerous Bundists. They hope to be hired there thanks to the influence of Bund leader Maurycy Orzech, who has a lot of money invested in this plant. As the scripture says, "Each of the faithful turns to the son of his art." Here the obvious meaning is this: they turn to fellow members of their party. Each man helps his neighbor as much as he can.

In front of the building at 80 Leszno Street where the Collegium used to be, now the offices of the German labor agency in the ghetto, once again there are thousands of people. (There is a violent stampede toward the closed doors.) This is where you get work cards proving that you're employed, that you work in a shop. The word is that people like that won't get deported.

Finally I get to my office on Grzybowska Street. More tumult: here people are trying to regularize religious marriages that haven't been registered with the marriage bureau. [The majority of Polish Jews at that time simply got married in front of a rabbi and didn't bother with a civil service.] Men who have found a job want to protect their wives. That means that they need to be able to show a marriage certificate. Such people wouldn't be deported, rumor has it.

In front of the Kehilla[20] and inside, once again there was much nervousness and agitation. Everyone wants a position, any job at all. It doesn't matter what kind. Just so that you can say, I'm employed. People use anything they can in this effort, any connection or pretext.... People with jobs won't be deported, or at least that's what they assure each other.

I go to Rabbi Yitzhak Meir Kanal's place...on number 6 Twarda Street. Here, too, I find enormous hoards of people. I ask someone what's going on. People are getting married. Young men who have a job in a workshop (or at the Kehilla) want to save unemployed girls. So everyone is getting married all at once. As fast as they can. All the Halutzim boys quickly marry all the Halutzot girls and all the Tsukunftist boys [members of the Bundist youth group] marry all the Tsukunftist girls. Young women who haven't yet found a husband try to find one among the crowd.[21]

AN ATTEMPT AT EXPLANATION

During the seven weeks of the summer of 1942, some 300,000 Jews (German sources give the figure of 310,322[22]) were taken to the train station, shipped to Treblinka and gassed. On the second day, when Czerniakow was told to sign a proclamation ordering a

20. Traditional name for the community; here it means the Judenrat.
21. Seidman, *Warsaw Ghetto Diaries*, 49–51.
22. Stroop, *The Stroop Report*, p. 3.

partial evacuation to the East, he decided to commit suicide and this act and his last letters bring out the truth (see chapter 4).

And the Judenrat continued its work. The Jewish police took care of most of the evacuation, and there was no resistance at all.

On September 13, after most of the Jewish Gestapo agents and members of the Judenrat and the Jewish police were finally either killed on the spot or shipped off to die in Treblinka, the Germans called off their "operation."

Thus the Germans were able to select and send to their deaths more than 300,000 people out of a population of over 400,000, using 200 Germans with no heavy weapons, a few hundred Baltic and Ukrainian auxiliaries and 2,000 unarmed Jewish cops. They suffered no losses and met no resistance. It is true that the Anti-Fascist Bloc, strongly motivated by the need to support the Soviet Union in its war efforts, had no arms, and their main component group, the Communists, despite their close links to the Polish Communists on the other side of the wall, could not get any because the latter, much less numerous than their Jewish comrades, were still unarmed themselves. But the ZZW, which was highly trained and relatively well armed, organized with a view to combat for two and a half years, did not fire a shot. The fact is that with the forces and weapons it had then, a strength similar to what it was to have in the April 1943 uprising to come, the ZZW, all by itself, could have overcome the unarmed Jewish police and pushed back – if only temporarily – the Germans and their auxiliaries, who were at that time much less numerous than they were to be in April 1943.

In juxtaposition to the four eyewitness accounts given above, various explanations – of various degrees of convincingness – can be put forward to try to explain this nightmarish and shameful passivity, although they cannot justify it.

In the summer of 1942, Germany was still going from triumph to triumph militarily. Except for Britain, the Soviet Union and the four neutral countries (Spain, Portugal, Sweden and Switzerland), all of Europe was either occupied, in the majority of cases, or under German puppet regimes such as those in Romania, Hungary,

Slovakia and Croatia. In Africa, the German and Italian troops under Rommel threatened Egypt and Palestine: they controlled all of North Africa, either directly or through the Vichy government. In the Soviet Union, the Germans had occupied the Ukraine, Byelorussia, the Baltic countries and the Crimea. They had taken millions of prisoners, and a segment of the population of those countries was so favorable to the Nazis that they volunteered to fight alongside them. The Germans had Leningrad under siege and were already in the outskirts of Moscow as they drove toward the Caucuses. Since the blitzkrieg occupation of Poland and the equally rapid capitulation of France, all the German offensives had been crowned with success with the exception of the decisive battle in the skies over Britain. German military power seemed unstoppable; there were resistance movements in many European countries but none even so much as dreamed of, let alone planned, an all-out attempt to take the cities. It seemed obvious that such a revolt would be smashed immediately and followed by horrific repression.

The Poles had a deeply rooted tradition of revolts and revolutions going back to the early nineteenth century. Traditionally and culturally, the main enemy was Russia, which had occupied most of Poland and its capital. Warsaw was twice partially destroyed in the wake of two nineteenth-century revolutions against Russia. The only model of success was the seesaw stratagem employed during World War I. After Prussia and Russia had been temporarily weakened in mutual combat, Polish independence was proclaimed in Warsaw, and when Russian troops, now sent by the Soviets, once again advanced on Warsaw, they were stopped and pushed back all the way to the Ukrainian heartland. Poland's military officers had all come out of that victory in 1920. All Poles were simultaneously anti-German, anti-Russian and more or less anti-Semitic. These three "antis" were only strengthened by the German atrocities, the Soviet stab in the back of the fall of 1939 and the atrocities that followed it, and the enthusiastic welcome of the Soviets and assiduous collaboration with them by a part of the Jewish population. Speaking in deliberate understatement, during a January

1940 cabinet meeting, General Sikorski presented the essence of the "three antis" in the following way:

> The Prime Minister stressed that under the Nazi occupation, the anti-Semitic mood declined considerably under the impact of the inhuman persecution of the Jews by the Germans. The Poles resent these persecutions. In the areas under Soviet occupation about 70% of the Jews behave with decency, while about 30% side with the Communists, often in a manner which for Poles is provocative. We have to ignore such provocations…[23]

The strategic plan, explicitly stated and supported by almost all concerned, was to procure weapons, get organized and wait, "arms at the order,"[24] according to the slogan at that time, while the two

---

23. Israel Gutman and Shmuel Krakowski, *Unequal Victims: Poles and Jews during World War Two* (New York: Holocaust Library, 1986), p. 39.
24. Thus dispatch no. 803, dated September 30, 1942, i.e., the end of the "transfer," sent to General Sikorski by "Grot"-Rowecki, aka "Kalina," commander-in-chief of the AK, reads as follows: "The National Party and other national groups [the Labor Party and the People's Party] and democratic groups [the WRN and the PS] call for reprisals by the Allies and do not foresee carrying out fighting within the country except if and when the enemy makes self-defense necessary. [Obviously they did not consider defending the Jews an act of self-defense.] The Democratic Party [recommends] Allied action and active self-defense with fighting in the forests. *National Thought* [a right-wing underground publication] [calls for] immediate action within the country without listening to the Government's advice. The Communist PPR is taking advantage of the prevailing sentiment in society to criticize the passivity of the official civilian and military opposition and is calling for people to join the Soviet partisans in the forests. This presents the danger of the situation blowing up against our will and of a mass struggle led by the Communists. Therefore I demand bombardments, reprisals against Germans in Allied countries and individual acts of reprisal against Polish traitors and Germans [or nearly anything else at all except for premature fighting]. Kalina." Bernard Mark, *Powstanie w getcie warszawskim* (Warsaw: Żydowski Instytut Historyczny, 1953), pp. 190–91.

    Here we have a commentary from an official source on the position expressed a year later by the new AK commander-in-chief, General Komorowski, alias "Bor," alias "Lawina," an opinion which, he says, is in agreement with that of the Government Delegate: "The commander-in-chief of the Home Army is convinced that at this historic juncture when the Nazi invader is about to flee from Polish territory after having defeated our State, humiliated us and destroyed us with barbaric brutality, and when our land is about to be invaded once again by our second enemy, the accomplices of the Germans in the destruction of Poland, the Soviets, who destroyed us in a barbaric fashion when they occupied our land and now bring with them the threat of the most ferocious enslavement, it is impossible to rest content with firing a few shots in the country and making a few diplomatic moves in London. The

giants bled each other, and until the time, very far off, true – but didn't we wait a century and a half last time, from the end of the eighteenth century until 1920? – when the Germans were defeated and the time came to rise up against them, liberate Warsaw from the Germans, and then defend it against the Russians. That was in fact what did happen in 1944: as the Soviet army drew within a few miles of Warsaw, the uprising was launched and the city was liberated with its bridges still intact. (The Soviets, remembering that they were, after all, Russians, and recalling what the Poles had done to them several times before, during the preceding century and in 1920, pulled back and gave the Germans the few months they needed to drown the insurrection in blood, evacuate the survivors and finish destroying the city.) But let's not get ahead of ourselves. Two years earlier, neither the Polish people nor the resistance had any intention of acting prematurely, since it would inevitably lead to a massacre. By April 1943, the Polish resistance had grown, but still kept to its strategic plan of double-edged resistance against both the Germans and the Russians. Meanwhile, 300,000 Warsaw

---

commander-in-chief of the Home Army believes that Polish soldiers must fight to liberate their country from the German and Russian invaders so that they can take part in the final victory; that it is their right and duty to be the masters in their own house along with the representatives of the Polish civilian administration, at a time when the Russians are about to penetrate their territory, and to represent before them and before the whole world the sovereign rights of Poland. It would be better if once the Russians were in Poland they would be forced to openly show their hostility to the representatives of the Republic instead of quietly pulling the soldiers of the Home Army from their hiding places. In fact, there can be no doubt about how the Soviets will behave. It seems impossible to keep clandestine a Home Army with more than 300,000 members, especially since pro-Soviet agents have already found out about much of it. Clearly, given the irreversibility of the tragic unfolding of events, we must at least behave in a way such that future generations will not be able to accuse us of cowardice…Our organization has grown a great deal and it will be impossible to keep it clandestine under Soviet occupation. In practical terms, I will reduce the number of officers and units that must be revealed to a strict minimum and I will strive to protect the others by dissolving them…In case of a second Soviet occupation, I am preparing, in the greatest secrecy, the core of a basic command structure and a clandestine organization that will be at your disposition. I will transmit the details after finalizing my decisions in this matter. In any case, this will be an autonomous network that is not linked to the main organization of the Home Army, which has already been largely compromised by Soviet agents. [Signed: Lawina 2100]." *Polskie sily zbrojne w II wojnie swiatowej*, vol. 3, *Armia Krajowa* (London/Warsaw, 1998), pp. 555–57.

Jews were murdered, Rommel was routed, and, above all, the German army turned back at Stalingrad, signaling the future total defeat of Germany for all to see. But during the summer of 1942, all these events still lay hidden in the future. During the summer of 1942, Poles did not want to see all of Warsaw go up in flames.

Within the parameters of their murderous madness, the Germans behaved with impeccable logic. So did the Poles, within the parameters of their unrealistic plan to save the country's independence by resisting both the Nazi Germans and the Russian Communists.

And the Jews? Berman explains the passivity of the Anti-Fascist Bloc by blaming the population as a whole for rejecting the very idea of action. Bednarczyk accounts for the passivity of the ZZW in much the same way. When asked why the ZZW took no action whatsoever, which contradicted its very raison d'être, Mendelson answers, "What could 300 people do when a mass of 500,000 completely lacked any will to resist?"[25]

It was not information that was lacking in the ghetto. People were well-informed about the fate of the Jews in the East, where more than a million were massacred, about the recent annihilation of other ghettos, about the fact that Treblinka had become operational and that the first convoys of people sent there from Warsaw were gassed to death as soon as they arrived. The German lies may have been very persuasive but they ultimately couldn't mask these incontestable facts. Their collaborators – the few dozen Jewish

---

25. "Höfle's operation, i.e., the deportation to Treblinka of about 300,000 people between July 23 and September 13, 1942, greatly disorganized the ZZW and led to the loss of more than 50 soldiers. Bednarczyk had previously informed us that this operation was in preparation (he had a permanent pass that let him come and go, which facilitated his work with us). We knew it was coming, despite the denials of Auerswald, who was in charge of the ghetto, and the Gestapo representative for ghetto affairs, Untersturmführer Karl Brandt. The Jewish Gestapo agents, among them Gancwajch, Sterfeld, Kohn, Heller, Grajer and Erlich, were also clearly up to something. But the ZZW was not in a position to stand up to the deportations. What could 300 people do when a mass of 500,000 completely lacked any will to resist? At that point no one dreamed that the deportations would be on such a large scale. It was not until afterwards that the Jews grasped the full extent of this tragic situation." Mendelson, "*Rozwoj i dzialanosc ZZW*."

Gestapo stooges, a few thousand Judenrat functionaries and 2,000 Jewish police – may have had their reasons for believing that they would survive, but, as it turned out, they were not much of a force to be reckoned with, as was evident as soon as the will to resist began to concretize after the mass deportation.

But there are also possible underlying reasons for their passivity which do not contradict the others given above. One is of a biological order and the other is cultural.

Famine stalked the ghetto from the start.

> According to statistics provided by the Supply Office, the food officially distributed by the Germans furnished an average of about 800 calories a day. These provisions contained about three grams of animal fat and about 20–30 grams of vegetable protein. They consisted of black bread, wheat and rye flour, potatoes, tiny amounts of butter and oil or lard, and sugar, and a bowl of soup.[26]

Of course tons of food were smuggled in daily, but only a part of the population could eat adequately, while the majority was always hungry and severely malnourished. During the previous year, 1941, 10% of the ghetto's population died, a great many of starvation. As is well known, malnutrition is accompanied by an insurmountable apathy.

Furthermore, there was a tradition that proved stronger than the danger of collective death – the sectarian struggles within the community between the religious Jews, the Bundists, the Zionists and the Revisionist Zionists.

For religious Jews, Zionism was evil incarnate. It has been proven beyond all doubt that they opposed any notion of armed resistance. Religious circles continue to abjure the Warsaw ghetto uprising to this day. In Israel, the anniversary of the first day of the

---

26. Emil Apfelbaum, ed., *Maladie de famine: Recherches cliniques sur la famine exécutées dans le ghetto de Varsovie en 1942* (Warsaw: American Joint Distribution Committee, 1946), p. 80.

insurrection is marked by a minute of silence; the great majority of religious Jews refuse to take part in this observance. "The major post-war anguish for ultra-Orthodoxy in the 1950s was that the God of history was a Zionist and they themselves were forced to move here and become dependent on the Zionist adversary. [...] In their view two interlocking tragedies had occurred: the Nazi Holocaust and the Zionist victory. [...] By the mid-70s, ultra-Orthodox thinkers, says Friedman, developed a theory 'demonizing Zionism and imputing to it responsibility for Holocaust.'"[27] In a book entitled *Those Burned in the Ovens Accuse*, one of these theorists writes that "the Zionist heroism" was a "goy solution" that defied "the will of the Wise Men," just as the Zealots had defied the rabbis when they rebelled against the Romans 19 centuries earlier, and that the Warsaw ghetto revolt, like that of the Zealots, had caused even more Jews to die. It was part of a more far-reaching Zionist strategy. Desperate because of the trickle of immigrants to Palestine, the Zionists are said to have deliberately provoked Hitler in the 1930s with the hope that a bloodbath would spur massive emigration.[28] According to Friedman, this book is considered authoritative in Orthodox circles (and on Holocaust-denial Web sites as well).[29]

To get back to the ghetto period: the Orthodox opposition to any plans for military resistance was one of principle, deeply rooted and subsequently reaffirmed. Considering the enormous influence of the religious Jews, which was intensified by these dramatic circumstances, it would seem that this is one of the reasons why the ZZW remained inactive. Paradoxically, although the Bund was traditionally an enemy of religion, its attitude reinforced this refusal to act. For many years, Nazi Germany and the Allies had been considered capitalist twins, Tweedledum and Tweedledee, and the Jewish proletariat, which the Bund claimed to represent, had no more reason to choose one over the other than to pick the

27. Friedman, cited in the article by Netty C. Gross, "Why Did God Do This to Us?" *Jerusalem Report* 11, no. 1 (May 8, 2000).
28. Sheinfeld, cited by Friedman in Gross, "Why Did God Do This to Us?"
29. Ibid.

plague over cholera. "Neither of these two imperialist countries have any interest in defending the working class."[30] After the attack on the Soviet Union, and the murder of more than a million Jews in German-occupied territory, the Bund finally did choose sides, but it continued to hold that solidarity with the Polish proletariat (represented by the Polish Socialist Party) claimed priority over solidarity among Jews.[31] Their hostility toward the bourgeoisie and the Zionists was so basic and intense that they denied not only the legitimacy of other Jewish movements but even their existence.[32] Even the most recent Bundist publications, a half-century after the fact, describe a wait-and-see policy.

> On July 23, 1942, after Adam Czerniakow's suicide... the Bund, the Tsukunft and the unions met...They decided to contact other organizations to discuss the possibility of an uprising. An activist should be sent to the "work camps" to investigate exactly what happened to the people sent there.[33]

Faced with the hostility of all the other Jewish movements, the

---

30. *Yugnt shtime*, January–February 1941. Many Bundists declarations with the same general content can still be read today. "Every time the reactionaries mount anti-Semitic demonstrations to attack the freedom of the workers' movement, Jewish nationalism reemerges, seeking to undermine our confidence and subvert the fighting spirit of the Jewish masses who are taking part in the overall fight against reaction. Jewish nationalism proclaims that we are in exile.... The Austrians, Czechs, Poles and Dutch are persecuted and oppressed. They have all suffered a fate similar to that of the Jews, even if they do have their own country." Georges Bensoussan, "*De la 'zone d'épidémie' au ghetto: La mort programmée d'un peuple Septembre 1939-Mai 1943*," in Seidman, *Warsaw Ghetto Diaries*, p. 386.
31. "At the first general meeting of the representatives of all the political parties in the Warsaw Jewish underground, in March 1942, the delegates were unable to reach a consensus of opinion or to agree to a common course of action. The representatives of the Bund were opposed to the formation of a separate Jewish resistance organization, and argued that activities should be coordinated with the Polish socialists." Gutman and Krakowski, *Unequal Victims*, p. 152.
32. Polish Jews had two representatives in the National Council (a sort of limited parliament in exile), Szwarzbart for the Zionists and Zygelbojm for the Bund. During the session of May 18–20, 1942, Zygelbojm officially demanded that he be recognized as the sole representative of the Jewish resistance on the grounds that apart from the Bund no other Jewish underground organization existed. See Gutman and Krakowski, *Unequal Victims*, p. 62.
33. Henri Minczeles, *Histoire générale du Bund* (Paris: Denoël, 1995), p. 415.

ZZW was organizationally and practically dependent on the Polish resistance, whose strategy, as we have seen, was to wait, "arms at the order."

The ZZW was caught in a vise. On one side, there was a Jewish population that had been made passive through malnutrition, Nazi manipulation,[34] the influence of the religious Jews who were stubbornly opposed to resistance, the ambiguity of the Bund and the hatred of the leftist Zionist groups, and on the other the Polish resistance, which had been kept in waiting by a policy whose aim was to await the moment to oppose a Soviet occupation. The ZZW did nothing more than seek to survive. During the "transfer," it lost 10% of its forces, while the ghetto as a whole lost almost 85% of its people.

34. January 14, 1943: "It was impossible to resist. We all thought that everyone would not perish, that some among us would be saved. Thus, how could anyone take the responsibility for endangering the lives of others, of their loved ones and the existence of the entire community? We knew all too well that the Germans applied the rule of collective punishment." Seidman, *Warsaw Ghetto Diaries*, p. 234.

CHAPTER 5

AFTER THE MASSACRE

The *Grossaktion*, the great extermination, ended on September 12, 1942. It resumed once more on the 21st, the eve of Yom Kippur, when another 2,000 Jews were sent to Treblinka: "The Germans called together several hundred Jewish policemen on the pretext that they were going to get medals and sent them and their families to Treblinka."[1] The ghetto's area was reduced, and the only ones authorized to reside there were registered "shop" workers. Some 35,000 people quartered around their workplaces were subjected to strict disciplinary measures in grotesque contrast to the context.[2]

---

1. Zuckerman, *A Surplus of Memory*, p. 245.
2. "Factory regulations: 1) Until further notice, work hours are from 7 a.m to 5 P.M. Lunch break: 12:30–1:30; 2) Attendance is to be registered by giving one's number at the entrance to the Werkschutz; 3) Each employee must give his or her number personally. All violations will be punished. Punishment for both the person to whom the number corresponds and the person who replaces him or her may include dismissal; 4) Unless management has sent them to another establishment, all employees must remain within the establishment located at 30 Gesia Street. Anyone who leaves this site without authorization will be immediately struck from the list of employees and their name will be sent to the staging camp (Sammellager). Authorization to leave the factory may be signed by Jozef Landau, L. Hereszkowicz and Aleksander Landau; 5) Any late arrival will be considered an absence and punishment will be a fine of 10 zlotys. This also applies to any unexcused absence. An absence of three days will result in the elimination of all services (bread, soup and other foodstuffs); any absence longer than that will result in being stricken from the list of employees; 6) All employees must strictly obey the instructions of their work team head or their superiors on pain of being stricken from the list of employees; 7) Smoking is strictly forbidden. It is also forbidden to loiter in the courtyard. Everyone must remain at their

In addition to these "legal" survivors, the ghetto's population also included roughly the same number of people in hiding who had no access whatsoever to "official" rations and lived illegally in supposedly uninhabited buildings. (Map no. 1 shows the shrinking perimeter of the ghetto, the manufacturing district, the brushmakers' neighborhood and the Többens district, and the so-called "free fire" areas.)

When almost 90% of the population had been removed, it was no longer possible to harbor illusions or hopes for survival. It was obvious to everyone that the Germans were going to kill them all quickly.

FOUNDATION OF THE ZOB

On October 28, representatives of the various leftist parties in the ghetto met and decided to found the *Zydowski Komitet Narodowy* (ZKN), the Jewish National Committee. The Bund, the Revisionist Zionist party and the religious parties did not take part.

On the following day, October 29, the ZKN founded the Jewish Combat Organization (ZOB).[3] But the new ZOB did not really come into existence until the night of December 1 when a meeting adopted its final by-laws and those of an additional political organization, the *Zydowski Komitet Koordynacyjny* (ZKK), Jewish Coordinating Committee. The ZKK was designed to act as an intermediary between the ZKN and the Bund and allow the latter to become part of the ZOB. Thus, the ZOB combat organization was subordinate to the ZKK, which comprised a federation of left Zionist organizations and the Communist Party, on one side, and the

---

work post as indicated by the team head and it is forbidden to leave that post; 8) Persons other than staff and employees are forbidden to enter the factory without written authorization. All violations of this regulation will be punished; 9) At the end of the work day, each employee must leave his or her post clean and in good order; October 29, 1942, The Management, *Fuer die Richigkeit der Uebersetzund* (signature illegible)." *Biuletyn ZIH*, nos. 71–72 (July–December 1969), pp. 162–63.

3. Another very small organization of the same name had been declared in the early summer but never became active – see chapter 2.

Bund on the other. This complicated and apparently absurd formal structure was deeply rooted in the political situation.

Here is an account of that meeting by Cukierman, General Secretary of the Coordinating Committee:

> There were three problems. One of them was in regard to the Bund.... The Bund did not want to be united with us in the same political organization and would accept nothing more than a coordinating committee.[...] This came from their traditions and their ideology, which crystallized back in 1897; they wanted to distance themselves from us because of the "sins" of Zionism and our desire to cooperate with "all of Judaism" [except the bourgeois and the Revisionists]. The Bund would not accept any ties other than to the two branches of the Polish Socialist Party.
>
> For our part, we did not want to resign ourselves to abandoning the Jewish National Committee (ZKN), which included all forces except for the Bund [and the Revisionist Zionist religious parties]. In light of this situation, we agreed to form the Jewish Coordination Committee (ZKK) with the Bund.
>
> The second problem had to do with the ZOB. The Bund agreed to cooperate with the ZOB only on the Warsaw level and not on a national scale. When the ZOB was first founded in July, we agreed that it would take action throughout Poland.... In order to unite with the Bund and involve it in our activities we created two commands. The first was a Warsaw command that included the Bund.[4] The second was a secret command whose authority extended to all the other cities; it included only Hehalutz and Hashomer Hatzair. It turned out that the existence of the ZKK and the ZOB facilitated the solution of the problem of cooperation with the PPR [the reconstituted Communist Party – this was the third problem]. The Jews and

4. The Warsaw command was a coordinating committee between various units that retained their respective political identies: Dror, five groups; Hashomer Hatzair, four groups; Communists, four groups; Bund, four groups; Akiwa, one unit; Gordonia, one unit; left Poale Zion, one unit; right Poale Zion, one group. Theoretically, these groups were simultaneously under the authority of both their own respective parties and the overall command.

> the Communists [of course this means Jewish Communists] wanted to work together but this was difficult for organizational reasons. There was no Jewish Communist Party that could act as a political agent for Poland (i.e., there was nothing like the Jewish section of the Soviet party), but simply a Jewish cell in Warsaw functioning as a subdivision of the Warsaw section, and another Jewish cell in Cracow, a component of the party section for that city. So there was no party body empowered to take up Jewish questions on the national level.... Thus, the [creation] of the ZKK resolved the problem of how to work with the PPR.... [5]

Thus, in addition to the two political committees (the National Committee, including the Communists, and the Coordinating Committee, which also included the Bund), there were also two commands: the Warsaw command, composed of the Communists and Bundists as well as the Zionist groups, and the national command, made up exclusively of Zionists and ignored by everyone else.

RELATIONS BETWEEN THE ZOB AND THE ZZW

Why did the ZOB and the ZZW fail to merge, despite the obvious logical and strategic advantages of fusing these two resistance organizations? The circumstantial reasons involved remain somewhat obscure, but the underlying conflicts were deep-rooted and intractable.[6]

Here are some examples of obviously unreasonable mutual criticism reported by Cukierman, who, as General Secretary of the Coordinating Committee, was in the thick of these quarrels:

> The Revisionists have begun to carry out their own propaganda

5. Zuckerman, *A Surplus of Memory*, p. 221–22.
6. Shmuel Krakowski, *The War of the Doomed: Jewish Armed Resistance in Poland 1942–1944* (New York/London: Holmes and Meier, 1984), p. 168.

> campaign and it has worried us quite a bit. We feared that it could leave the door open to Jewish Gestapo agents, who had stayed behind in the ghetto even after the deportation of most of the police and other collaborators on the eve of Yom Kippur, after the *Neila* prayer. [...]
>
> Another source of disagreement between us and the Revisionists was their demand that the commander-in-chief be one of their comrades. [Cukierman does not name that person, but other sources, as we have seen, cite Apfelbaum, Frenkiel or Rodal, the three leaders of the ZZW.] They claimed [...] that they were professional military men. None of us, not the Bundists nor the PPR members, wanted to accept that kind of a demand. [...]
>
> Our orders were to keep our arms hidden in case of a search. But in their apartment, we saw their arms in full view. [...] This was not somewhere in the mountains or in a forest, but right in the city. And this was how a movement that claimed to be underground was acting. We had never seen anything like this before. Of course that does not take away from the Revisionists' contributions to the Jewish struggle, but their behavior was overbearing and inappropriate for the circumstances. [...] [Thus the ZZW is accused of recruiting, of wanting to be in charge, of making ostentatious preparations – these are pretexts rather than reasons.]
>
> The general staff [of the ZOB] met nearly every day. At one of these meetings it was decided that I should be named secretary of the ZKK. This proposal was presented to the ZKN forum. The Revisionists alone were opposed. But they would have been against any candidate who was not one of their own.[7]

The "bad company" argument used by Cukierman – the accusation levelled against the ZZW that they associated with rightist Polish organizations – is also put forward by Jaworksi, Edelman and Ringelblum. The latter also points to what he considers

7. Zuckerman, *A Surplus of Memory*, pp. 226–29. This is the only known reference to the idea that the Revisionists were part of the ZKN and/or the ZKK.

a suspiciously apolitical stance. Bronek Jaworski, a ghetto survivor, writes:

> [A] political coordinating committee was created to link up the Zionists and the Bund. [Jaworksi was a Communist leader.] Comrade Lejbgott represented the PPR [Communist Party] on this committee…; the Revisionists were not allowed to join because we knew they were in contact with reactionary Polish military circles, and nothing good could come from that; we informed the ghetto of this in numerous leaflets.[8] [These leaflets have not been located.]

Bernard Mark cites Ringelblum:

> The ZOB's platform was anti-fascist, whereas the ZZW limited itself to the issues of resistance and fighting. The unity discussions proved fruitless because the ZOB was willing to accept the ZZW's soldiers in its ranks only on an individual basis and not as a group. Further, the ZOB had misgivings about certain people the ZZW was in touch with on the "Aryan" side, contacts which went beyond both the GL [a Communist armed resistance organization] and the AK [the military organization of the Polish government in exile in London].[9]

We have only one eyewitness account that represents the ZZW's point of view, but it confirms the substance of the disagreements:

> From the beginning, I hoped that there would be only one combat organization. But after two meetings with Ziwia Lubetkin, who represented the Zionist far-left, and Mordechaj Anielewicz, who had become commander of the ZOB, it was obvious that this was never going to happen. We Revisionists thought it reasonable that in order for the revolt to be successful, the person who led it had to be the

---

8. Bronek Jaworski, "*Informacje Bronka Jaworskiego*," Jabotinsky, W (8), no. 41, and ZIH Archives, no. 5016, p. 2.
9. Bernard Mark, *Walka i zaglada warszawskiego getta* (Warsaw: Wydawnictwo Ministerstwa Obrony Narodowej, 1959), p. 149.

> most capable in military terms. The other group insisted that it be headed by a political leader, and obviously they meant someone from their camp. What's more, they wanted the Betarites to be admitted to the organization individually and not as a group.[10]

Consider this recent commentary by Edelman who confirms the allegations of "bad company," militaristic pretensions and an apolitical stance:

> Why didn't the ZOB establish relations with the ZZW [...] a paramilitary organization of the "Revisionists" as they were called, after the name of one of the rightist groupings in the Zionist party? Actually, there were efforts to establish relations. But the whole thing was very complicated. They had some dubious relations with far-right Polish groups on the Aryan side, it seems. [Thus Cukierman, Jaworski and Edelman rest content with repeating rumors.] In addition, they felt that as a military organization, they should be in command. We didn't trust them because among the ZZW cadres there were some people whose political activities in the ghetto we knew very little about. One day in the spring of 1943, we had a rendezvous with the ZZW in a building at 42 Nalewki Street. Three of us went: "Marian" (Mordechaj Anielewicz, the ZOB commander), "Antek" (Icchak Cukierman, my best friend, head of the Dror) and me. They threatened us with their weapons. They demanded that we put the command of military action in their hands. But we were armed too. What does that mean? Just what you think it does. But I won't go into details because that would not be very encouraging. On another occasion, we decided to pull off an "eks" against a supply company, or, in other words, to raid it and expropriate money for the underground resistance. Of course, they found out, I don't know how, and went into action ten minutes before we did. They

10. Wdowinski, *And We Are Not Saved*, pp. 78–79.

> wanted to take the money. A real firefight broke out, but they were nine to our forty, so we got the better of them.[11]

Thus the highly centralized ZZW, theoretically apolitical but in reality made up to a large degree of "Revisionist" volunteers, had a professional officer corps, and in their possession a relatively large quantity of arms (see Krakowski, appendix 4) that were used by well-trained people. It seems that the two organizations made some mutually unacceptable demands. The ZOB, a federation of politically homogeneous groups, is said to have refused to incorporate the ZZW units into its ranks. Using the ZZW's association with Polish rightists as their justification, the ZOB demanded that the ZZW be dissolved and that its members join the ZOB on an individual level. The ZZW is said to have demanded that the commander-in-chief and officers be chosen entirely on the basis of military competence, without any attempt to strike a political balance. Since it was the only group to have regular army officers and non-coms in its ranks, who had been sharpening their skills for three years, this would have given the ZZW complete control.

No matter what degree of responsibility we assign to each of them for the failure of the negotiations, the fact remains that the merger never took place. The two organizations prepared for and fought the battles of January 18–20, 1943, completely independently of one another.

THE BUILDING OF NEW TUNNELS

The ZZW prepared for regular warfare, relying on fortified positions and heavy firepower.[12] In its view, the main problem was how to maintain contact with the outside world so as to obtain munitions and reinforcements and, if necessary, leave the ghetto to continue

11. Rudi Assuntino and Wlodek Goldkorn: *Straznik: Marek Edelman opowiada* (Cracow: Znak, 2000), pp. 66–67.
12. Mendelson, "*Ci, ktorzy byli z nami*," *Argumenty*, no. 15 (April 15, 1973): 775.

the fight in the forests. (Actually, two different plans coexisted. Lieutenant Leon Rodal, commander of the 1st company stationed at Muranowski Square, called for dying at their posts; another plan was to escape into the woods after an initial period.) The Gestapo had discovered the tunnel in the western part of the ghetto, which crossed Okopowa Street at Gesia and led to the Jewish cemetery. Another tunnel, under the Church of the Blessed Virgin, had become inaccessible due to the shrinking of the ghetto and could not be fully reactivated. "The ZZW technical department [...] dug a tunnel leading to a bunker from the church, and another from the church and under Leszno Street to the abandoned houses on the other side of the street."[13]

This new route was long and inefficient. Consequently, priority was given to the construction of two new tunnels, under Karmelicka and Muranowska Streets. The Karmelicka Street tunnel started out from under number 5 in the "free fire" zone of the ghetto and went to number 4, the Carmelite hospital. Part of this passageway went through the sewers. "As soon as the plans drawn up by the Works department were approved by the general staff, Zwi Federbusz was named project chief. He was a real hero, both because of his capacity for work and his outstanding courage. He carried more weight than any ordinary mortal could."[14] This tunnel was protected and run by the independent platoon lead by Lieutenant Mendelson.

The Muranowska Street tunnel presented far more serious technical difficulties but it was the more important of the two. It led out of number 7, a large and particularly well-fortified building, which in turn was the center of a whole fortified area, defended by the 1st company, and went to number 6, on the other side of the wall.

---

13. Lazar, "The Jewish Military Organization," p. 27.
14. Ketling, cited in Lazar, "The Jewish Military Organization," p. 29; Bednarczyk confirms this: "Mendelson's...independent platoon...protected the passageway through the sewers from 4 Karmelicka Street on the Aryan side to number 5 of that same street in the ghetto." See Bednarczyk, *Zycie codzienne warszawskiego getta*, p. 85.

Ketling-Szemley describes the construction:

Work on the 50-foot tunnel took about three months, from August through September 1942. Crossing Muranowska Street at an angle, it connected the ghetto with the Aryan quarter, beginning in the basement of the building at number 7 and ending at number 6 on the other side of the street. On the odd-numbered side, rising right along the sidewalk, was a red brick wall with iron spikes and pieces of broken glass on top, artificially separating the two quarters of the same city that had been like two parts of the same living body. The streetcar ran through the middle of the street; beyond that lay a few buildings, and behind them, so near and yet so far, was the wide world that looked – deceptively – so free.

This was the world that was supposed to be made accessible by the tunnel under Muranowska Street, dug with stubbornness and sacrifice. It was toward this world of freedom, threatening because it was unknown and all the more foreign because of its very proximity, that the enthusiastic youth turned their eyes. Their watchword was this: put an end to the inertia and passivity of their own people and throw daring and bravery into the wheels of the machine of destruction that was almost on top of them.

The construction work had to be well hidden from the curious glances of the innumerable people who constantly trooped through the building's courtyard. In fact, as the Jewish population was shifted around inside the shrinking perimeter of the ghetto, they seemed to move in waves like some unchained natural element. This created all sorts of unpredictable difficulties for the construction of the tunnel. The entrance was scarcely a meter wide and only a few people at a time could pass through. And it was essential to hurry, because every day brought more disturbing reasons to fear that the complete liquidation of the ghetto was at hand. The latest "operation" in July had left no doubt about that.

At first, specialized engineers directed the work. The excavated dirt and the water that leaked into the tunnel had to be hauled out in buckets in the middle of the night. The hard paving stones of the street sunk deeply into the ground made the earth below almost impossible to dig into. There was no question of using modern earth-moving equipment because of the need for silence, and so the ground had to be burrowed using little more than bare hands. Then, midway through, they ran up against a water pipe. The specialists declared that it was impossible to continue. We can't get around it, they said, and, and we can't get through it. The pavement above was in danger of collapse and there was an underground stream below.

The specialists stopped working.

But the ordinary people did not. About 60 of them kept working, people whose efforts were determined by their goal and not the other way around. Szlamek, a young man about 20 years old, exceptionally gifted at all sorts of things, was the heart and soul of this team and the initiator of the plan to build the tunnel. His enthusiasm, energy and self-sacrificing spirit won over the others. He was tireless at his work. Although he could hardly read, those who knew him acclaimed his poetic talents. A self-taught virtuoso, he played the piano and composed songs. Although he was not a professional, his technical knowledge was far greater than that of the expert engineers. This very special man became the hero of the tunnel. No obstacle could stop him; once it was started he was determined to see this project through to the end. It was the crowning point of a life that was admirable as it was brief, cut short as he courageously fought the Germans during the liquidation of the ghetto in April 1943.

This tunnel enabled me to enter the ghetto for a meeting with representatives of the Jewish organization [the ZZW], previously arranged in December 1942. Now it was early January 1943. The tunnel could only be used at night. To enter, you had to show up at the concierge's lodgings before curfew and wait for the right moment to go down to the basement. This meant crossing a fairly wide courtyard, after nightfall, in the pitch dark, when the building's residents would no longer come downstairs. Actually, the entrance to the tunnel was in the basement, which had been made into a shelter. After you lifted the trapdoor camouflaged under a layer of hard earth, you crawled on all fours into the tunnel, which was lit by electric lights and equipped with quilts.

Inside the ghetto, in an apartment situated at number 3 or 5 Muranowski Square,[15] the organization's leaders and several armed soldiers were waiting for me. Their commanding officer gave me a regulation report on the military situation. That made a good impression on those attending the meeting. My personal satisfaction was all the greater because I was able to announce to my comrades in arms that I was in a position to meet their requests, although only partially. Although I was not able to bring them an answer from the "competent Polish authorities" – the time was too short to wait for that – I was bringing with me explosives [...] Molotov cocktails and military manuals. I spent the night familiarizing the members of the Jewish organization with the explosives and flammable materials supplied, training them, etc. I left the ghetto the next day at dawn. In the following months I was to take the route I have just described many times until it was destroyed in April and May 1943. Meanwhile, our cooperation became closer and closer until it became real and lasting.

Whether out of cowardice or cupidity, the concierge of the building at 6 Muranowska Street refused to allow the tunnel to be used anymore. He was persuaded to give up his job in return for 30,000 zlotys, and was replaced by one of my subordinates, a sailor, Kazimierz Ozdobinski, who had the necessary character and qualifications.[16]

The tunnel facilitated many excellent combat actions, such as the execution of five Gestapo stooges and the burning down of the workshops producing SS uniforms. [...]

During long nocturnal conversations, and my daytime walks

---

15. No! At number 7, which is what was originally written in the Polish manuscript and then crossed out.
16. A resident of this building describes him as being of Russian origin: "In August 1942, there was a concierge who had rented the apartment on the fourth floor to Jews. This concierge soon left us and was replaced by a Russian, Gorecki-Szalapa." Alicja Kaczynska, *Obok piekla* (Gdansk: Marpress, 1993), p. 74.

> through the ghetto in disguise and wearing an armband, I learned innumerable fascinating details about Jewish life, among them the story of how the tunnel was built.
>
> This was how I made good on my promise of cooperation between Poles and Jews in the struggle against the Germans.[17]

The ZZW's three functioning tunnels were used for bringing in provisions, transporting arms and ammunition, and taking out people who wanted to seek refuge on the Aryan side. The ZOB had no tunnels, probably because its links with the Polish resistance were recent and not very strong; their relations were not marked by any mutual confidence or cordiality. Pro-ZOB historians accuse the ZZW of "cowardice," as if flight were their only goal....

But the ZOB did use these tunnels on occasion. "The general staff decided to send Zygmunt Fryderych, a Bundist, and me, to contact our comrades on the Aryan side. We used the tunnel dug by the ZZW (the Revisionists)."[18]

KARSKI'S VISIT

At the Bund's request, the Muranowski tunnel was even used by the government's special messenger, Jan Karski.

Dawid Landau, a ZZW member, recalls:

> One day, Sawek Bekerman told me to go to headquarters. Moryc Apfelbaum and one of the Lopata brothers were waiting for me there. They ordered me to take a man through the Muranowska tunnel. We had just barely finished digging it, after enormous complications

17. Janusz Cezary Ketling-Szemley, "*Wspomnienia z walki dzialalnosci* ZZW...," ZIH, no. 4469; Bednarczyk dates the tunnel to January 1943 (see Bednarczyk, *Zycie codzienne warszawskiego getta*, p. 90), while Ketling claims he used it for the first time at the beginning of January 1943, but also says that the tunnel was finished in October 1942 (see footnote 74 in Bednarczyk). There are numerous other descriptions of the Muranowska Street tunnel, all in agreement on the basic points.
18. Simha (Kazik) Rotem, *Memoirs of a Warsaw Ghetto Fighter: The Past Within Me* (New Haven/London: Yale University Press, 1994), p. 43.

> and difficulties. Midway we had run into several pipes and we were forced to go over them, which brought the tunnel near the surface...At that time I didn't know the man but I clearly remember having waited for him outside and not on the Aryan side of Muranowska Street, as Thomas Wood wrote in his biography. When Karski showed up, accompanied by another man [the Bund leader Feiner], I went into the courtyard and they followed. Another ZZW member whose name I can't remember covered us from behind. We went through the tunnel in that order. I think Karski stayed in the ghetto for about two hours. Then we were called to take him out again via the same route.[19]

Jan Karski crossed occupied Europe to London, where he reported on the situation to the Polish government, and, at its behest, to the British government. Then he was sent to the United States, where he had a long conversation with Roosevelt and gave a series of lectures meant to alert the American public to the situation of the Jews in Poland. This is his description of his visit to the ghetto:

> On orders of the Delegate of the National Government in London and the Home Army, before I left Poland, a meeting was organized for me with two men who were then leading the work of the underground Jewish movement and had held prominent positions in Jewish society before the war. One was the head of the Zionist organization [A. Berman?], and the second the leader of the Bund [L. Feiner]. [...]
>
> We met at nightfall in a large unoccupied and half-destroyed house. The fact that both of them had come meant that what they wanted to communicate through me to the Polish government and the Allied governments was not of a political nature and not limited to the special interests of each of the two groups. This meeting was meant to express what the Jewish population as a whole wanted to

19. "David Landau: The Man That Fought the Germans in Their Arms Uniform," *Publications of the Museum of the Combatants and Partisans* 8, no. 10 (April 1995): 83– 84.

communicate, to express the feelings, demands and recommendations of a population that, again as a whole, was dying.

What I learned during these meetings and what I saw with my own eyes afterwards staggers the imagination. I am familiar with history. I know quite a bit about the development of nations, about political systems, social doctrines, methods of conquest, persecution and extermination; I also know that never before in the history of humanity, never in the sphere of human relations, has there ever been anything even comparable to what happened to the Jewish population of Poland.

These two men made an unforgettable impression, not so much as individuals, but as personifications of the collective suffering and extreme nervous tension of a desperate struggle. Both of them lived outside the ghetto but the use of secret passageways made it possible for them to enter and leave the "quarter" whenever they wanted. Once inside the ghetto they looked, acted and talked just like the other inhabitants. When their work took them outside the ghetto walls, they were able to change their appearance so successfully that they could pass the most rigorous visual inspection. Especially the Bundist leader, who with his courtly white mustache, abundant hair, healthy complexion, imposing height and vigorous and dignified air, could easily pass for a Polish "nobleman."

A well-known judge before the war, he was considered an expert in criminal law. The German authorities thought he was the owner of a department store, rich, respectable and notable for his composure. I did not understand just what an enormous effort it was to play this role until one day when he walked through the ghetto with me. Suddenly the impression of wealthiness and self-confidence vanished as if someone had waved a magic wand. The well-off Polish businessman suddenly changed into a Jew, one among thousands of emaciated Jews, worn-out, hungry, tortured and persecuted by the Nazis with an inhuman zeal.

As we spoke in the night-time quiet of the Warsaw outskirts, the first thing I came to understand was the totally desperate nature of their situation. What these suffering Polish Jews were going through was the end of the world. There was not the slightest possibility of escape for them or their people. But this was only a part of their tragedy, only one of the causes of their desperation and anguish. These two men had no fear of death; they had already resigned themselves to see it as almost inevitable. But at the same time, they were bitterly aware that no satisfactory outcome for them was possible in this war, no hope that would have rendered the thought of death less painful. This I understood almost as soon as the Zionist leader began to speak.

– You non-Jewish Poles are lucky, he began. Of course you suffer, too; many of you will perish, but your people will continue to live. After the war Poland will be reborn. You will rebuild your cities, and some day, when enough times passes, your wounds will heal. Your country will arise again from this sea of suffering, tears, rage and humiliation, but the Polish Jews will have ceased to exist. We will be dead. Hitler will have lost the war against the representatives of humanity, justice and good, but he will have won his war against the Polish Jews. No, that will not be a victory, he added. The Jewish people will have been murdered.

Our conversation and the attempt to explain their situation had scarcely begun when the Zionist leader, holding his face in his hands and shaking with sobs like a child who has just been beaten, burst into a fit of rage:

– What good is this conversation? What good will it do if I live longer? I should go to the Germans and tell them who I am. When all the Jews have been murdered they won't need any leaders…But it doesn't do any good to talk to you about it. Someone from the outside cannot possibly understand. You don't understand it either. Even I don't understand why my people are dying and I'm still alive.

The older man tried to calm him down, putting one hand on his shoulder while nervously clenching and unclenching the fingers of his other hand.

– We have a job to do, he said, and our time has almost run out. We have to get down to business.

It took a moment for the Zionist leader to get a hold of himself. Finally, he smiled sadly and asked me to excuse him.

I told him that he had no reason to apologize and still less to worry that I had taken his emotional reaction badly. I grasped the situation.

– I'm here to help you if I can, I added. Soon I'll be in London and I'll have the opportunity to meet with the Allied authorities.

– Really? asked the Zionist leader, in a voice tinged with hope. Do you think you'll be able to meet with Roosevelt and Churchill?

– Maybe. If not, certainly with at least someone close to them. We have a mission to accomplish in the name of the underground Polish resistance and I will be accredited by the Polish government in London; my opinion will have an official character and you must give me an official message to send to the outside world. What do you want me to tell them?

They hesitated a few seconds as if they were weighing what to say in their minds, as if they were carefully choosing their words so as to best express their deepest feelings, to best explain their situation and their appeals. With his hands resting on the table as though this gesture helped him concentrate, the head of the Bund spoke first:

– We want you to tell the Polish government, the Allies and their leaders that we are powerless in the face of the German murderers. We cannot defend ourselves and no one here in Poland can defend us. The underground Polish authorities can save a few individuals but they can't save the masses. The Germans are not trying to enslave us, as they have with other nations; we are being systematically murdered.

– That's what people don't understand, the Zionist leader added. That's the hardest thing to make them understand.

I nodded my head. The Bundist continued.

– Our people as a whole will be exterminated. Perhaps a handful can be saved but the three million Polish Jews are doomed. There is no force here in Poland that can stop that from happening, not the Jewish resistance nor the Polish underground resistance. Put the responsibility for this on the shoulders of the Allies. You must do something so that no League of Nations leader can say he didn't know that in Poland we are being murdered, and that only outside aid can do any good.

This was the solemn message I took out to the world. They impressed it upon me so well that I could never forget it. With full knowledge of their situation, they told me that more than 1.8 million Jews were dead. These two men held no illusions. They feared that the way the League of Nations would react to this news was all too predictable: they wouldn't be able to believe it, they'd say that these numbers were exaggerated and unreal. Therefore I had to be ready to argue my case, to convince them, in short, to do everything I could, marshaling eyewitness reports and evidence, hammering at the truth until it became impossible to deny.

They had prepared for me a precise statistical study of the number of Jewish dead in Poland. I needed a few further details.

– Could you tell me, I asked, the approximate number of people in the ghetto who were murdered?

– German orders concerning the transfers make it possible to give you a very nearly exact figure, answered the Zionist leader.

– Does that mean that every single person who is transferred ends up dead?

– Every single one, the Bundist leader confirmed. Of course the Germans pretend otherwise. Even now, when there is no longer any room for even the slightest doubt, letters come from people we know are dead, happy letters telling their families and friends that they are working, that they're in good health, eating meat and white bread. But we know the truth and with our help you can see it for yourself.

– When did the transfers start?

– The first orders date to July. The German authorities demanded that they be presented with 5,000 people a day, supposedly to be sent to work outside of Warsaw. They were shipped straight to death camps. Later the daily quota was raised to six, seven, and finally 10,000 people. When the Germans ordered Czerniakow, the engineer who was chairman of the Judenrat, to provide 10,000 people a day for "work," he committed suicide. He understood what that meant.

– How many people have been "transferred" in all?

– More than 300,000. There are still more than 100,000 people left but the transfers are continuing.

I turned white. This was in early October 1942. In two and a half months the Nazis had committed 300,000 murders in one single quarter in Poland. The message I was to take to the world was a description of slaughter on an unprecedented scale. And this report had to be based on facts I myself had verified.

My interlocutors suggested that they take me into the Warsaw ghetto so that I could see with my own eyes the tableau of the annihilation of a people, so that I could watch them as they drew their last breath. They were also to take me to one of the many death camps where Jews were tortured and murdered by the thousands. The words of an eye witness would have more impact than those of someone relaying second-hand reports. At the same time, they warned me that if I accepted their proposal I would be risking my life. And further, after a visit like that, the visions of horror I would witness would haunt me for the rest of my days.

I told them that I absolutely had to see all this for myself. I hoped to reach the other side very soon and have the opportunity to report the facts to the rest of the world, the countries that were still civilized. If I didn't personally confirm the information that I was to transmit, then I couldn't consider myself up to the task incumbent upon me.

We agreed that they would make the necessary arrangements so that I could visit the ghetto and the camp as soon as possible. After that I was to come back to this house to continue discussing how best to present the situation of the Jews to the world. When I was about to leave, they very warmly wished me good night, standing like two battered shadows in the half-light of the candle, their voices conveying the confidence that they had in me and in the success of our enterprise.

When I came back the next time, neither the place nor the people had changed any more than the events that they reported. It would be difficult to imagine a more appropriate place for our meeting: an abandoned house in ruins, the deep silence interrupted only by our own voices and the wind, which constantly threatened to blow out the candle throwing rough, pale patches of light on the night around us.

We briefly took up the question of my visit to the ghetto, mechanically going over the details of how I was to dress and behave, as if we wanted to get rid of the subject as quickly as possible and go on to something more substantial. I ended by asking the two men what they would like me to say to the English and American authorities if they were to ask me how they could help. Their response was both bitter and realistic. They spoke as though they were only too aware that most of their proposals would come to nothing, that there was no hope that they would be implemented, but nevertheless they had to put forward the only measures that could end the suffering of their people.

The Zionist leader was the first to speak:

– The only things the Germans understand are force and violence. German cities should be bombarded mercilessly, and every time leaflets should be dropped to inform all Germans about the fate of the Polish Jews. They must be told that the German people will suffer the same fate both during and after the war. We are not in favor of massacring Germans and we hope that doesn't happen. But that threat is the only way to stop German cruelty, he went on. If accompanied by a demonstration of force, such a warning can scare the German people so much that they'll pressure their leaders hard enough to make them change their policies. Nothing else can have that kind of effect.

– We know, the Bundist leader added, that it will never be possible to put such a plan into effect and that the Allies will never make it a part of their strategy, but there's nothing else we can do. The Jews and those who want to help them cannot limit themselves to looking at this war solely from the point of view of military strategy. Tell the Allied governments that they must issue a formal notice to the German government and people, saying that if the persecution of the Jews continues then it will be answered by massive reprisals and the systematic destruction of the German people as a whole.

– I understand you, I responded. And I promise you that I will do everything within my power to give them your message and make them conscious of what you've told me.

– We want even more than that, the Zionist leader said. Hitler has announced that all Germans, no matter where they may live or their views, constitute a single racial group. He has gathered them all into a single army to dominate the world. He is waging all-out war against civilization and his avowed aim is the complete destruction of the Jewish people. This situation has no historical precedent and only unprecedented methods can deal with it. Everywhere the Allies can do so, in the United States, England and Africa, they must begin publicly executing every German they can grab. That's what we demand.

– But that's utterly inconceivable, I responded. That kind of demand will only unnerve and terrify the very people who feel sympathy for you.

– Of course, the Zionist leader shot back. Do you think I don't know that? We make that demand because it's the only possible way to respond to the way the Germans are treating us. Even in our wildest dreams we understand that these demands will never be carried out. And yet these are our demands. We are putting them forward so that people will understand how we feel in the face of this situation, so that they will understand how helpless we are, how desperate, and how little we expect from the Allied victory under these circumstances.

They both fell silent for a moment as if they were waiting for the seriousness of their situation to sink in. I began to feel overwhelmed with fatigue and nervous excitement. As time went by, these two desperate figures, pacing up and down the dark room where each step echoed for a long time in the deep silence, looked more and more like ghosts. The depths of their anguish, suffering and despair could never be expressed, and yet it was reflected in their eyes. They whispered or rather spoke in low tones, wheezing, and yet I had the impression that they were crying out. I felt like I was witnessing an earthquake; as though with a terrible sound the earth were opening up before me to swallow up a part of humanity, as though I could hear the screams and cries of the damned falling into the abyss.

– It can't be, they said in their wheezing voices, raising their clenched fists as if to threaten all those on the other side. It's just not possible that the democracies would accept the idea that there is no way to save the Jewish population of Europe. If American or English citizens can be rescued, why can't there be a mass evacuation of the Jews, at least the women and children, the old and infirm? Offer the Germans an exchange. Offer them money. Why can't the Allies pay a ransom for the lives of a few million Polish Jews?

– But how? How could they do that? I asked, moved by the desperate and disturbing quality of their suggestions. What you ask for is incompatible with any military strategy. How can we give the enemy money? How can we give them back soldiers they would send back to the front lines to fight against us?

– Exactly. Everyone tells us that these proposals run counter to the Allied war strategy. But a strategy can be changed, it can be modified as circumstances make necessary. Let it be modified so that it can include the saving of some, at least a small percentage of the Jewish people. Why does the world allow us to be killed? Haven't we made a contribution to culture and civilization? Haven't we worked, fought, shed our blood? Why does the world fight for everyone else? Why doesn't anyone say that the strategy and tactics have to be changed in response to the methods the Germans are using against the Jews?

I leaped up.

– What plan of action should I suggest in your name to the Jewish leaders in England and America? They have a certain influence over the waging of this war. They can help you.

The Bundist leader came up to me and without a word squeezed one of my shoulders so tightly it hurt. I was awestruck by his wild, wide-open eyes and thoroughly shaken by the immensity of the pain reflected in them.

– Tell the Jewish leaders that this matter can't be dealt with by political or strategic means. Tell them that they have to make the earth shake to the core and wake the world up. Only when the world opens its eyes will it see and understand – maybe. Tell them that they must find within themselves the strength and courage necessary to make sacrifices of the kind never before required of any statesman, sacrifices as painful and unique as the fate of my dying people. That's exactly what they don't understand. There is no historical precedent for the objectives and methods of the Germans. The democracies must react in an equally unprecedented fashion; in response, they have to choose methods that no one has ever even heard of until now. If they don't do that, their victory will be only a partial one, a purely military victory. Their methods will not protect the people being swallowed up by the Nazi extermination plan. Their methods won't protect us.

He stopped speaking, and it was only at that point that he released my shoulder from his grip. He paced nervously up and down the room. Then he stopped right in front of me. He spoke slowly, thoughtfully, as if each word were torn from his soul.

– You asked me what plan of action I suggest to the Jewish leaders. Tell them to go to every major institution and government office in England and the United States. Tell them not to leave until they have been unambiguously assured that a decision has been reached, that measures will be taken to save the Jews. They must refuse to eat or drink. Let them die a slow death before the eyes of the whole world. Let them die. That's the only way to awaken the world's conscience.

I fell back into a chair. I was trembling with chills and the blood was pounding in my temples. I stood up and got ready to leave.

– One more moment, said the Zionist leader. We didn't want to tell you this but I think that you should know. Our demand that foreign leaders make this kind of sacrifice is not an act of cruelty on our part. We intend to make the same sacrifices here ourselves. The ghetto will rise up in flames. Instead of dying a slow death we'll go down fighting. We will declare war against the Germans and it will be the most desperate declaration of war the world has ever seen.

For a short instant the leader of the Bund seemed terrified but he immediately leaned over to me and confirmed what his comrade had said. He spoke in a very low voice, as if he feared being overheard by someone who had their ear to the other side of the wall, or as if the wind might carry his words throughout the world and thus give away the plan for the insurrection to the Gestapo.

– We are organizing the defense of the ghetto, he said slowly through clenched teeth, not because we think we can defend it but so that the world can see our desperate struggle as a demonstration and a reproach. Right now we're engaged in conversations with your high command [the AK command] about the arms we need. If we receive weapons, the units in charge of the transfer are going to get a bloody surprise one of these days.

– We will be able to find out, the Zionist leader added, if we Jews can still win the right to die fighting instead of under torture as Hitler has decided. [...]

[In London], I was to meet with a leader of the Bund named Szmul Zygelbojm. He had worked in the underground Jewish movement in Poland until 1940 and been a member of the Warsaw ghetto Judenrat. If I recall correctly, he had even been imprisoned by the Nazis as a hostage for a period of time. [...]

At first sight, Zygelbojm looked like the kind of man I had often met among the Jewish leaders. With the hard, distrustful gaze of a proletarian, he was the sort of self-made man who was not about to let himself be taken in by fine words and who smelled lies everywhere. Life had undoubtedly been hard for him when he was young; perhaps he had worked as an errand boy for a tailor or as a street sweeper. "I had better be careful," I thought to myself.

– What do you want me to talk to you about?

– About Jews, my friend. I'm Jewish. Tell me everything you know about the Jews in Poland.

– Are you authorized to receive a report on the information I gathered during joint meetings with the Zionist and Bundist leaders?

– Yes. I am the Bund representative on the National Council and I was one of its leaders in Poland. [...]

Later: "Are you Mr. Karski? I have been sent to tell you that Szmul Zygelbojm, member of the National Council and Bund representative in London, has committed suicide. He left a note saying that he had done everything he could to help the Jews in Poland but without success; since all his brothers and sisters were dying he had decided to join them. He left the gas on in his apartment."[20]

ARMS AND MEN

Both combat organizations began to recruit widely in the months following the deportation. For the ZOB, this became especially the case in early December.

> It was [...] about that time, in other words, mid-September and early October, that approximately 150 semi-trained people joined the ZZW. At that point the total number of fighters reached about 400. [There is a problem here: if there were 400 before the deportation, 50 lost in the course of it and 150 new recruits, that would make 500.] These soldiers were divided into three companies, and the fourth was to be formed in mid-April 1943. [...] Even at that point many hundreds of youth declared that they were determined to wage armed struggle against the Germans after the failure of the political compromise put forward by the brave Adam Czerniakow. [Here the term "brave" clearly refers to Czerniakow's suicide during the second day of the deportation and not his politics.] It was also at this time, in mid-October, when the ZOB was formed, organized by the ZKK (Jewish Coordinating Committee), itself created in October as an inter-party

20. Jan Karski, in Wladyslaw Bartoszewski and Zofia Lewinowa, *The Samaritans: Heroes of the Holocaust* (New York: Twayne Publishers, 1970), pp. 385–96; 399.

> organ representing various social and political groups. Therefore the most recent volunteers joined the ZOB.[21]

During October 1942, the ZOB sent a representative from the Aryan side, Arye Wilner, alias "Jurek," also mandated by the ZKN. He had – not without some difficulty – made contact directly with the government delegation and the AK commander-in-chief.[22] A document dated March 3, 1942, and signed by "Waclaw" (Henryk Wolinski) reads:

> On 2/12/42 I put the Bund representative Mikolaj in contact with the ZKN representative, Jurek. On that occasion Jurek gave me the by-laws of the KK [Coordinating Committee] and the ZOB, which represented the Jews in Warsaw as a whole. The KK had adopted these statutes during the night of December 1 in the ghetto. Mikolaj dropped all his objections to the ZKN's right to represent all the Jews before the Polish authorities and the two representatives of the Jews, Mikolaj and Jurek, now jointly represent the KK, in accordance with the powers granted them by its statues. [...]
>
> The two KK representatives (Jurek and Mikolaj) emphasized the importance of the ZOB's immediate need for arms supplies. [...]
>
> Mikolaj and Jurek ask for:
>
> 1. More weapons, because the ten handguns they have received are not enough to organize armed resistance or carry out anything but individual actions. [...]
>
> 2. Help in buying weapons; for their part, they confirm that they

---

21. Mendelson, "*Rozwoj i dzialanosc ZZW*."
22. "'Jurek' asked to establish contact between the representatives of the Jewish population and the country's civilian and military authorities so as to unite and subordinate their actions and obtain military aid for the ZOB. This contact was established on the basis of the two ZKK declarations...signed by 'Jurek' and 'Mikolaj' (Feiner, the Bund representative) and addressed to the commander-in-chief and the Government Delegate. Commander in Chief 'Grot' (Stefan Rowecki) responded to the Jewish delegation in his order of 11/11/1942. He had been informed of that declaration." AK Archives, cited in Mark, *Walka i zaglada warszawskiego getta*, p. 155.

> can raise the necessary money for this purchase. (My opinion on this: we should be the ones to buy them in order to control them.)[23]

In a message sent to London on January 23, 1943, "Kalina" (General Rowecki) wrote:

> Finally, Jews from various communist groups are asking us for arms. […] On a trial basis I have given them a few pistols. I'm not sure what use, if any, they will make of them. I won't give them any more.[24]

The practical results were not much: 20 revolvers, some of them unusable. There were also some small-scale black market purchases, it seems. We will come back to the ZOB's lack of armaments in the next chapter.

The ZZW's situation, according to concurring testimony from both sides, was incomparably better. Its main source of free arms since the beginning, the KB, continued to provide them by numerous means. Further, another Polish resistance organization under the AK, the PLAN (*Polska Ludowa AK cja Niepodleglosci* – Polish Popular Action for Independence), also bought weapons for the ZZW (see chapter 6) and got them in through the tunnels.

The following is a report of the first meeting between the PLAN and the ZZW, held without the knowledge of the KB, which is not even mentioned:

> Our meeting was to take place at 11 A.M. in Targowek, which was far away, somewhere near the Brodno cemetery. I remember that I didn't have much time. The meeting had been suggested only a few hours before I was supposed to leave Warsaw, and I hadn't yet gotten ready for my departure. I don't remember the exact date. It was toward the end of December 1942 when it was very cold. Frequent

23. Cited in Mark, *Walka i zaglada warszawskiego getta*, pp. 208–209.
24. Ibid., p. 117.

German police patrols made it difficult to travel. I knew nothing whatsoever about the people I was about to meet for the first time or their organization. There were few houses in that quarter and our meeting place was unpleasant; if this rendezvous turned out to be a trick, it would have been difficult to defend. All this made me have serious doubts – I had good reason to turn down the proposed meeting. But nevertheless I didn't hesitate for long. This meeting, I was assured, was to be with people who had put everything they had and all their spiritual strength into fighting the Germans. The three people who were my inseparable guards and I all took up our weapons and went to where we had been told that the meeting would take place.

The nature of the situation I found when we got there was exceptional and unprecedented. The building where my first meeting with ZZW representatives took place, located far from other houses, looked more like a large parking garage than a home. In a low-ceilinged, dark room, filled with army cots covered with a large quantity of grenades, pistols and ammunition, I found a number of young Jews in civilian clothing. Only the handguns and grenades at their belts, their leather boots, attitude and energetic movements revealed that they belonged to a military organization.

The reasons for their coming were laid out to me by Pawel, the head of the delegation. Also taking part in the discussion were Michal, Montek and Feliks, members of the Jewish organization, all under the age of 30, judging by their appearance.

The representatives of the Jewish military organization explained that they wanted to become a part of the Polish liberation movement that existed outside the ghetto. The leadership of this movement should take into account the organization's forces and make use of its technical and military resources in the ghetto in an insurrection against the Germans. Declaring their loyalty to the Polish state and the underground Polish authorities, they expressed a desire for help in terms of training and buying arms. During this long and exhausting discussion, the representatives of the Jewish organization informed me that all previous efforts to obtain aid for the ZZW from the Delegation of the Government in London had been fruitless. Since they felt that this situation was more the result of a lack of conscience on the part of a few individuals than the considered policy of the institutions in question, they had decided to give it one last try. [This is misleading, since the ZZW representatives hid from the military leader of this resistance organization, the PLAN, the fact that they had close and long-standing relations with another organization, the KB. Such a ruse was all the more risky in that both organizations were united, although fairly loosely, it is true, under the umbrella of the AK. But it succeeded: they were able to acquire arms from both sources, on a cash basis from the PLAN and free from the KB.] At the same time I was also told that they represented the Zionist movement and that many of them had undergone military training in Palestine [obviously this was a tall tale]. They wanted to continue the policy carried out by Jabotinsky, the head of the Zionist movement who had received aid from the pre-September 1939 government on numerous occasions, they claimed, and they hoped that under the present changed conditions, and at a somewhat different level, they could count on the support of the Polish people and authorities. I explained that while I had no mandate from the government delegation to enter into decision-making discussions on this matter, I was willing to accept the mission of facilitating the realization of their plans. Without being able to guarantee success, I promised to do everything in my power to see that their legitimate request was satisfied.

After agreeing on our next meeting, and having been invited to visit the ghetto, I asked them to explain to me how and under what conditions they had been able to leave the ghetto and reach such a distant site.

The house where we met was occupied by a trolley car conductor who had handed it over to the Jewish organization for a price. The arms and provisions bought in the city were brought here. It also served as a meeting place, and the supplies were transported from here into the ghetto. The delegates themselves had left the ghetto via an underground tunnel they promised to show me very soon. Earlier

> that day, they had succeeded in acquiring a lot of weapons, and now they had to get them into the ghetto as quickly as possible.
>
> To this end, two or three days before the meeting I have just described, a group of well-armed people headed by the organization's leader, Pawel [different writers describe the leader variously as Pawel Frenkiel, Apfelbaum or Rodal], had left the ghetto in the middle of the night. Since they were out in the city, and numerous and well-armed enough to deal with any danger, their leader had decided to take advantage of the situation to make contact and personally look into the possibilities for cooperation [...] with the Polish military and civilian authorities. Thus, by chance, they happened upon me.
>
> The little house/garage situated in a remote Warsaw suburb had been transformed into a fortress that could be defended at any time.
>
> I was very impressed by the attitude of the members of the Jewish organization, their fanatical thirst for combat and the enormous risks they had decided to take to defend their cause – all this bore testament to a high level of social consciousness and a sense of responsibility in their work. I was also very impressed by their ease and familiarity in the face of danger, which exercised an irresistible attraction over me.
>
> And so, when we said goodbye, I promised them – and myself as well – that I would do everything possible to help them in all their plans and undertakings.
>
> I felt that now we had confidence in one another and would not disappoint each other.[25]

In addition to the arms furnished by the KB and the PLAN, the ZZW continued to acquire weapons on the black market. In this regard, Ringelblum explains:

> Before my very eyes, an ex-Polish army officer sold weapons for a quarter of a million zlotys and was given a 50,000 zlotys down

25. Ketling-Szemley, "*Wspomnienia z walki dzialalnosci ZZW...*"

payment; also bought were two machine guns for 40,000 zlotys and a large quantity of grenades and bombs.[26]

THE FIGHT AGAINST THE COLLABORATORS

The execution of traitors was one of the tasks that obsessed the leaders of the two resistance organizations during this period. According to Cukierman, the fight against Jewish collaborators was first taken up by the ZOB, while Bednarczyk claims that the ZZW executed Gestapo stooges even before the "transfer operation" in the summer of 1942.

Here is the former's account:

> We had begun to act. [...] The police working for the Germans did most of their recruitment among assimilated circles. The majority of them were graduates of the elite schools and universities. Many of them were lawyers. [...] The bulk of the Jewish police spoke Polish, and a few of them spoke Yiddish. The Judenrat people came from the same background. Szerynski, the police chief, was a converted Jew. After our assassination attempt, he was replaced by Lejkin, a lawyer. Because he was short, the Germans called him "little Napoleon" and praised his brutality. [...] So after we became active again we decided to liquidate Lejkin[27] because Szmerling [Szmerling had changed his name to Szerynski] had disappeared from view. Later we tried to get rid of Szerynski again when it turned out that he was only wounded during our first attempt in August, but after the January revolt he killed himself. Since I'm not privy to the secrets of the human soul, I don't know why he did it. Maybe it was fear, maybe it was because he saw Jews fight while he, a converted Jew, was sending them to their death. [...] The names of the three people who carried

26. Ringelblum, *Polish Jewish Relations*, p. 170.
27. "This is to inform the public that following the indictment of the leadership, officers and functionaries of the Jewish Order Police – public notice of 17/08/42 – the death penalty has been carried out against Jakub Lejkin, deputy police chief, on 29/10/42 at 6:10 P.M." Mark, *Powstanie w getcie warszawskim*, p. 109.

out the attack are known. Lejkin was killed in broad daylight. […] That made a strong impression. […]

The second man to be condemned to death was Israel Fürst. […] He was the liaison between the Judenrat and the Gestapo. […] As far as his previous organizational membership is concerned, Fürst was a Revisionist. […] The Revisionists were no less loyal to their nation than we were. And when one of them did something against the Jews […] usually it was outside the ghetto. Finally we found out that from time to time, toward evening, Fürst would return to the ghetto and that he lived in the same group of buildings where our organization was located. […] As he approached his house […] Fürst got a bullet.

Mention should also be made of Anna Milewicz [a Gestapo agent], who had been a member of Hashomer Hatzair, and was liquidated by the Revisionists. […]

The Germans had created a so-called underground group called Zagiew. This was a group of assimilated Jews who had put out a number of issues of a magazine or a newsletter in 1941–42. It disappeared and then reemerged at the end of 1942–early 1943. They constituted themselves as a combat group and put out leaflets. We began to investigate who these people were. It turned out that they were a group in the pay of the Gestapo. In the course of this investigation, we obtained conclusive evidence from the brushmakers but the Revisionists cooperated with them. [This sentence is ambiguous in Polish. Did the Revisionists cooperate with the ZOB brushmakers? Or are they being accused of having cooperated with Zagiew, a Gestapo Trojan horse? Further, it is known that the ZZW executed members of that organization on at least three occasions.]

Another incident took place in which the revisionists killed a number of Germans. The Germans were in plain clothes, so of course they were agents. We contacted the Revisionists to explain to them that they shouldn't do things like that in the ghetto again, because in the end someone always had to pay the price for that kind of action.[28]

---

28. Zuckerman, *A Surplus of Memory*, pp. 244–47, 324–25, 330.

Here is what Bednarczyk has to say about this:

> The ZZW intelligence unit carried out a constant fight against the traitors at 13–14 Leszno Street. They had found out – with my help and participation – that a provocateur organization called Zagiew had been set up by the Gestapo. This organization recruited young patriots with a fighting spirit, so that later they could be forced, on pain of death, to betray their people by carrying out work against the Jews. The ZZW wiped out Zagiew three times and each time it was reconstituted by the Gestapo.
>
> There were certain strategic spots in the ghetto, areas around the gates and near the walls, that were used as observation posts around the clock by the intelligence unit. In general, our people were stationed in cafés, restaurants and other places where they could keep watch over them without being noticed. There were many of these observation posts. The intelligence unit also carried out liquidation operations. One of these, the biggest, took place at the end of May or early June 1942. After having observed the Zagiew gang, which included people of the "13" group, I figured out that they had a food storage depot on Elektoralna Street. [...] Through the ZZW's intelligence men I laid a trap for them, using our own hideout located in the grocery store on 6 or 8 Elektoralna Street. Immediately after their first shipment of contraband (of course every Zagiew shipment got through), all of their organization's members held a party that night. There were 11 of them, including three women. When their drinking had reached a peak, they were surrounded by the ZZW intelligence platoon. With the aid of Mendelson's platoon they tied them up and gagged them, and drove them in a rickshaw to Karmelicka Street, where they were court-martialed. Their treason wasn't hard to prove, since all of them were carrying identification provided by the Gestapo, service pistols and permits to carry guns. After they were duly judged, they were killed and their bodies buried in a basement. A report was sent to the OW-KB. When Chaya Blumberg was executed in a market by "Garbaty" and "Rudy," that made a big impression. [...] In the spring of 1942, two other Zagiew

> members were killed on Karmelicka Street. [...] I led that action myself, and Zelwanski and "Balbina" also took part. These Gestapo agents had been drinking with us at the Sztuka, and once they were drunk we offered to buy them a meal at Szulc's restaurant on Karmelicka Street. We walked with them arm in arm while discreetly patting down their guns. Then, on Karmelicka Street, we pushed them into a building entrance where ZZW men stabbed them and took their weapons. During roughly the same period, another Gestapo agent, Branstein, was killed. Makower and I were there.
>
> In June 1942, just after the big action when the 11 Zagiew members were liquidated, a second lieutenant whose name I can't remember was killed. [...] There were other executions of traitors and the pace of them increased between March and July 1942, and then from January to April 1943.[29]

Thus, it is well established that the ZZW was very active in executing collaborators. But even this activity gave rise to criticism and conflict. Here is a criticism of the ZZW by Cukierman, who confirms the ZZW's anti-collaborationist activity:

> Among those sentenced to death, including the Germans' "best" servants, mention must be made of Fürstenberg, executed by the Revisionists. This incident sheds light on the role they played. Fürstenberg, a high-ranking officer in the Jewish police, very clearly deserved to die. At that time he feared for his life and was trying to redeem himself by promising to find us arms and, of course, weapons were very important to us. That's why we hesitated and were in no hurry to sentence him to death. That's when the Revisionists showed up and killed him. I don't feel that the elimination of Fürstenberg was a big sin. But this incident proves that there was no cooperation between us and the Revisionists. Fürstenberg knew what we did to Szerynski, Lejkin and Fürst; he knew that we weren't fooling around. To save his own skin he had begun to get us some

29. Bednarczyk, *Zycie codzienne warszawskiego getta*, pp. 63–64.

> weapons. We had totally reliable information about this. Fürstenberg could obtain them through the Polish police. And even better, he didn't ask for payment.[30]

So allegedly, according to the ZOB, the ZZW killed Gestapo agents and their Jewish stooges, but they didn't do it in the right way. When someone keeps bad company...

SUMMARY

Relatively speaking, during the *Grossaktion*, the ZZW did not lose a significant amount of men or arms (50 dead, according to Mendelson). Recruitment had been facilitated by a new spirit of resistance: 150 new recruits had brought the total number of fighters up to 400 on the eve of the January days. Two new tunnels (on Karmelicka Street and Muranowski Square) had been dug. In addition to the arms furnished without charge by the OW-KB, the ZZW had established ties with other organizations belonging to the Polish resistance.

In the months following the deportation, the ZOB was founded within a broad political framework, and the ZZW grew. The two organizations could not reach an agreement. The Jewish population, reduced by 90 percent and now considerably younger, lost all hope, while the Judenrat and the Jewish police lost all authority.

30. Zuckerman, *A Surplus of Memory*, p. 323.

CHAPTER 6

THE RESISTANCE OF JANUARY 1943

On January 9, 1943, Himmler visited the ghetto, surrounded by armored cars. This presaged a new catastrophe in the near future. In fact, he gave orders that the ghetto be liquidated as soon as possible.[1] Two days later, he ordered that 8,000 Jews be deported immediately: "There are still 40,000 Jews, of whom 8,000 must be shipped out within the next few days."[2]

THE LEAFLETS

A few days after Himmler's visit, the ZOB and the ZZW printed out appeals for armed resistance. The following is a mid-January 1943 ZOB leaflet:

> During the last few weeks, rumors have circulated about letters supposedly received from Jews expelled from Warsaw who are said

1. "Confidential! 1) I order the creation of a concentration camp in the Warsaw ghetto; 2) All Jews in Warsaw shall be transferred to this camp; Jews are forbidden to work for private companies; 3) The private factories currently located in the ghetto will be transferred to the concentration camp (State-owned factory); 4) The Warsaw concentration camp, including its companies and inhabitants, shall be transferred to the Lublin area as soon as possible, but in such a way so that production does not suffer; Himmler." Tatiana Berenstein, Artur Eisenbach, Adam Rutkowski, eds., *Eksterminacja Zydow poskich w okresie okupacji hitlerowskiej* (Warsaw, 1957), doc. 169, pp. 323–24.
2. Letter from Himmler to Krüge on January 11, 1943, in *Nuremberg Documents*, the Pohl trial documents, no. 1882.

> to be in a work camp near Pinsk or Borujsk. Jewish masses! Do not believe this nonsense! It is being spread by people in the pay of the Gestapo! This is an attempt by the bloodthirsty murderers to pacify the Jewish population so that they can carry out another transfer without difficulty, without risk to the Germans and with a minimum of effort. They don't want the Jews to build bunkers and resist. Jews, don't repeat these lies – don't help these agents! All the Gestapo murderers will have to pay! Jewish masses, the time is coming, you must be ready to resist. Not a single Jew should climb into the freight cars. Let those not in a position to fight actively carry out passive resistance – let them hide. We have just learned that in Lwow, the Jew Order Police acted alone in carrying out the deportation of 6,000 Jews. This won't happen in Warsaw. The shooting of Lejkin is the best proof of that. Our slogan is: Let us all prepare to die like men![3]

Another leaflet, by the ZZW, declared:

> Prepare to act! Be on the alert! Let us rise up to fight!
>
> Our aim is the awakening of the nation. We want to cast our watchword before all of society: Awaken and fight! Do not lose hope in the possibility of salvation. You should know that salvation does not lie in going passively to our deaths like sheep. It lies in struggle.
>
> He who struggles to save his life has a chance to save it. He who resigns himself in advance to not struggling is lost in advance. What awaits him is a shameful death in the Treblinka smothering machines. Awaken, my people, and fight! Cease this shameful acceptance that "we are doomed to die." That's not true! We too have the right to live! We must know how to fight for this right!
>
> It's not hard to live when life is graciously given to you. It is harder to live when they want to snatch your life away! Awaken, my people, and fight for your life! Let each mother become a lioness

3. Cited in Mark, *Powstanie w getcie warszawskim*, pp. 119–20.

defending her cubs! Let fathers cease to go along with the death of their children. Let there be no repetition of the shame of the first act of our perdition! Enough resignation! Enough resignation and lack of faith! Enough of our slavish souls!

Let the enemy pay with his blood for each Jewish life taken! Let each home become a fortress! Awaken, my people, and fight! Your salvation lies in fighting! He who struggles for his life can save it!

We are rising up in the name of the struggle for the life of the unarmed masses whose salvation we seek! It is not for our own lives that we want to fight! We will not have the right to save ourselves until after we have fulfilled our duty!

As long as the life of a single Jew is in danger we must be on the alert and fight! Our watchword: Let not one more Jew die in Treblinka! Enough traitors to the nation!

Unconditional struggle against the occupier until the last drop of our blood!

Prepare to act! Be on the alert![4]

To demonstrate the moral superiority of the ZOB, Israel Gutman, a survivor of the Warsaw ghetto and a leading historian of the Holocaust, wrote:

> This clearly shows the difference between the two combat organizations. The ZOB leaflet makes no reference to the possibility of being saved and surviving. The authors of this leaflet promise nothing; rather, they point out that there is no way to avoid death. The only choice is determining the type of death: passive or active. The

4. The Polish ZIH original of this document is undated. It is referenced as part of the Ringelblum archives (cf. ZIH, Ring. index no. II/333). But the text is the same as that cited by certain sources (Mark, Gutman, Lazar) as an appeal of January 1943. We have a typewritten text dated February 1943 (cf. Odezwa ZZW 1943 [1943 ZZW Appeal], ZIH, index no. 230/113), whose content is identical to that of the January appeal. Is this a mistake or was there a new public opinion campaign by the ZZW that included the reprinting of the leaflet? Cited in Mark, *Powstanie w getcie warszawskim*, pp. 120–21.

> authors of the ZZW leaflet present struggle as though it offered the possibility of survival; they introduce an element of hope.[5]

This subtle criticism is an excellent example of excessive zeal in the ideological struggle. But nevertheless, it is unfounded. The following contemporaneous ZOB leaflet, dated January 18, 1943, which Gutman does not cite, declares, "You can save yourself by fighting." It reads:

> Jews!
> The occupier is beginning the second act of our destruction.
> Do not go to your death without resisting!
> Defend yourselves!
> Take up an axe, a crowbar, a knife! Barricade yourselves in your home!
> Let them have to take you like that… [ellipsis in the original]
> You can save yourself by fighting!
> Fight back![6]

THE RESISTANCE OF THE ZOB

On January 18, 1943, at 7 A.M., the German forces – 200 SS men and their auxiliaries, 800 troops from the Baltic countries and the Ukraine – entered the ghetto. There were no visible preparations and the attack was a complete surprise.

When it began to resist, the ZOB had little at its disposal. Z. Lubetkin, a leading member of the ZOB, recalls, "We began the January revolt with few arms and few grenades. The group under the direct leadership of Anielewicz had a total of five pistols and five grenades. Cukierman's group, with 40 people, had four pistols and six grenades."[7]

---

5. Gutman, *Zydzi warszawscy*, p. 306.
6. Cited in Mark, *Powstanie w getcie warszawskim*, p. 122.
7. Krakowski, *The War of the Doomed*, p. 180.

On the first day, the German and Jewish plant managers encouraged the population to voluntarily present themselves at Umschlagplatz for shipment: not to a death camp, they said, but to work camps. This, of course, was once again a lie, because all Jews, whether they surrendered voluntarily or not, were sent to Treblinka to be killed. The Judenrat seconded these appeals in its own name and ordered its own employees to report to Umschlagplatz.

Very few people volunteered. The Germans and their Baltic and Ukrainian auxiliaries, and "a small number of the Polish blue police"[8] (this time, the Jewish police did no more than help, due to their diminishment in number at the end of the Great Deportation, and perhaps because they were discouraged by the assassination attempts on their chiefs) began to use force to round up not only the "illegals" living in "unauthorized" (i.e., officially unoccupied) buildings but also the "legal" employed factory workers. The armed resistance began with the waging of partisan warfare.

A ZOB member recalls:

> Wednesday, January 20. At noon, Mordechaj [Anielewicz] shows me the seized weapons, a carbine and a parabellum semiautomatic. We disarmed a German SS man and took his weapons. [...] M. describes the battle at the corner of Zamenhof and Niska. He was in the middle of a group of Jews [being taking to Umshlagplatz]; when he raised his hand, that unleashed the fighting. Some of the SS men fell, others fled, losing their helmets and even their guns. Then the Germans burned down the house where M. and his group were barricaded. But they were able to escape.[9]

The ZOB had very few weapons: 20 pistols furnished by the Polish resistance (10 in December 1942, 10 in January 1943),[10] a small

8. "A small number" could be construed as a compromise between a concern for the truth and a desire to minimize Polish participation on the part of Bednarczyk, *Zycie codzienne warszawskiego getta*, p. 80.
9. Hersz Berlinski, alias Jelen, in Mark, *Powstanie w getcie warszawskim*, p. 121.
10. "We have received from the AK scarcely a few dozen guns and that was not enough to arm the men in our unit." Zuckerman, *A Surplus of Memory*, p. 255. This is confirmed by the higher levels of the AK, as has been seen in chapter 5.

quantity bought on the black market, and an even smaller amount supplied by the GL [Gwardia Ludowa, People's Guard], which at that point was itself still in an embryonic stage and unarmed. In total, some 30 handguns and a similar number of grenades.

THE ZZW'S RESISTANCE

The ZZW had one weapon per soldier, thousands of grenades and several dozen automatic weapons. With the single exception of the light machine gun T. Makower used at the corner of Smocza and Nowolipki,[11] the ZZW did not use its heavy arms or automatic weapons, and did not send companies or even platoons into action but satisfied itself with actions by individuals or five-man units, using small arms exclusively. Mendelson recounts:

> The fighting in the Warsaw ghetto began with the so-called January action that took place January 18–21, 1943. More than 400 soldiers of the ZZW grouped in three companies, as well as my own platoon, took part in this battle. The well-trained and well-armed ZZW soldiers bore the brunt of the fighting. [There is plenty of bad faith on both sides – numerous witnesses concur that the ZOB fought hard as well.]
>
> The German troops were under the command of Oberfürher Ferdinand von Sammern-Frankenegg, head of the SS and police in the Warsaw district. The Germans intended to remove a third of the remaining Jewish population in Warsaw, about 20,000 people. [This figure, also given by Bednarczyk, is not confirmed by any other source;[12] the previously cited order by Himmler refers to 8,000.] But they were met with armed resistance. The operation was car-

11. "Except for one occasion at the corner of Smocza and Nowolipki streets…where a machine-gun was used…(I have verified this: it was T. Makower who was shooting), the ZZW did not use automatic weapons." Bednarczyk, *Zycie codzienne warszawskiego getta*, p. 83. I have found no confirmation of Makower's action.
12. "They were given the task of removing 15–20,000 Jews from the ghetto, i.e., a third of the ghetto's population…." Bednarczyk, *Zycie codzienne warszawskiego getta*, p. 80.

ried out by 200 German SS and 800 Latvians and Lithuanians. The German appeals for people to voluntarily surrender themselves at Umschlagplatz, and the encouragement in this regard by German factory managers, were in vain. The round-ups in the streets and apartment buildings had little effect because the people were hiding out in all sorts of places, including the underground bunkers under construction at that point. Many SS were killed or wounded during these round-ups, forcing the German command to change tactics. They began sending patrols made up of some ten men and avoided dispatching smaller units to prowl the streets. Groups of Jews taken by surprise were marched to Umschlagplatz, but the soldiers escorting them were attacked along the way by ZZW units. [What about the ZOB?] Many hundreds of people were able to escape during ambushes. We adopted the tactic of attacking the Nazis by surprise and avoiding frontal engagements so as not to expose our troops. It was forbidden to use automatic weapons. Each platoon was under orders to defend its own perimeter and carry out surprise attacks against the Germans. Thanks to this approach to combat, the ZZW fighters suffered very few losses. These four days of fighting served as a harsh training period for the resistance forces. My platoon and I found ourselves in a densely-populated industrial and residential area bounded by Karmelicka, Leszno, Smocza and Nowolipki Streets, which included the large Fric Schulc plant, the Hoffmann and K.G. Schultz workshops, and, nearby, the Hallman firm. Tadeusz Bednarczyk provided essential aid in leading the ZZW forces overall. He spent four days with us in the ghetto supervising the execution of the orders concerning how to fight. Our tactics were proven correct because they wore down the Germans. They were only able to arrest 6,000 people, including the sick taken from the hospital, and on January 21 at noon they halted the incursion and left the ghetto. The operation cost them more than 10 soldiers killed and dozens wounded, not only by bullets but also the stones, knives and hammers used by unarmed ZOB soldiers and civilians. Our own losses were minimal, a few dead and about 10 wounded. Actually, our sentries warned us in time when the Germans were approaching and told us how many there were, so that we could either stage an ambush, or, if the aggressors were too numerous, retreat elsewhere or go down into the bunkers. The ZOB's losses were many times higher than ours. Fighting took place all over the ghetto. The ZZW 1st and 3rd company and all the ZOB's soldiers took part.[13]

A FEELING OF VICTORY

On the fourth day, January 21 at noon, the Germans withdrew after killing more than 1,000 Jews in the ghetto (the official statistic given by the Judenrat is 1,171)[14] and deporting 5,500 to Treblinka, according to their own figures. Since the total number of victims was declared to be 6,500,[15] well short of the goal of 8,000 set by Himmler, it is probable that von Sammern deliberately exaggerated these numbers. During this operation, several dozen ZOB fighters were killed (Edelman says that 80 percent of the ZOB's forces perished)[16] and the ZZW lost about half a dozen soldiers.[17]

But the unfolding of events was very different from the previous summer:

> Thursday, January 21. [...] Today is very different than yesterday. Today yelling and kicking is not enough to make people go to the transfer train station, to make them come down from the third floor and line up. Today they have to [...] take care when they're looking for people, because a Jewish fighter might spring up from nowhere and open fire. They climb the stairs slowly [...] and blockade every house.[18]

---

13. Mendelson, "*Ci, ktorzy byli z nami.*"
14. Mark, *Powstanie w getcie warszawskim*, p. 294.
15. Figure given by Stroop: "In January 1943, another resettlement operation was carried out, which encompassed a total of 6,500 Jews." See Stroop, *The Stroop Report*, p. 3.
16. Marek Edelman, *Getto walczy* [The ghetto fights], (Warsaw: Bund Central Committee, 1945), p. 47.
17. "The ZZW suffered half as many losses as the Germans...ZZW soldiers killed a dozen Germans and Baltic troops." In Bednarczyk, *Zycie codzienne warszawskiego getta*, p. 83.
18. Berlinski, cited in Mark, *Powstanie w getcie warszawskim*, p. 207.

The Germans withdrew without having met their objectives. It is not possible, however, to deduce how much of the Jews' success was due to the respective fighting of each of the two organizations, or to the passive but fierce resistance of civilians, as well as the increasingly desperate situation of the German army under General von Paulus at Stalingrad.

But the ghetto's people did not know that the immediate operation had only limited the Germans' objectives, and falsely believed that the revolt and passive resistance alone had prevented total annihilation. This feeling of victory played a major role in the preparations for the April events.

THE MYSTERY OF THE ZZW

The ZOB was taken by surprise, not only by the German operation itself but the timing of its unleashing. "Only five groups were able to go into action. The others, taken by surprise [...] couldn't get to their arms caches."[19]

The ZZW, for its part, kept most of its soldiers quartered in barracks, and yet it seems to have been only minimally active. Bednarczyk gives this explanation: "[A]n open, frontal engagement...cannot take place under such conditions. [...] The ZZW waged this battle in the form of urban guerrilla warfare, considering it a kind of real-life drill. [...] The ZZW fought above all near the clandestine sites where its soldiers were barracked and its arms were stored."[20]

This is confirmed by the only surviving ZZW officer. The ZZW's strange behavior – the engagement of only a small portion of its forces, the failure to use heavy weapons or even light automatic weapons – could be seen as the result of orders from the OW-KB, represented in the ghetto by Bednarczyk, which may have believed it necessary to camouflage the real strength of the Jewish resistance

19. Edelman, *Getto walczy*, p. 30.
20. Bednarczyk, *Zycie codzienne warszawskiego getta*, p. 82.

in view of a future decisive battle. But in the context of a German operation, which the ZZW command had every reason to believe could continue without interruption until total extermination, this explanation does not seem credible.

Yet I cannot help suspecting that their competition with the ZOB, who were poorly armed and poorly trained but politically predominant, may have played a role in the ZZW's approach to this battle.

At any rate, the judgment passed by each of the two organizations regarding the other's actions demonstrates equal bad faith on both sides. In Bednarczyk's book – which was published in 1995 – out of the six pages devoted to the January resistance, there are 22 lines discussing the ZOB, including the following: "[T]he documents do not paint an accurate portrait of the actions and as a general rule attribute them to the ZOB."[21] Gutman goes one step further – in a book published in 1982, out of 12 pages only two lines refer to the ZZW: "At this time we do not have any data concerning the activity of the ZZW during the January deportation."[22]

21. Bednarczyk, ibid., p. 83.
22. Gutman, *Zydzi warszawscy*, pp. 314–15.

CHAPTER 7

LAST PREPARATIONS

The January victory transformed the mood in the ghetto. People became convinced not only that resistance was possible, but that it could also be effective.

The urgency of the situation was felt by all, because everyone was certain that the Germans were preparing themselves to finish the massacre. But each individual was faced with three options: fleeing to the "Aryan" side, hiding in the ghetto and armed resistance.

FLIGHT

The flight option required close Polish accomplices, a "good" appearance and a perfect command of Polish with no tell-tale accent, and money. The various routes and options available by which to leave the ghetto included: the sewers,[1] the ZZW tunnels, the columns of Jewish workers who went out daily (an adult could slip into their ranks – although he or she would be killed instantly if discovered) and the garbage trucks driven by members of the Polish resistance led by the OW-KB.

1. This is how my parents and I escaped in February 1943 – the crossing took a dozen hours.

The Sewers

Zajdler Wladyslaw Zarski, a KB officer who was to play a very important role in the uprising, recalls:

> April 1943. Warsaw was under high pressure. In the face of their defeat, the Germans were determined to bury millions of human lives under the ruins of their military power, no matter what. A crazed terror paralyzed traffic in the city. The red wall encircling the ghetto divided streets and buildings. Behind this wall, surrounded by a cordon of SS men armed to the teeth [this is a bit of poetic license – the wall was guarded by Jewish, Polish and German police], thousands of people were dying of hunger, disease and Nazi bullets.
>
> The Jews had joined underground organizations such as the ZOB, the ZZW and others. The Jewish combat groups had made contact with the Polish underground organizations.
>
> Inside the ghetto itself, there were Polish organizations that transferred Jews and helped them. They got them papers and money and provided the secure contacts that enabled them to survive. One of these groups was headed by Henryk Iwanski, alias "Bystry," who had several bases in the ghetto [...]. [In the ghetto the KB acted only through the ZZW and at its request; it had no base of its own there.] The preparatory meeting on 32 Senatorska Street was scheduled for 10 A.M. I was one of the first to arrive. "Bystry" explained the situation to us: we were to smuggle arms into the ghetto; a large quantity. Three boxes of "Filipinka" grenades "Bystry" had made on the Saint-Stanislas hospital grounds, a few rifles, submachine guns and pistols. All these arms had to be brought in through the sewers, since the other transportation routes had been exposed. Our guide was to be "Tomasz," who knew the Warsaw sewers like the back of his hand. We discussed the details of this mission and set a date for the arms shipment.
>
> On the appointed day we were all there. Meanwhile, another group had taken the weapons to the apartment of "Bystry" at 36a Zlota Street.
>
> The building's concierge, Mateusz Przytulski, was engaged in a

conversation with "Skierko" in the building's archway, as if this were a normal day, while closely watching the street. The whole shipment was to leave the entrance in a few moments. "Bystry," "Sep"-Kowalski, and, off to the side, Professor Mateuszczyk, stood in front of the building on 49 Zlota Street, the latter rubbing his hands nervously. "Tomasz," wearing rubber boots and leaning on a lever, was next to an open sewer manhole in the courtyard of the building on 49 Zlota Street.

I stood alongside Konstanty Piotrowski near a hand truck loaded with packages and covered with a tarp. With a Vis pistol in my belt and my coat open, I waited.

"Bystry" slowly pulled out a handkerchief, took off his hat and wiped his forehead. This was the signal to get started.

As I pushed the cart it got stuck in a pothole. I pushed harder and headed towards the sewer manhole.

The boxes were ready to be lowered. They were wrapped in long pieces of rope so that they could be brought down more rapidly.

I was right next to the manhole cover. We took off the tarp and carefully climbed down with our load. "Bystry," "Tomasz" and "Skierko" were already in the sewer; "Sep" and I guarded the rear. The last package disappeared into the depths of the sewer. I was the last to climb down; the guard remained outside.

We each took up our package and followed "Tomasz." He led the way, lighting the ground with a torch. Anyone who has ever ventured into a sewer knows how "nice" it is: the stinking mud under our feet, the wet, slippery walls, the water dripping down our collars…

Finally the signal: Careful, be quiet! We had arrived at our destination. The exit was at 4 Karmelicka Street. An underground passage had been dug between the building's basement and the sewer manhole, camouflaging the exit from undesirable eyes.

When we came to a low-ceilinged, windowless cellar, I recognized Boruch Federbasch [Federbusz], a porter by trade and head of a platoon in the Polish army. Beside him were Chaim Goldberg, Moryc Apfelbaum and Henryk Sobelsolen. Boruch shook our hands and asked, "How was it, tell me how was it in there?"

"Shitty," I replied, which was the truth.

"Do you think I can't smell?"

We put the packages down and went into another cellar. There were a lot of people. They were "preparing" the group we were to take with us on our return trip.

We could barely see people's outlines by the torch light. Somewhere off in a corner a baby was crying. But aside from that it was almost completely quiet; people were whispering to one another.

A woman wrapped up in scarves came up to me. Her pale face and shining eyes were terrifying by torch light. Her hollow cheeks made her face seem all the more pale.

– Are you going to take us, she asked. I'm bringing my little girl. I beg you to take us far away from this hell.

I felt my throat tighten. All I could see were her great big frightened eyes which were intensely fixed on me. I first cleared my throat, and then said,

– Of course, madam.

She grabbed my hand.

– That's good, that's good, she said.

Meanwhile, "Bystry" was explaining to them in a low voice how to proceed and in what order to go down through the manhole. [...]

Somewhere, in some corner, a woman was sobbing silently. A man could be heard trying to reassure her. "Sh! Sh! Maybe I'll get out next time and we'll be together again. Come on, get a hold of yourself...."

A final salute, handshakes and we went back into the sewer. If walking loaded down with crates of arms had seemed difficult, this time it was horrible. The children began to cry and their mothers tried to calm them. We constantly had to halt and reorganize. We took turns carrying the children on our shoulders. You couldn't walk for very long stooped down as we were trying to avoid banging our heads on the ceiling. Every dozen steps or so, our backs aching and heads spinning, we had to stop and rest again.

Janina Sonnenberg and her two little children, Ruchla Dudek

and Rojza, her 12-year old daughter Anna Guminska and her son Moryc, were part of this group, among other people.

The whole lot ended up in the apartment of "Bystry"; from there, after the necessary preparations, everyone would be taken to our safe houses.

That night I slept at the concierge's place. The next morning, washed and cleaned off, I went to 32 Senatorska Street where I gave a report on the operation to "Tarnawa." I informed him of the date set for the next evacuation. Unfortunately, this was our last operation.

On April 19, 1943, flames, gunfire and exploding grenades announced to the city of Warsaw, and later the whole world, the beginning of the last stage of the genocide.

The ghetto launched its last, hopeless struggle. The fighters had only one way out: to die fighting for the human dignity that fascism had trampled underfoot.[2]

Tunnels

Bednarczyk writes:

> The ZZW had taken advantage of the period before the insurrection to strengthen its fortifications for the coming battle. Two more tunnels leading to the Aryan side were dug [one under Muranowski Square, the other under Karmelicka Street], so as to bring in aid and assure an escape route. Emphasis was placed on reinforcing the positions on the odd-numbered side of the square. These positions provided extremely important protection for a new underground passage under the square between number 6 Muranowksi Square on the Aryan side and the building at number 7, and the first company's headquarters. Construction on this tunnel began at the end of January 1943. [This date seems wrong; since Ketling writes that he used it in January 1943 and that it had been finished in October 1942, and Karski used it as early as October 1942 – see chapter 5.]

2. Wladyslaw Zarski-Zajdler, "*Ostatni transport*," *Express Wieczorny*, no. 95 (April 20–21, 1968).

Inside, it was as high as a man is tall and wide enough so that two people could get by each other. The enormous quantity of earth dug up was carried into the cellars of abandoned neighboring buildings. It was very difficult to find enough timbers to shore up the ceiling and prevent it from falling in. These problems were finally resolved and even the weight of tanks did not make it collapse. The tunnel had to be built to meet high standards because the ZZW command wanted to be able to use it to evacuate their units to the forests in the future after the fighting was over, if it decided to do so. But at the same time the command also entertained another plan to do the opposite – to refuse to evacuate after the main battle and continue fighting until the last bullet and the last soldier. It was in light of this latter option that the fortifications at 7 Muranowski Square were reinforced. This plan was formulated by Lieutenant Leon Rodal, who as commanding officer of the first company was in charge of this area. He supervised the building of "chimneys," the barricading of ground-floor windows, and the construction of many shafts between cellars, attics and the floors between. He prepared well-situated shooting stands in the ruins of the house at 11 Muranowski Square. Piles of rubble stretched for several meters into the square itself. The building at the corner where Bonifraterska Street met the square was also buttressed and adapted for the purposes of combat. Rodal had not neglected to provide the area with a secondary escape route through the sewers and coming out on the Aryan side. But this exit was not used during the uprising.

The ZZW dug a fourth passageway between numbers 4 and 5 Karmelicka Street, under the grounds of the Evangelist hospital, tunneling part of the way and making use of the sewers for the rest. [This is the passageway referred to in the previous eyewitness account.] You went from the passageway into the sewers through an opening situated in the upper part of the sewers. This opening had doors on both the tunnel side and the sewer side, which meant that either comings and goings had to be highly synchronized or that it had to be guarded on both sides at all times, because the doors closed tightly, from outside and inside the sewers as well. Someone had to close one door after the last man passed through and someone else had to open the other. This passageway was built in the fall of 1942. It was used to bring in arms and get people out. Lieutenant Mendelson (and his platoon) were in charge of operating it and evacuating the ghetto's inhabitants. He had inside help from Sister Elzbieta, who worked in the hospital. Between November 1942 and April 1943 much of the aid that the OW-KB sent for the ZZW and the ghetto came through this route. It was also used to bring in arms, munitions and the bulk of the food and medical supplies stocked up for the insurrection.[3]

The Garbage Collectors

Teodor Niewiadomski, responsible for one of the garbage trucks, recounts:

> In 1940, Mayer, who was at that time head of the *Zaklad Oczyszczania Miasta* [ZOM, Municipal Sanitation Department], set up a separate transport unit, the *Dzial Wywozu Smieci* [Garbage Collection Service], called the DWS, to be run by Skowronski.
>
> Alfred Hebich was this service's most trusted man. He was a freshly-minted Volksdeutsch [a Pole or other non-German individual who acquired the privileges of the master race thanks to the discovery of a German ancestor, no matter how distant] and loved to "devour" Poles, always on the alert for treason to his new fatherland.
>
> Übermensch Hebich [...] did not speak a word of German, which sometimes made for burlesque situations, especially when he was trying to speak with native-born citizens of the Reich.
>
> Hebich was from Warsaw and worked for the ZOM before the war. His municipal job allowed him to buy a house in Jelonki. In 1942 or '43, as a reward for faithful service, the Germans gave him a luxury apartment on Natolinska Street, decked out with fine furniture from the ghetto. [...] In addition to the veteran truck drivers

3. Bednarczyk, *Zycie codzienne warszawskiego getta*, pp. 90–91.

of the Municipal Sanitation Department from before the war, the Garbage Collection Service also took on new recruits at that time, young men who were obviously in the underground or hiding their origins.

At the end of 1940, after the ghetto was walled in, German sanitation "experts" got the idea of only allowing "Aryans" to pick up the waste generated by German-owned enterprises in the ghetto, or in other words, the sweat shops. The Jewish company owned by Heyman [elsewhere Niewiadomski says that the owner's name was Pinket] formerly in charge of this job was now restricted to Jewish waste.

At first two sealed trucks were allocated for Aryan trash. It was a unique opportunity – one that could not be passed up – to establish a "legal" connection with the ghetto through which arms, food, construction materials, etc., could be brought in, and finished products and Jews smuggled out on the return trip.

The OW-KB command did not fail to leap at this opportunity. Following their orders, I began working for the ZOM in August 1941, after escaping from the IVA Stalag (Hoyerswerde). Thus I became involved in the efforts to help the ghetto.

The first major problem that had to be solved was how to get rid of the sealed trucks used in the ghetto. They were not much use for carrying merchandise and no good at all for evacuating people. The truck drivers wrote up reports commenting that it was impossible for them to haul bulky loads.

The DWS management eventually replaced these trucks with open-dumpster vehicles, which finally allowed us to really get to work.

The gas-operated engines that powered these vehicles were also to our advantage, since carrying the bags of wood fuel made it easier to sneak in weapons and ammunition hidden in them.

I had two places where I could make contact with the OW-KB command. The first was in the courthouse building on Leszno Street, and the second was a bar on Madalinski Street, across from the ZOM.

The place was a real greasy spoon where no one but garbage men hung out. They called it "the broom bar."

It was an ideal place to discuss business deals regarding waste with any sort of value at all. Neighborhood gardeners came to buy garbage to fertilize their fields, and these deals provided the DWS employees with a little extra income.

The Germans avoided the place, since even its appearance from the street was not inviting. Its signature odor, a mixture of brandy and dubious bar food, tended to keep customers from staying too long.

But all of these factors made the establishment highly conducive for clandestine work, such as organizing discussions, picking up reports, passing on orders, etc.

To be chosen for this work, a man had to be trustworthy, ready to do anything, and well aware that he would be risking his life every day. Most of them were members of the secret group organized within the ZOM headed by Witold Bednarczyk.

The secret OW-KB unit in the ZOM comprised two sections, each of them corresponding to a garbage truck crew.

Using the name "Bicz," I led one of these sections. Perhaps I was chosen to head a truck section because I had escaped from internment under the Germans three times and spoke German, which was important in terms of daily contacts with the German police in the ghetto. Further, as chief of a reserve platoon and a Stalag escapee, I had to take a job in a quiet company, someplace that did not stand out.

It was up to Bednarczyk [Witold], with the help of Szabelski, a DWS office worker, to choose reliable people who would be issued passes by the Germans. The two crews of garbage men worked throughout almost the entire period of the ghetto's existence, until Hebich turned me in.

Roman Siedlecki, who still lives in Warsaw today, was one of the members of the second team. I don't remember the others. He was caught in a round-up on "Black Sunday" in January 1943 and rescued from a convoy on its way to Majdanek.

The ZOM underground unit received its orders concerning tasks to carry out from a OW-KB officer whom I knew as Lieutenant "Tadeusz." His last name, Bednarczyk, was the same as Witold's; apparently they were related.

I often met Lieutenant "Tadeusz" in the bar on Madalinski Street where later he gave Witold Bednarczyk and myself packages of weapons that he had hidden nearby. This was also where he passed along the instructions for the evacuation of people from the ghetto.

The two operations were carried out by both crews, while theoretically my unit had sole responsibility for transporting arms and munitions.

During the approximate year and a half that I was involved, we brought between 200–300 Jews out of the ghetto.

The evacuation operation mainly concerned Jewish intellectuals. It was organized in the following manner: as a recognition sign, the head of the truck section would be given half an envelope or postcard with the address of the contact point in the ghetto and a name. The person to be evacuated had the other half. The date on the card or envelope was the day of the person's evacuation.

This postcard or torn envelope was not only a recognition sign. As the part with the stamp, it was meant to serve as an alibi in case of a police search, which happened from time to time. The crew chief would explain that he was a dedicated amateur stamp collector, an explanation that seemed credible.

The evacuee was to have an Aryan "Kennkarten" and the other half of the torn card or envelope, which fit perfectly with the first half.

We would go into the ghetto with a partial load, usually garbage. Underneath were planks meant to protect the person who was to be evacuated from the ghetto. We also hid all sorts of goods for the ghetto under these boards. The wood was meant to protect the person from direct contact with the garbage and allow air to circulate freely. The garbage piled above provided 90% protection against the curiosity of the German police, who were deathly afraid of typhus and thus gave the job of rapidly inspecting the trucks to the Jewish police and later the Baltic and Lithuanian collaborators. [Is it patriotic discretion that leads Niewiadomski to omit mention of the Polish police, the "blues"?] The latter could always be bribed, even with the worst rotgut brandy.

The Jews were evacuated to temporary way stations, which, for security reasons, were located near the ZOM's premises. The first was in the old cellars of the Krolikarnia building, and the second on Dolna Street.

Because of shifting substrata, the Dolna Street building had partially collapsed before the war. Under the ruined part lay some abandoned basements I knew about.

This place was home to a Jew who had lived there from the time of his evacuation from the ghetto until the uprising and later the liberation of Warsaw. His forged papers bore the name of Ludwik Modiewski, an identity he later kept. (After Liberation, Modiewski was a founder of the *Klub Inteligencji Pracujacej* [Working Intelligentsia Club] on Mokotowska Street.)

Sometimes we would transport Jews from the contact point to the cardboard factory on Zajaczkowska Street, and later, from there, after taking on a load of cardboard, to the tarpaper factory on Syrena Street.

From what I know, from that point they were taken by train along with roofing tarpaper as freight being sent to "building companies" in the East, to the Soviet Union or to the partisans operating in the eastern reaches of Poland.

We carried arms and ammunition into the ghetto, sent by the OW-KB for the ZZW. We would pick up the weapons on the Aryan side of town, from a number of houses where the trash cans were permanently installed and not of the movable, metal kind. The liaison agent would put a canvas bag full of munitions or disassembled automatic weapons inside, and watch over the place until the truck arrived and the crew took the package out.

One such liaison agent was disguised as a street sweeper, the kind of person often seen during the period between the two wars, whose job was to sort through the trash cans and take out any objects that might have some value.

This kind of pick-up most often took place at the building on 4 Mazowiecka Street, where the concierge was a sworn member of the OW-KB. Another place was the building on 21 Chmielna Street.

As I mentioned previously, on Madalinski Street, Lieutenant "Tadeusz" handed me some less bulky packages.

Yet another anecdote also has to do with the trash cans on the Aryan side. Especially during the early days of the Occupation, it was common to find grenades, handguns, ammunition, bayonets, etc., abandoned in them, probably because of some sudden danger. These discoveries were like a gift from heaven. After informing the organization about these weapons and cleaning and fixing them up, I often took them into the ghetto. They were handed over to officers of the Jewish organization [the ZZW] at previously-agreed spots communicated to the heads of the "truck section." Among the men who received them, two are still alive, one in Israel and the other in Warsaw.

I can recall the addresses of the buildings where we delivered arms packages: Nowolipie Street near Smocza Street, Leszno Street next door to the church, Orla and Grzybowska streets near Zelazna, and Mila and Karmelicka streets.

In December 1942 [there is a mistake in the Polish text: this took place in December 1941 – in December 1942 both the children and Korczak were dead], our trucks brought wrapped Christmas presents from the Aryan population for the children at Janusz Korczak's orphanage in the ghetto. One of the men who organized this operation was "Bartosz"-Leon Glowacki, who had a butcher shop then. He still lives in Warsaw today. In addition to organized aid, such private initiatives were numerous. We organized the transportation of food, especially tin cans. "Bartosz" took part in this as well. These cans were picked up during the phony unloading of garbage at Smolarek's horticulture company. After one of these operations, the latter's son, Kazimierz, was killed by the Germans.

"Bartosz"-Glowacki also took care of bringing the population food supplies during the uprising. At that time he was in the quartermaster corps in the Mokotow neighborhood. I was a member of the company led by Lieutenant "Judym."

In late 1942, construction materials began to be brought into the ghetto to build bunkers and fortifications.

Around that time the Germans began to search the garbage trucks more and more regularly, which depressed many crew members. Some of them exhibited signs of nervous depression; they were sick of seeing bloodshed and countless corpses. The Ukrainians and the Letts [once again Niewiadomski neglects to mention the Polish "blue" police] became increasingly difficult and our comrades lost their reflexes. We were afraid that our fellow crew members would sink into total depression.

We couldn't let that happen. But at the same time it was hard to see how they could be replaced, because that would mean training other people and above all getting ghetto passes for them, which might have raised suspicions among the Germans, especially Hebich.

On February 1, 1943, that weasel Hebich finally succeeded. More precisely, he found me out. First he called the Gestapo and then he tried to hold me for them in the enclosed ZOM compound. I fought with him; I wanted to shoot him but my gun jammed. Finally I escaped from his grip and fled outside the ZOM, leaving in his hands my leather jacket with my forged papers inside. These documents were used to issue a warrant for my arrest, which was published in the Gestapo bulletin and the *Kryminalpolizei* in March 1943.

My successful escape made it possible to save the whole ZOM cell.

After being nominated by Witold Bednarczyk, I was summoned to be awarded the Cross of the Order of Virtuti Militari (fifth class) for my overall military activity and the aid given to the ghetto.

While speaking of the ZOM cell led by the OW-KB, mention must be made of another underground organization under the aegis of the AK, which also operated within the ZOM.

The *Spoldzielnia Pracy Odbudowa* [Reconstruction Work

Cooperative], founded after the 1939 surrender of Warsaw by Stefan Starzynski, the city's mayor, also worked out of the ZOM grounds on Madalinski Street. Its official function as part of the ZOM was to provide support for the DWS by sending its own employees to do municipal upkeep and maintenance work. Actually, this was a cover, a means through which people with an "uncomfortable" political past and Jews hiding out on the Aryan side could get an *Arbeitskart* [work card]. This made it possible to save a great many people, including, for example, the Jewish engineer Rotsztein, who survived the Occupation because he could present papers showing he was employed by the Odbudowa.

Aleksander Cesarski, a left-wing activist before the war, also used this "service."

Taking advantage of its relationship with the Philips company on Karolkowa Street, the Odbudowa obtained radio parts to be sent to the ghetto. Its work in general was coordinated by Piotr Wisniewski, alias "Piotr," who is still alive.

Finally, I'd like to give some details about one of the actions, a story I already mentioned, the evacuation of Ludwik Modiewski.

As I recall, it was in the summer of 1942.

The day before I was given, as usual, half of a postcard with the ghetto address of a Jew whom our garbage truck team had orders to take to the Aryan side. In the back of the truck, buried under garbage, we were carrying bags of cement meant to be used in the construction of the bunker on 9 Mila Street. We entered the ghetto without the slightest problem by showing, like always, our permanent passes. The collaborators did a superficial inspection watched over by the German police, who were already pretty drunk.

We began our shift by unloading and then taking on a load of garbage at the Szulc factory on Leszno Street. There was more than enough to hide the ghetto refugee we were picking up that day. We went to the address we'd been given.

I gave Modiewski a careful look, as I always did, to try and get an idea of what I could expect from the person we were dealing with, because their mood played a decisive role in the choice of an appropriate transport tactic.

He was short in stature and middle aged, and his good accent and careful way of speaking indicated that he was from an educated background.

I was not told his real name, only that which appeared on his Aryan identification papers. In this regard, our orders were clear: do not seek any information about the past of the person to be evacuated.

Modiewski was frightened. I was afraid when the person to be evacuated was of this sort, because their courage was a factor that determined half our chances of success. I tried to converse with him so as to distract his mind from the possible dangers that lay ahead. We went onto the street together and walked toward the truck that was waiting for us.

As we walked, Modiewski was looking around as if to say his farewells to this place so infested with evil, where death lay waiting everywhere.

When he saw the truck filled with garbage, Modiewski reacted with disgust and took a step back. He wanted to call the whole thing off. I tried to explain to him that he wasn't the first person to be brought over to the Aryan side under such conditions. Finally I succeeded in persuading him. We placed him in our specially-designed and so often used hidden compartment under the garbage.

We headed back to the street that lead to the checkpoint. As we drove along, we were stopped, as usual, by starving Jewish children who knew us well as the frequent and long-standing visitors to the ghetto that we were. They knew that we always carried modest packages of food for them, often our own breakfast. As usual, we gave out the food to a few of them, accompanied by the squeals of those left out. We didn't notice that someone was watching this whole scene very closely. We stopped in front of the roadblock.

It was our unlucky day. Next to the crossbar, surrounded by collaborators, stood the German called "Frankenstein." Out of the corner of my eye I also noticed Rotholc, the famous Szapsio Rotholc, a well-known boxer in the 1920s and '30s, the Polish featherweight champion who had often represented his country in international bouts. In those days quite a few Germans had occasion to experience the formidable efficiency of this very popular figure's fists.

He just stood there, at a good distance from the German police. He seemed tiny and puny as he all but disappeared under his enormous Jewish policeman's cap. Along his leg hung a club, a symbol of the dubious power awarded him by the Nazi oppressor.

It was truly our unlucky day because "Frankenstein" had seen us giving out food. Rumor had it that he never ate breakfast until he had killed several Jews. Completely drunk that day, he stopped our truck in front of the crossbar, shouting, "*Halt! Wo ist der Mullkasten-Führer?* (Where is the leader of this garbage can?)" Inwardly I laughed at the idea that the Germans even had a *Führer* for garbage cans!

"*Ich!*" I answered, trying to stay calm while showing my pass for the ghetto.

"No, *ja*," he said. I had the impression that he was calm and everything was going to be all right. But I was worried about Modiewski. I hoped he would hold out, that a movement or unnecessary noise would not give away his presence in the hideout under the garbage.

"Frankenstein," weaving back and forth on his legs and stinking of alcohol, asked me in a voice of feigned friendship and solicitude, "*Hast du Hunger?* (Are you hungry?)" "*Nein*," I answered quickly.

This time he screamed: "You're lying! You're lying! I saw you, you and your Polish swine, feeding those Jewish vultures. You must be hungry!"

He was sputtering with rage and screaming so loudly that his companions stepped back, as though they were afraid of this irresponsible drunk. Grabbing Rotholc's nightstick, he began to rain blows down on my head.

I tried to protect myself with my hands so as to limit as much damage from this beating as possible. Luckily, he was drunk and his blows were neither accurate nor hard enough to kill me. I fell down and pretended to have passed out. As I was lying on the ground, he kicked me as hard as he could, and screaming, "*Weg mit dem dummen Polacken!*" he ordered his cohorts to throw me on top of the trash. He raised the crossbar himself. The road to the Aryan side was open.

A pail of cold water from a nearby well brought me back to my senses. But my head hurt far too much to touch. I was stunned and only half-conscious.

A last task still remained undone – to deliver Modiewski to the contact point. We drove toward Dolna Street. At the corner of Dolna and Pulawska, we noticed several uniformed officers and plainclothesmen acting suspiciously – by their attitude, we could tell that they were members of the secret police, the Kripo. There was nothing left for us to do but continue on to the *zwalka*, that is, the garbage dump on the slope behind Saint Michael's church.

The *zwalka* was a relatively safe spot. After making a sign that indicated that the truck was broken down, as a pretext for leaving it in this location, we got Modiewski out that evening and delivered him into the hands of the people who were waiting for him.

I didn't see Modiewski again until 1945 when I ran into him by chance on a street in Warsaw and told him the details of his ill-starred "departure" from the ghetto. He had never suspected a thing; he hadn't seen or heard any of it. The worst thing he had to endure that day was the horrible stench of garbage and the time that seemed to last forever.[4]

---

4. Teodor Niewiadomski, "*Z pomoca dla warszawskiego getta*," *Kultura*, no. 161 (April 21, 1968): 254. Here is some further information supplied by Niewiadomski on another occasion: "The real work and most heroic actions of OW-KB sanitation workers began when the Warsaw ghetto was sealed. Shortly afterwards, Hebich summoned the author of these memoirs to make an announcement. Because I could speak German, for many weeks I had been his teacher as well as his right-hand man, and recently I had been promoted to the position of truck crew chief. Now Hebich told me that the 'king of the garbage men' himself, Schilling, had decided to send two trucks into the ghetto every day to pick up waste. The *Übermensch* had become so consumed with racist hatred that they had chosen to apply the Nuremberg laws to the harmless trash and garbage that up until then had been picked up by a Jew named Pinkert who had enjoyed a monopoly on this business. Hebich accepted the author's suggestion that the two trucks with OW-KB teams aboard be sent into the ghetto. That very day, memos to this effect were sent through 'Bewit' and Lieutenant 'Bednarz'

HIDEOUTS IN THE GHETTO

In retrospect,the idea of hiding out in the ghetto seems like an illusory solution, because we know that the Soviets would not liberate Warsaw until two years later, on January 18, 1945. But early 1943 saw the defeat of the Germans in Africa and Stalingrad, so there was hope of a rapid Nazi collapse.

The hope of Nazi defeat and the terror inspired by life on the "other side" were both strong arguments in favor of hiding out in the ghetto itself. Hundreds of underground hideouts were constructed and equipped with varying degrees of sophistication depending on the means of those who built them.[8] Some contained toilets, kitchens, several entrances, a connecting passageway to the sewers and a communications link via a clandestine phone line. We will come back to this in the chapter on the uprising.

THE ORGANIZATION OF THE ARMED RESISTANCE

The ZZW

In addition to their ideological and cultural differences, the two armed resistance organizations also diverged on practical matters. The OW-KB regularly supplied the ZZW with arms – a total of more than 1,000 grenades, more than 300 pistols and dozens of automatic weapons (two heavy machine guns, three light machine guns, ten automatic rifles, ten submachine guns, 20 combat rifles and 20 carbines).[9] The resistance group PLAN, which also belonged to the AK but was not specifically responsible for supporting the Jews, helped the ZZW buy arms; as a result, the ZZW bought a heavy machine gun, a dozen rifles, a few dozen handguns and grenades.[10] In terms

8. See chapter 8.
9. Bednarczyk, *Obowiazek silnejszy od smierci*, p. 123.
10. "The existence of the tunnel under Muranowski Square was an additional source of strength for the ZZW – through it, on the eve of the uprising we provided 1,200 Walter 7.65 mm semiautomatic pistols and ammunition [Obviously, this figure is either a gross exaggera-

of automatic weapons, Mark estimates that the unit quartered on Muranowski Square alone had two machine guns (one light and one heavy) and eight submachine guns.[11]

The ZZW's forces had grown steadily from 300 soldiers in September 1942 to 400 in January 1943, then to 500 in April.[12] The social and political barriers which had greatly restricted ZZW membership from autumn 1939 to the deportations of the summer of 1942 were lifted,[13] and smugglers, porters and shopkeepers were now granted membership. During this period, the organization's insistence on remaining apolitical made it possible to take in volunteers of every political stripe, including Marxists, and every walk of life. Few of these new recruits had sufficient military training, but among its ranks the ZZW counted 20 officers and twice as many non-coms. Trained veteran soldiers constituted 60 percent of the total.

Ringelblum recounts:

> [...] I visited the ZZW's arsenal. It was in an improvised barracks located in an abandoned and now "off-limits" building at 7 Muranowski Square, in a six-room apartment on the second floor. In the

---

tion or a typo], all obtained through purchases [...] Thus we transported...on the eve of the uprising two Maxim machine guns with 2,000 rounds of ammunition, five combat rifles and many pistols." Janusz Cezary Ketling-Szemley, "*Przyczynek do historii mojej walki i wspozpracy z Zydowskim Zwiazkiem Walki Wyzwolenczej na terenie ghetta warszawskiego w latach okupacji*," Jabotinsky, W (8) 25, pp. 26–27.

11. Mark, *Powstanie w getcie warszawskim*, p. 16. This figure is consistent with the overall numbers published by Krakowski (see below and appendix 4).
12. The figure 500 is that given by Mendelson and Bednarczyk. Mark, who did not take part in these events himself, but who after the war had access to a great many firsthand accounts, puts the number of troops at 400. See Mark, ibid., p. 10.
13. "[T]he Revisionist branch (supporters of Jabotinsky, from Jewish families that were well-off before the war), did not join the ZOB but instead founded the Jewish Military Union (ZZW). Among its ranks were many men who had performed their military service in the Polish army. Thanks to its numerous contacts with the Aryan side, the ZZW acquired a large quantity of arms. Unfortunately, these weapons were not suitably used by the ZZW at Muranowski Square during the uprising. In reality, they were wasted." Michal Jaworski, "*Refleksje w 50 rocznice powsatnia w getcie warszawskim*," *Wojskowy Przeglad Historyczny*, no. 1 (1993): 143; for more memoirs see idem, "*Plac Muranowski 7: Fragment wspomnien*," *Biuletyn ZIH*, no. 2 (1974): 90.

> command room, there was a top-of-the-line radio receiver able to tune in to news broadcasts from all over the world, and some typewriters. These officers, with whom I talked for many hours, carried pistols at their belts. In the main rooms there were coat racks hung with every conceivable weapon – automatic rifles, regular rifles, pistols, strings of grenades, bags of ammunition and the German uniforms that were to prove so useful during the April fighting. There was a constant hubbub in the command room, just like in a real army headquarters. Orders were being sent to the barracks where the future fighters were quartered. Reports came in about the expropriations of the well-to-do that were carried out to buy arms for the ZZW. I witnessed the purchase of weapons from an ex-Polish army officer for a quarter of a million zlotys. He was given 50,000 zlotys as a downpayment. The lot included two automatic rifles for 40,000 zlotys and a large quantity of grenades and bombs. I asked why this place was not more secret. The answer given to me was that there was no reason to fear that soldiers would talk and any undesirable visitor, such as a policeman who might wander in, would never get out alive.[14]

Ringelblum's somewhat naïve enthusiasm – "just like in a real army headquarters" – is certainly not a result of sympathetic feelings towards the ZZW, since a page earlier he calls its fighters "fascist soldiers, in the Italian style."[15]

Following, in counterpoint, is another description by Ringelblum of a ZOB gathering place:

> The apartment, with two rooms and a kitchen, was on 32 Swietojerska Street [...]. The fighters could not go outside; food was brought to them there. The entrance was through the attic of adjacent buildings. You had to give an agreed-upon knock at the door. Three women fighters were there. They prepared meals and carried out dangerous

14. Ringelblum, *Polish Jewish Relations*, pp. 169–70.
15. Ringelblum, ibid., p. 169.

> missions for the ZOB. The discipline and order were exemplary. They belonged to the left Poale-Zion group and had already carried out many successful expropriations so as to arm the ghetto.[16]

Let us get back to the ZZW and see how Mendelson recalls this period:

> The period between mid-September 1942 and mid-April 1943 was devoted to intensive preparations for the battles to come. The three companies were practically no longer clandestine. The soldiers were stationed in barracks, and worked on fortifying defensive positions or guarding the permanent passageways, the tunnels and sewers, that made it possible to supply the ghetto – for instance, the first company at 7 Muranowski Square (the tunnel to the "Aryan" building at 6 Muranowski Square) and my own platoon on 5 Karmelicka Street (the underground passageway to 4 Karmelicka on the grounds of the Evangelist hospital).
>
> Acquiring arms and food supplies and evacuating people from the ghetto had become far more difficult. The sealed ghetto was all but empty. The remaining population was cooped up behind the gates of the tiny ghetto sweatshops that belonged to various German companies. All the streets were deserted. Gestapo patrols shot at people for the slightest excuse. It was very dangerous for people in civilian clothes to travel inside the ghetto, even with an official pass. For this reason, Bednarczyk now used people in uniform as intermediaries to carry out his work of organizing aid for the ZZW, such as the Polish policemen from Captain Zmudzinski's cell,[17] or,

16. Ringelblum, ibid., p 126.

17. "I declare that during the Nazi occupation, in my capacity as chief of the Tenth and Eleventh police stations of the PP [Polish police], I carried out clandestine work as a member of the OW-KB, the unit led by comrade Tadeusz Bednarczyk, alias 'Bednarz.' In addition to protecting the places used by the OW-KB general staff (for example, General Sikorski's secret mailbox and the apartment of his wife and daughter at 5 Gorski Street, and the offices of the CKON used by the engineer Ryszard Swietochowski at 61 Marszalkowska Street), my clandestine duties also included helping to hide and protect members of the underground movement, and to help save, hide, supply with food, transport and protect Polish citizens of Jewish nationality, many of whom were able to survive thanks to this work. My work as

more often, firemen who could drive into the ghetto in case of a real or pretended emergency. Thus it was possible to transport the grenades and long weapons that were particularly lacking in the ghetto. The ZOM trucks were another ideal means of transportation. Hidden under the garbage, arms, ammunition, medicine, food, cement and other items could be smuggled into the ghetto, and, coming back, people could be brought out to safe houses. The main organizer of this heroic operation was Teodor Niewiadomski,[18] who, along with his crew, and using his garbage truck, evacuated about 200 people from the ghetto between fall 1941 and February 1, 1943. I was present when he was given responsibility for the rescue of most of these escapees, with a special identification sign for each of them that came from Bednarczyk. [...][19]

According to information at my disposal, we received, free of charge [...] two heavy machine guns, three light machine guns, more than 10 automatic rifles, 10 submachine guns, about 40 combat rifles, more than 300 pistols, ammunition, grenades and explosives.

---

a member of 'Bednarz' unit was under Major 'Bystry'-Henryk Iwanski, as I was to learn later. Signed Tadeusz Zmudzinski-'Orlin.' [Followed by the annotation: "I declare that 'Orlin'-Tadeusz Zmudzinski, a captain in the reserves, helped the Jews following my orders through the intermediary of Bednarz, and that he saved many people." Signed: "'Bystry'-Henryk Iwanski, ex-commander of the special units for the protection of Jews."] In Tadeusz Zmudzinski, "*Oswiadczenie*," February 1962, Archives ZIH, no. 6112.

18. "I hereby declare having recruited and sworn in [to my unit] in August 1941 Teodor Niewiadomski, platoon leader in the Polish Army reserves. He was a member of the ZOM unit [Municipal Sanitation Service] under leadership of Witold Bednarczyk. Starting in mid-1940, this unit was part of my OWN unit, assigned to protect the offices of the general staff of the OW-KB and the CKON and help the Warsaw ghetto. Niewiadomski was made the chief of the truck crew that went into the ghetto daily. Using the cover of his job as a garbage collector, Niewiadomski helped take arms into the city of Warsaw and take weapons, ammunition and grenades into the ghetto. In addition to firearms, he took in construction materials for building bunkers, medical supplies and many radio transmitters. On his way back, he brought out people selected by the ZZW. In a secret compartment under the garbage he brought out about 200 people between fall 1941 and the end of January 1943. During one of these operations Niewiadomski was beaten by a German policeman, following which he was ill for a long time and permanently disabled. In early February 1943, he was found out in his workplace by a ZOM employee, the Volksdeutsche Hebich. He was forced to give up his job and, wanted by the Gestapo, to leave town. He thus ceased to work in my unit and was transferred to Lowicz to continue his underground work there." Tadeusz Bednarczyk, "*Oswiadczenie (o Niewiadomskim)*," August 16, 1969, Archives ZIH, no. 6575.

19. Mendelson, "*Rozwoj i dzialanosc ZZW*."

Furthermore, we bought more than 100 pistols and ammunition with the money obtained from collaborators in the sweatshops after a slight amount of pressure. During the uprising itself, the OW-KB gave us some 15 rifles and a constant supply of ammunition, which enabled us to keep fighting longer. Behind the names of these major military organizations that came to the aid of the ZZW (all of which subsequently joined the OW-KB) were human beings, made of flesh and blood, fierce patriots who, motivated by the need to come to our aid, added to the ordinary dangers they faced – the death penalty for any help to the Jews – and especially military support. In addition to arms, they provided us with food, medicines, help in organizing and training. The quantity, the weight and so on given in numbers would make quite a chart, but it is hard to imagine, today, the efforts and the number of people involved just to get a pistol, a rifle or a little food into the ghetto. Because the need for food was so great, every Pole who came into the ghetto for military or other reasons always brought some with him.

Here I would like to sketch the portrait of a few soldiers of the OW-KB and of the organizations of which it was comprised, those who deserve the most credit for the aid they brought to the ZZW. Since the work carried out by Bednarczyk and Petrykowski has been described elsewhere [...], I will not go into it further here, especially since these two men are so modest themselves. Further, Bednarczyk is well known to readers as a journalist and historian, thanks to his many publications. Tadeusz Niewiadomski, a soldier (sergeant) in the "Bednarz" (Bednarczyk's) unit, who, as head of the sanitation workers group, came into the ghetto in his garbage truck for more than a year and half – until they were found out on February 1, 1943 and wanted by the Gestapo – is also well known to readers. In special compartments on the bottom of the truck, he courageously smuggled many rifles, many dozen pistols, grenades, ammunition and food into the ghetto, along with cement for building bunkers and fortifications, and he even got people out the same way.

Captain "Orlin" (Tadeusz Zmudzinski), a member of "Bednarz" unit, commanded a group of policemen (a platoon and a half). He was the police chief at the Tenth station of the Polish police, and his assistant, Second Lieutenant Ryszard Stolkiewicz (a comrade of Bednarczyk), was extremely helpful in the protection of the OW-KB and the CKON's headquarters and in getting arms into the ghetto. Policemen carried arms and ammunition into the ghetto in broad daylight and left them there before leaving via a different checkpoint so as not to be recognized and caught. During the uprising, many policemen belonging to that unit fell in battle alongside their Jewish comrades [I have found no confirmation of this and don't believe it]. Stolkiewicz was murdered in his apartment on Mokotowska Street, and many other police officers caught by the Germans were sent to concentration camps. Wyhowski, a captain in "Bednarz" unit and chief of the Eleventh station of the Polish police, was also killed. The police played an important role in rescuing people who were hiding on the Aryan side and moving them to other safe houses by pretending that they were transporting prisoners, and if necessary, hiding the Jews they were protecting in the police station. [The two examples given here have been confirmed but there are a great many accounts of Jews who were arrested by the "blue" police.] Zmudzinski even had a basement especially set up for that purpose, and further, he used it to store large quantities of food to be shipped into the ghetto. He was in charge of organizing the ZZW general staff's investigations service, and he personally trained its core members. Often he himself was forced to hide at the place of "Orlin."

A third soldier from "Bednarz" unit who rendered tremendous services during the Jewish support operations was Stefan Woszczyk. At that time, he owned a garment workshop on 2 Nalewki Street, a place called the Simons Arcade, where he stored arms that Lieutenant "Bednarz" was having sent to the ghetto. Further, since his shop was not far from a ghetto exit, it also served as a temporary hiding place for Jews coming out. By agreement with other Polish manufacturers in his field, and as part of his economic and social activities, he was supposed to supply the ghetto with cloth, so as to raise its productivity and allow its inhabitants to make some money.

The shipment in and out of raw materials and finished products was organized in a variety of ways. Some of the goods went by way of the station of the first firemen's company on Nalewki Street (who were Skala-KB soldiers), others went via various official shipments to the ghetto, or thanks to a counterfeit pass, or by bribing the German police on duty in front of the entrances through the ghetto walls. Woszczyk added packages of military material or food stuffs and medicine skimmed from the supplies being sent to the North Warsaw section of the Polish Red Cross (headquartered on 2 Nalewki Street), which was organized by Bednarczyk.

The ZPN soldiers gave the ghetto a large quantity of weapons. This operation was run by Lieutenant-Colonel Stanislaw Szopinski, and the shipment, organized by Bednarczyk, went through the sewers. Further, Szopinski hid a number of Jews with ZPN units in the field. When the ZPN joined the OW-KB in November 1941, he became the head of the general staff's unit II and played an important role in the liquidation, on the Aryan side, of the Jewish Gestapo stooges of the Zagiew organization whose existence in the ghetto had been discovered by "Bednarz" in 1940. In his capacity as security chief for the Delegation of the Warsaw region, Szopinski acquired information that was extremely valuable for the ghetto and its security, which he sent to the ZZW through "Bednarz."

Major military and food supplies were sent to the ghetto by the Skala-KB soldiers, who were firemen by profession, particularly those of Nalewki's unit I and Mirow's unit IV on Chlodna Street. Unit I was led by Lieutenant-Colonel Drozdzenski. [...] But the favorite shipment route of Lieutenant "Bednarz" was through unit IV. Michal Pogorzelski, then a lieutenant and the commander's assistant, was the head of the cell in charge of ghetto shipments. A part of the fire station complex extended into the ghetto (the same was true for unit I), separated from the odd-numbered side of Elektoralna Street by no more than a wooden partition wall. The storage facilities for the firemen's provisions were adjacent to this wall. Every night, as darkness fell, boards would be removed from the wall and large quantities of people and goods would be sent through (including raw materials going into the ghetto and finished products in the opposite direction), along with food and military supplies.

Upstairs in the firehouse, Lieutenant "Bednarz" organized preparatory meetings for the education and training of the ZZW high command [...]. The work went almost as smoothly as in a normal institution, with no danger of the Germans barging in. Lieutenant-Colonel Michal Pogorzelski, who died a few years ago, was the heart and soul of these meetings. One of the most active of the non-commissioned officers was Augustyn Jaworski, now a colonel. I myself often took part in these meetings with OW-KB officers, including from the Skala-KB. In 1941–42, I used the fire station to have several hundred people evacuated from the ghetto and transferred to hideouts on the Aryan side, even though at that point the courthouse on Leszno Street was a relatively easier exit route. But you had to look respectably Aryan. During the uprising, in April 1943, I witnessed the enormous support the firemen gave the insurgents, resulting in the death of many of them. During the last days of the ghetto, they were the source of the ammunition sent not only to our units but also the ZOB, as was the case throughout the whole time of the uprising. The firemen had the same advantage as the policemen – their uniforms and official access to the ghetto facilitated their aid operations. In the same way, the permanent pass held by Tadeusz Bednarczyk, the overall organizer and leader of the ghetto support operation, in his capacity as a tax office employee, authorized him to come into the ghetto every day and facilitated his clandestine work. It was thanks to these means that the operation was able to be so effective. Yet, a pass was not enough to keep someone from dying, a risk they ran every day. Only a profound commitment and a powerful humanitarian spirit could have motivated these people to involve themselves in such all-consuming and dangerous work. They often even used their own money to come to the aid of the ghetto. For example, Tadeusz Makower and his brother wore Bednarczyk's suits. Bednarczyk helped them financially, and others as well. This attitude was common among all the OW-KB soldiers who took part in this work.

> Now I would like to recall the names of a few soldiers of the W unit that belonged to Zbrojne Wyzwolenie. [...] The W unit, undermanned and with no reserves of its own, brought in arms and supplies directly from the main depots of the organization itself. This operation was not led by the unit's commander, the hospital administrative director Nosarzewski, but by Jan Skoczek, his assistant. Small quantities of arms were brought by Skoczek himself, sometimes with the help of his wife Wanda or soldiers from his unit, non-coms working at the hospital as stock handlers, like, for example, Marian Kowalski, who on his own had hidden a few weapons in September 1939, and Henryk Iwanski, Pudowski, Lejewski and others. The W unit and the Zbrojne Wyzwolenie were active in getting people out of the ghetto and finding them hideouts on the Aryan side. On behalf of the ZZW, Wladyslaw Zajdler and others also took part in the arms shipments.[20]

The ZOB

The ZOB officially came into existence at the end of 1942, that is, less than six months before the launching of the insurrection. It had practically no experienced military officers and few weapons – 90 pistols, 500 defensive grenades, 100 attack grenades, 15 kilos of plastic explosives, detonators, a light machine gun, a submachine gun, all arms furnished by the AK,[21] mainly between January and April, as well as guns bought in small quantities. The ZOB also made incendiary Molotov cocktails in its own workshops. The Communist resistance movement, known as the People's Guard, was still in an embryonic stage and in January 1942 possessed, in Warsaw, 24 pistols and a similar number of grenades.[22]

The various Polish organizations had finalized their consolidation into a single body, the Home Army (AK). For obvious reasons, the AK had more in common with their comrades-in-arms, the

20. Mendelson, "*Oni byli z nami.*"
21. Krakowski, *The War of the Doomed*, p. 176.
22. Bednarczyk gives similar figures. See Bednarczyk, *Obowiazek silnejszy od smierci*, p. 137.

ZZW officers, and felt closer to them both politically and culturally speaking than to these ZOB newcomers, who were often Marxist and all very leftist, and even worse, were suspected of having neither the means nor the desire to fight. After long and complicated negotiations, the AK furnished the ZOB with ten pistols in December 1942, and another ten in January. This, along with a few black market acquisitions, constituted the ZOB's entire stock of armaments during the January events, which succeeded in changing the attitude of the Poles somewhat. As badly armed and trained and as few as they were, the ZOB members fought and won, with the efficacious but niggardly and unenthusiastic aid of the ZZW. In February, the AK was slightly more generous, giving them 70 pistols, 500 grenades and 15 kilos of explosives.

In total, at the time of the uprising, the ZOB had at least 500 soldiers,[23] who were trained for a period of six months maximum, but most had less than three months of training (January 21–April 18), since the big influx of recruits into the ZOB was in January 1943, after the victorious defensive battles. They were armed with handguns and/or grenades, but had neither automatic arms nor officers or non-coms.

> In April 1943, at the beginning of the uprising, the ZOB had about 500 people, as did the ZZW. [This estimate seems exaggerated in regard to the ZZW; 400 would be a more realistic figure.] Here I must emphasize that the two organizations worked together despite the ZOB's baseless demand that the ZZW be subordinate to it. We could not accept that, if only because we had been fighting alone in the ghetto for three years. Further, the ZZW was well trained and armed

23. A count of the ZOB's forces remains controversial. Edelman, *Getto walczy*, puts them at 220, which surely represents an underestimation, since the names are known of 220 people who died in combat and another 60 who got out of the ghetto. An estimate of 500–600 would seem more consistent with eyewitness accounts and the judgment of historians. Perhaps Edelman is only taking into account those fighters who had firearms, in which case the figure would seem likely.

> while the ZOB hd neither officers nor weapons nor training, which it continued to ask the AK to provide.[24]

In addition to the two organizations whose preparations have just been described, some "unorganized" forces also readied themselves. Almost all of the bunkers were built by individual initiative. Some of their inhabitants had bought weapons for their personal self-defense. They did not spring into action until the Germans attacked their particular bunkers. The number of people thus involved, their armament and their combat effectiveness (most likely not very high) – all this remains unknown until this day and will never be known.[25]

In this situation, as the battle approached, the two combat organizations dropped their clandestinity. The Judenrat shared power

---

24. Mendelson, "*Rozwoj i dzialanosc* ZZW": "If we generally accept the higher number mentioned, it is possible to assume that the arms held by the ghetto were as follows: a few thousand grenades and Molotov cocktails, a few hundred pistols, no more than twenty-five submachine guns, no more than ten machine guns [the ZZW had eight], and twenty mines." Krakowski, *The War of the Doomed*, p. 178.
25. "[...] In late March 1943, I learned that a certain engineer named Goldman, in a discussion with ZZW representatives about his enlistment in the organization, had mentioned the building of an underground passage leading from the brushmakers' district to the Aryan side. I demanded that he be contacted. I had a number of conversations with him. In fact he and his men had dug a narrow and rather jerry-rigged tunnel. It seemed that two Polish army officers belonged to his group; the engineer said that he himself was also an officer. Our discussions did not go very well. I demanded that the tunnel be turned over to the ZZW and that the group join the ZZW. He let things drag on and did not show a great enthusiasm for struggle in the ranks of the ZZW. While emphasizing his esteem for the ZZW, he admitted to me that he was in the midst of discussions with the ZOB, but added that he had no intention whatsoever of joining up with them because its units had no military character and its soldiers as well as the organization itself lacked discipline. He demanded that he and his group be helped to make contact with the units in the forests, in exchange for which he would hand over the tunnel. As a military man, he could predict in advance a rapid, total and useless defeat of the insurgent units. Consequently, all he was interested in was fleeing straight to the forests and not fighting. Because of the gravity of the situation, in mid-April 1943 it was decided to evacuate this group to the forests. I informed engineer Goldman that this decision had been made. But he put off the evacuation for two days and we were taken by surprise by the uprising which began April 19, 1943. As late as April 18, I tried to hurry him up by telephone, demanding that he make contact through the ZZW. He did not do so and our channels were broken off." Bednarczyk, *Obowiazek silnejszy od smierci*, pp. 91–92.

with them, at a minimum, and even helped finance the resistance organizations.

Relations between the Two Organizations

The discussions between the two organizations which had dragged on uselessly for several months finally resulted in a geographic coordination, which obviously was based on the fortifications already built and the location of the bunkers and passageways, particularly those underground, which made up a tightly-linked network.

The Communist leader Walewski (who nonetheless fought alongside the ZZW) recalls:

> Relations within the ghetto, especially those between the ZOB and the ZZW, did not improve. Clearly the ZOB sought complete hegemony in the ghetto. It obviously did not want to admit to the existence of other military forces in the ghetto, such as the ZZW and other armed fighting groups that were not in contact with the ZOB. It sought to ignore the fact that the ZZW, better armed and more efficaciously organized, with better contacts on the Aryan side (for example, a Polish resistance captain helped provide training), with strong fortifications, was unquestionably a military force to be reckoned with in the ghetto. [...] Once again I had to appeal to Gutkowki, who after much effort succeeded in getting the ZOB to agree to such a meeting.
>
> There were more and more meetings while time was running out. Out of fear of a German surprise attack, I went to the ZZW high command to once again suggest a temporary agreement with the ZOB that would mainly concern defensive operations in case of a German attack. This plan turned out well. A provisional agreement was signed between the ZZW and the ZOB providing for the division of the ghetto into two military sectors. [Nowhere else have I found any reference to a signed agreement or to the central role Walewski attributes to himself.][26]

26. Ryszard Walewski, "*Protokol*," November 25, 1948, Jabotinski, W (8) R5, pp. 540–41. He

It was decided that open areas, such as Muranowski Square, which faced the major artery Nalewki, and the relatively broad streets like Smocza, through which the Germans brought prisoners to the Pawiak jail, would be assigned to the ZZW, since they could only be defended with heavy weapons. The two organizations adopted different strategic approaches, based essentially on their capabilities. The ZOB planned light, mobile, broadly dispersed units, while the ZZW concentrated its forces so as to dispose of sufficient firepower in strategic locations and mount a sustained defense of its Karmelicka, Leszno and Muranowski tunnels.

The general staff, led by Apfelbaum, with his personal security platoon, was located at 10 Mila Street. Close by on Muranowski Square was the first company commanded by Rodal and also nearby, on Muranowska and Niska Streets, the third company commanded by Weisstok; the second company under Federbusz, on Nowolipki Street; the fourth company, the most recently formed and unequipped, commanded by Frenkiel and Mendelson's independent platoon on Karmelicka Street. Thus two zones, especially the area around Muranowski Square in the central ghetto, as well as the quadrangle formed by Nowolipki, Leszno, Smocza and Karmelicka Streets in the Többens-Schultz industrial area were strongly held by the ZZW (see map no. 2).[27] The Leszno tunnel was

---

writes a few lines previously, "[...] In consistently following that line [of conduct], we [the Communist group lead by Walewski] submitted to the ZZW, which was the second military organization and our immediate neighbor, a proposal for cooperation. This time an agreement was reached rapidly. We remained an independent military unit, under the ZZW general staff, with our own organizational apparatus and our own group and field commanders. A new period of underground work began. We expanded our activities and took part in certain ZZW operations. I was present when Fürstenberg, the Ordnungsdienst inspector, was given the death penalty. [...] Our arms were repaired in Brauer's machine shop; we also used the ZZW workshop on Gesia Street. On the grounds of Brauer's shop we had a bunker equipped with an entrance to the sewers. Thanks to the ZZW's direct tunnel, we now had easy access to the Aryan side. Jurek Plonski, then 15 years old, took care of transporting our arms from the Aryan side into the ghetto. Many times a week he came into the ghetto and then left for the Aryan side carrying the mail and our reports." Ibid., pp. 539–40.

27. This organizational chart is based on the writings of Mendelson, the only ZZW officer who survived, and those of Bednarczyk, who was the coordinator for the ghetto for the OW-KB and later other Polish resistance organizations as well.

Frenkiel's responsibility; the Karmelicka tunnel was Mendelson's; Rodal was in charge of the Muranowski tunnel. The two main battles would take place in the central ghetto, and later the ZZW would retreat from the central ghetto toward the industrial zone. In the brushmakers' district, the ZZW only had small units that would fight alongside the ZOB.

CHAPTER 8

THE UPRISING

On February 16, 1943, Himmler issued an explicit order:

> An overall plan for wiping out the ghetto must be submitted to me. In any case, it is necessary that this space taken up until now by 500,000 subhumans, which will never be suitable for Germans, disappear from the face of the earth, and Warsaw, a city of one million, a place of constant disorder and diversion, must become that much smaller.[1]

On April 6, 1943, the resistance received word that a definitive German operation was imminent.[2] This time, the attack was not a surprise. Here is Mendelson's description:

> It was Bednarczyk who on April 6, 1943, brought the order of alert to our high command. The ZZW confined all its troops to quarters, and the ZOB followed suit, though only partially. But the German

1. "Himmler Orders the Destruction of the Warsaw Ghetto, February 16, 1943" in Yitzhak Arad, Yisrael Gutman and Abraham Margaliot, eds., *Documents on the Holocaust: Selected Sources on the Destruction of the Jews of Germany and Austria, Poland, and the Soviet Union* (Jerusalem: Yad Vashem, 1981), doc. 134, p. 292.
2. "The OW-KB first received word that the Germans were preparing for the definitive destruction of the ghetto. On April 6, I communicated the order by 'Tarnawa' for armed mobilization to the ZZW command. This information was then communicated to the ZOB by Apfelbaum." Bednarczyk, *Zycie codzienne warszawskiego getta*, p. 95.

> attack was put off until April 19. [...] In total, standing up to them in the ghetto were a thousand fighters, the soldiers of the ZZW and the ZOB.[3]

Those ZZW soldiers not yet confined to their barracks were called to quarters, and the weapons were distributed. The remaining fortification work was speeded up. A complex system of sentries was set up; they were camouflaged and linked to their command centers.

On Sunday, April 18, the day before Passover, a ring of troops surrounded the ghetto. On the 19th, at dawn, around 6 A.M., the German troops – about 2,000 strong according to the Stroop report[4] – marched into the ghetto through the gate at Nalewki Street.

Thus began a battle that was to last several months. For the sake of clarity, we will divide the battle into three phases: that of the front, the partisans, and the ruins.

THE FRONT

This phase lasted nine days, from April 19 to April 27. The first few hours were marked by the defense of the triangle defined by the intersection of Nalewki-Gesia and Mila-Zamenhof streets,[5] both held by the ZOB, and Muranowski-Nalewki crossroads, held by the ZZW.

The Two Ambushes

The German troops advanced in tight columns, singing as they moved up Gesia and then Zamenhof Streets, after having entered the ghetto through the Nalewki gate (see map no. 2).

3. Mendelson, "ZZW *w walce*," *Kronika*, no. 20 (May 16, 1970).
4. S. Krakowski's analysis of this report concludes that Stroop slightly underestimated the number of his troops (see appendix 4).
5. The Germans renamed some ghetto streets because they could not tolerate the thought of any prominent Jews, even dead, being honored. Thus Zamenhof became Dzika and Majzels Street, Kupiecka.

> According to Sammern's plan, the central ghetto was to be attacked first. [...] The workshops and the brushmakers' districts were to be left alone, because the Germans expected to see the Jews in those areas surrender and go to the trains of their own free will. Sammern had planned [...] that one part of these forces would halt on Nalewki Street [...] and the other would turn up Gesia Street, and from there, Zamenhof, the avenue parallel to Nalewki.[6]

The ambush was set up at the corner closest to the gate, at Gesia-Nalewki-Franciszkanska. The fighters allowed the head of the column to go up Gesia Street before attacking it from three sides. "The ZOB fighters greeted the Germans with a hail of grenades, Molotov cocktails and rifle fire; the one and only automatic rifle did not fail. The Nazi bandits fled."[7]

Shortly after, the column that had been sent further north, along Zamenhof Street, was attacked from four sides. The fighters allowed the Jewish police at the head of the column to pass, and then opened fire. The Germans and Ukrainians took shelter in the building entranceways amid great disorder. "On the faces of people who only yesterday were depressed and terrorized, there was a strange expression of happiness [...] the ghetto was defending itself."[8]

According to Jewish sources, the Germans suffered heavy losses, including a burned-out tank, and withdrew from the ghetto. This is confirmed by General Stroop himself: "The tank (only one tank) and the two armored cars used in the assault were attacked with Molotov cocktails. The tank caught fire twice. This attack caused the units engaged in combat to withdraw. Losses: 12 men (6 SS and 6 Trawniki)."[9]

---

6. Mark, *Powstanie w getcie warszawskim*, pp. 19–20.
7. Memoirs of H. Berlinski (member of the ZOB general staff), quoted in Mark, ibid., p. 21.
8. Memoirs of J. Manski, quoted in Mark, ibid., p. 23.
9. Stroop, *The Stroop Report*, daily report, April 20, 1943 (first report). The Trawniki men were Ukrainians, Lithuanians and Latvians, volunteers trained at the Trawniki military school.

M. Anielewicz, head of the ZOB, wrote to his second-in-command, Cukierman, who was on a mission on the "Aryan" side:

> [...] Something had happened which goes beyond our wildest expectations: the Germans fled twice. [The first time at about 7 A.M. on the 19th; when was the second? The book does not say. – MA] One of our units held out in combat for 40 minutes and another for more than six hours. The mine set under the brushmakers' district exploded. So far we have lost only one man, Jechiel. He died beside the machine gun, the heroic death of a soldier. [...]
>
> Starting tonight [the letter is dated April 23] we will go over to partisan warfare. During the night, three of our units will go out with the following two tasks: reconnaissance and seizing arms. I must tell you that handguns are worthless; we have hardly used them at all. We need grenades, automatic rifles and explosives. [...]
>
> Out of all the units in the ghetto, only one man was killed, Jechiel. This, too, is a kind of victory. [...] During the day, we burrow into our hideouts.[10]

Late in the morning on the first day, the ZOB's two strongholds were evacuated and its fighters retreated, some of them into the bunkers, the rest toward the interior of the ghetto.

The six-hour battle that Anielewicz speaks of took place at the Nalewki-Gesia intersection; this defensive position was later abandoned in the face of the German counterattack organized by Stroop, who reports:

> I arrived in Warsaw on 17 April 1943 and took command of the grand operation on 19 April 1943 at 0800 hours. The operation had already

10. Zuckerman, *A Surplus of Memory*, p. 357 commented on the machine gun: "Among other things, Mordechaj [Anielewicz] wrote, 'I must tell you that pistols are worthless.' In the translation, it says that Jechiel died beside the machine gun. In fact, we had no machine guns at all. In the original, it said 'automatic weapon' and I translated it as 'machine gun,' because Berman wanted it that way, so it would have more of an impact. I must say that this version of the letter here is not the original, but it is closest to the original (except for the 'machine gun')."

begun that same day at 0600 hours. [Stroop had been named head of the Warsaw police and was assigned responsibility for the destruction of the ghetto on the 17th. He preferred to take command after seeing the start of the operation, perhaps as much out of prudence as courtesy to von Sammern.] To prevent the Jews from escaping, the borders of the former Jewish quarter were secured from the outside by a barricade before the start of the grand operation. This barricade was maintained from start to finish of the operation and was reinforced at night.

The Jews and Polish bandits [Here Stroop is mistaken or lies to lessen the Jews' merit; at this point, the morning of the 19th, there were no Polish fighters in the ghetto] succeeded in repelling the first penetration of the Ghetto by ambushing the participating units, which included tanks and armored cars. [Stroop's predecessor, von Sammern-Frankenegg, was panicked by this defeat and told Stroop, who was still at his hotel, that all was lost and that they had to call for emergency air support.] During the second attack, at about 0800, I committed the attack units to various predetermined battle sectors with orders to sweep the entire Ghetto. The enemy was forced to withdraw from roofs and from strongholds above ground into basements, bunkers and sewers. The sewer system was dammed up below the Jewish quarter and flooded to prevent escape into the sewers. Most of this plan, however, proved illusory when the Jews blew up the cutoff valves. Heavy resistance was encountered on the first evening but was quickly broken by a special battle unit. During further operations, the Jews were driven out of their furnished nests of resistance, sniper holes, etc. During 20 and 21 April, the greater part of the so-called remaining Ghetto came under our control and resistance within these blocks could no longer be termed very substantial. [...][11]

The Two Flags

Stroop's report is filled with constant triumphalism even though

11. Stroop, *The Stroop Report*, p. 4.

he knew that real pitched battles still lay ahead. The truth emerges in the following lines of his report:

> The main Jewish fighting unit, which was intermingled with Polish bandits, had already withdrawn during the first or second day to the so-called Muranowski Square. [This vague "or" represents a departure from the report's overall tone of extreme precision; obviously this is an attempt to make the period of "significant" defense seem shorter.] [...] Their plan was to entrench themselves in the Ghetto by every means in order to prevent our penetration. [Thus he clearly confirms from the start that Muranowski Square was defended with particular fierceness.] The Jewish and Polish flags were hoisted on top of a concrete building in a call to battle against us. [...] But both flags became the booty of a special battle unit on the second day of the engagement [i.e., April 20]. During this skirmish with the bandits, SS Second Dehmke was killed when the hand grenade he held was triggered by enemy fire, exploded and injured him fatally.[12]

This brief paragraph contains both facts and lies. This time, there really were some "Polish bandits," although not very many. On April 19, a group of five KB soldiers led by Sergeant Jozef Lejewski, alias "Garbarz," delivered ammunition, grenades and weapons (four submachine guns) to the ZZW. They remained until the 20th. During the fighting, "Garbarz" and another soldier were wounded and two more were killed.

> [...] On the orders of Major "Bystry," along with four soldiers, I took part, arms in hand, in the ghetto uprising as part of Lieutenant Kalmen Mendelson's unit, on the ghetto side of Muranowska Street [...].[13]

---

12. Ibid., p. 5.
13. Jozef Lejewski, "*Oswiadczenie*," December 2, 1959, Archives ZIH, no. 5794. Here is a contradiction I cannot resolve: we have written that Mendelson's unit was in charge of the Karmelicka Street tunnel and that the Muranowski tunnel was guarded by the company under Rodal; therefore, how could Lejewski, who exited through the Muranowski tunnel, have

The two flags could be seen from most of "Aryan" Warsaw, and inspired much commentary in underground publications and even the Polish press in London.[14]

Here are two accounts by witnesses who were not involved in the ideological conflicts among Jews. The first is by W. Bartoszewski: "19 April. From the roof of a building on Muranowska Street flies a white and red flag alongside a white and blue one, both quite visible beyond the ghetto walls from Bonifraterska Street."[15] The second is from A. Kaczynska:

> [...] I recall April 19, 1943 [...]. As we approached Muranowska Street, I became increasingly worried because of the loud noises coming from the ghetto on the other side of the wall. In the house, everyone already knew that an uprising had begun in the ghetto. On the roof of the building facing us we could see people coming and going, all of them carrying guns. Then we witnessed an outstanding event: on that roof, a blue and white flag and a white and red flag were raised. We all shouted, "Look! Look! A Jewish flag! The

---

fought with Mendelson? Iwanksi confirms the role played by Lejewski-"Garbarz": "During the period from April 19–26, the unit led by Sergeant "Garbarz" entered the ghetto three times. Each time they carried a quantity of arms and ammunition that they shared with the ZZW." Iwanski, "*Czy mozna bylo ratowac ludzi...?*"

14. A survivor, J. Eisner, has described his part in hoisting these banners. See *The Survivor of the Holocaust* (New York: Kensington Books, 1980), pp. 177–81. He says that the Polish banner was raised many hours after the Jewish flag, which has not been confirmed by other eyewitnesses. But these two flags were not the only ones described. B. Mark, ZIH director since these archives were founded and the author of many articles and two books on the ghetto uprising, writes, "The partisans hung, in very visible places, the white and red banner, the red flag and the white and blue." See Mark, *Walka i zaglada warszawskiego getta*, p. 257. The multiplication of banners and especially the addition of the red flag were part of the generalized rewriting of history in Communist Poland. But Mark describes the April 19 battle for the flags at Muranowski Square, and in his report on April 20 there is no red flag and the ZZW is clearly mentioned, ibid., p. 258. The daily communiqués issued by the ZKK (Jewish Coordination Committee) make no mistake about the flags. Communiqué no. 3 of April 20, 1943 informs us that "on one of the buildings on Muranowska Street, the Jewish fighters raised two flags, the white and red, and the white and blue," but neglects to mention the ZZW – which it fails to mention in any of its daily reports – to the implicit advantage of the ZOB: "The ZOB, which unites all the active elements of Polish society, opposes [...]." See "*Meldunki sytuacyjne dzienne z powstania w getcie*, 20, 21, 22, 23, 25, 28 *kwiecien* 1943," AAN Archives, file 202/XV–Z 2.
15. Bartoszewski, *1859 dni Warszawy* (Cracow: Znak, 1974), p. 390.

> Jews have taken Muranowski Square! […] We could see two young men, teenagers […]. They had reason to be proud. The Jews of the Warsaw ghetto were the first in the entire world to dare to revolt against the German enemy! This cruel occupation will finally come to an end. […][16]

In the Stroop report, there is a particular problem concerning the death of Dehmke, or rather concerning the duration of the battle of the two flags. According to Stroop, the flags were taken down on the second day of the fighting, i.e., April 20. The report was written after the end of the *Grossaktion*, in May, at Himmler's request. But in Stroop's daily teletyped reports published along with Stroop's overall summary, Dehmke is said to have died on the 22nd. These daily teletyped reports are more convincing than the summary written in May, since, like the others, they were written in real time, in this case on the 22nd, late in the day:

> Progress report of the Ghetto operation on 22 April 1943. Report on operations up to 1200 hours already submitted today by earlier teletype message. […] SS Second Lieutenant Dehmke of the SS-Cavalry Reserve Division dead; enemy hit a hand grenade he was carrying.[17]

Did Dehmke survive for two days? Or did the defense of the flags, and the battle of Muranowski Square more generally, last longer than Stroop says, until the 22nd or even longer, after the death of Dehmke, as the following suggests?[18]

In one of a series of conversations with a fellow inmate during his trial, Stroop said:

---

16. Kaczynska, *Obok piekla*, p. 67.
17. Stroop, *The Stroop Report*, daily report, April 22, 1943 (second report).
18. This hypothesis was discussed by Mark in 1959: "In his daily reports, Stroop wrote that Dehmke died on April 22 […]. It is possible that he was wounded on the 20th and did not die until the 22nd. It's also possible that the battle of Muranowski Square […]." see Mark, *Walka i zaglada warszawskiego getta*, p. 286.

> Those flags flew over a concrete building. They were a constant affront. In the course of dangerous fighting to pull them down, an SS cavalry lieutenant, Otto Dehmke, was killed. The grenade he was holding was triggered off by a bullet. […] Those flags had tremendous political and psychological importance. They unified Poland in a way nothing else could. Hundreds of thousands of people were inspired by the sight of them or the knowledge that they were there. A flag is as much a weapon as a hundred guns. They realized that, and so did we. I'll never forget the *Reichsführer*'s voice [Himmler] shouting over the phone, "Get those flags down, Stroop, whatever the cost. [...] I instructed my duty officer not to wake me before seven o'clock the next morning under any conditions. "I won't talk to anyone," I insisted. "No one, *Herr General*?" "No one, with two exceptions. Wake me if the SS *Reichsführer* calls or if you get word that those flags are flying over the ghetto again."[19]

Thus, as evidence that the battle of Muranowski Square lasted one day, there is Stroop's post-battle report. As evidence that it lasted three or four days, in addition to the date of Dehmke's death, there is the casualty report in Stroop's teletype of the 22nd, his teletype of the afternoon of the 22nd, and his account while sharing a prison cell.

There are three other firsthand accounts that support the claim of a prolonged battle: Bednarczyk, who was in the ghetto, if not a participant in the battle itself, and two other eyewitnesses.

In writing about Muranowski Square, Bednarczyk recalls:

> A powerful two-day long battle […] in the afternoon of the 20th […] two [German] infantry battalions took part in the battle […]. But their superior firepower and superior technology (the use of tanks), as well as the German's greater military experience, finally took their toll. Carried away with enthusiasm, the ZZW soldiers tried to

19. Kazimierz Moczarski, *Conversations with an Executioner* (Englewood Cliffs, NJ: Prentice-Hall, 1981), pp. 133–34, 139.

> mount a frontal assault, and suffered major losses. The exhaustion of the previous day's battle also made itself felt. The Jews were losing ground and slowly withdrew. [How long did that take?] [...] This retreat was made inevitable by unsustainably heavy losses and the shortage of ammunition, which, because of lack of experience and in the heat of battle, they had used a little too freely.

A little later in this text, Bednarczyk writes, "After three or four days of positional warfare, the lack of ammunition forced the insurgents to adopt a mobile defense. [...]"[20] Two days? Three? Four?

Three months later, after he had left the ghetto, L. Najberg wrote a diary that contained a day-by-day description: "[...] Muranowski Square [...]. During the first, second and third days of the uprising, in these buildings there was a battle for every floor, every room, every inch of stairwell. The Germans fought ferociously to grab the two flags flying over the roofs of these buildings."[21]

Walewski also attests to a prolonged battle:

> I myself was near Muranowski Square, where for three days [i.e., April 20, 21 and 22 plus the afternoon of the 19th, or three days including the 19th?] positional warfare took place without interruption, and where despite the enemy's overwhelming superiority in terms

20. Here is the rest of the quotation: "[...] [A] ZZW unit (about 30 men) left voluntarily through the tunnel to 6 Muranowski Square, and camouflaged the entrance." Bednarczyk, *Zycie codzienne warszawskiego getta*, pp. 99–100, 102; Krakowski wrote, "The ZZW units fighting in this sector (Muranowska Street) were forced to abandon the positions they had. A group of about 20 people went through the tunnel to the Aryan side." See Krakowski, *The War of the Doomed*, p. 195. This departure of a very small percentage of the ZZW's forces was to be widely used against it.
21. Leon Najberg, *Ostatni powstancy getta* (Warsaw: Żydowski Instytut Historyczny w Polsce, 1993), p. 72. Here is another eyewitness account: "The second day [...] [i.e., April 20], there was [...] a very fierce battle at Muranowski Square. The unfolding of events there has also been described by Halperin: 'The Germans stepped up their attack against the positions held by the Betar fighters. Tanks and armored cars came down the street and opened fire mercilessly against this Jewish combat group. The fighters' situation also became increasingly difficult because of the loss of contact with the combat organization [the ZOB]. The Germans began to set fire to the buildings on Muranowska Street and the rebels were forced to leave a burning building and run into the neighboring building, all under the constant fire of German machine guns.'" In Gutman, *Zydzi warszawscy*, pp. 376–77.

> of material [...], they could not push into Muranowski Square. I remember some moments in particular. One of them has to do with the machine gun, which held the enemy in check for, I think, two days, despite their tanks, their armored cars, their flame throwers, their light artillery, the sappers, the SS [...].[22]

The Germans reacted to the strong resistance in the area around Muranowski Square by making it the focus of their attack. The resistance units fought to defend the flags and the tunnel, which was their vital link to the "other side." This made the battle there particularly fierce from the very start. Despite their losses, the ZZW units were relatively well armed, and after the enemy occupied the square, they were able to launch a counterattack and retrieve the positions the Nazis had demolished and burned.

An argument Stroop used later weighs in favor of a three-day battle:

> Muranow Square [...] was ferociously defended by the Jewish fighters. Submachine gun and machine gunfire made access impossible. The day before he died [i.e., the 21st?] [...] Dehmke, known as a talented officer, was put in charge of taking the building in question with his shock troops. But the explosives and incendiary bottles thrown by the defenders, as well as their concentrated gunfire, made it impossible to carry out this task. It was not until the following day [the 22nd?] that we succeeded in penetrating the building. The defenders withdrew over the rooftops. [...] Dehmke, who was below [...] succumbed. [...] I think that with the exception of two or three killed, all the defenders succeeded in escaping.[23]

At his trial in 1950, Stroop suggested that the resistance around the two flags was even more protracted:

---

22. Ryszard Walewski, "*Relacja na procesie Stroopa: Warszawa 1951*," Jabotinsky, W (8) R5, p. 9.
23. Cited in Michel Borwicz, *L'insurrection du ghetto de Varsovie* (Paris: Gallimard, 1966), p. 218.

> The insurgents launched a ferocious attack [...] from the concrete building where Dehmke was killed. [Therefore, the afternoon of the 22nd, at the earliest, or later?] For a long time [Just how long was it?] it was impossible to get into it, even though no one lived there anymore. We met fierce resistance at Muranowski Square [...]. We suffered losses.[24]

Below is another, more complete account, furnished by Walewski in 1948, emphasizing the violence and the duration of the fighting.

> [...] This organization [the ZZW] had its main garrison at 7/9 Muranowski Square, where its headquarters and its high command were located; this was also where most of their troops were barracked. In the basement of this building, under a cement slab, a bunker had been built [...] containing all the facilities necessary for defense and living, as well as a passage to the "Aryan" side. In addition to this building, ZZW units had been positioned in the first buildings [from numbers 7 through 21] of the odd side of Muranowska Street. [...]
>
> Muranowski Square and the surrounding buildings were stuffed with ZZW units. Two buildings especially, at 7/9 Muranowski Square and at the corner of Muranowski Square and Nalewki Street, were particularly well fortified. Throughout the battle, our contact with the Aryan side was uninterrupted. From there we received ammunition and a machine gun that had been placed on the roof of one of the buildings on Muranowska Street. Thus we controlled Muranowski Square and the outlets of the neighboring streets. The only machine gun in the ghetto [this is untrue – we know that the ZZW had several machine guns] kept the powerful German army operating in the central ghetto at bay. Despite violent attacks and the use of tanks and automatic weapons against us, the enemy could not take our positions. On the contrary, from time to time we went on the counter-attack and succeeded in snatching their arms, destroying their material and inflicting human losses on them. The

24. Ibid., p. 219.

> fact that beside the machine gun we had hung two banners – one white and blue and the other white and red – provoked a veritable Teutonic rage. They attacked more and more violently; the quantity of arms used was increased and new units were sent in against our positions. But our defense was also more and more ferocious. We defended these flags, symbols of the struggle and protest of a ghetto that even as it died was subjecting the "invincible" German army to a public slap in the face, a slap even more painful for the enemy because all of Warsaw saw it or knew about it. This gave us comfort and renewed our courage and energy to continue fighting. It also let us believe that our lives would leave a mark on the other side of the ghetto wall even after we were dead.[25]

Thus, the retreat of "the bulk of the forces toward Muranowski Square" took place "on the first or second day" – there is quite a lack of precision in the Stroop teletype cited above. This means April 19 or 20. Actually, we now know that it was on the 19th, and that the battle lasted for three days or more, which means until April 22 or 23. At any rate, it is certain that on April 23, the square went up in flames.

> April 23 [...] the houses burned like matchboxes, with hissing, crackling and the din of rafters collapsing. The ghetto's last inhabitants ran amid the fires and the buildings searching for safety. Mothers with babies in their arms bent over double trying to protect their

25. Walewski, "*Protokol*," pp. 537, 544–45. In his testimony at the Stroop trial, Walewski paid homage to the People's Guard, the GL (whereas he never mentioned the AK or the KB) and the Soviet Union, which was understandable at that time. Further, he was a Communist and led a Communist group that was part of the ZZW. "I'd like to get back to the first day of the insurrection. We at Muranowski Square foresaw the possibility of an attack from behind, from the Bonifraterska Street side. There the Nazis broke through a wall and set up machine guns and artillery. We were sure that the attack would begin at any minute. Later, I learned that right then and there the GL saved us twice. They threw grenades at the Germans, probably to keep them from attacking us. [...] [And a month later, when the fighting was almost over, Walewski tells us, enthusiastically:] The night of May 13 brought about a new factual and psychological situation. During that night Soviet aircraft appeared over the skies of Warsaw. That had a great, very great influence, in increasing our faith in the struggle. [...]" Walewski, "*Relacja na procesie Stroopa*," pp. 11–13.

> children from the bullets and the flames. Old people who walked with difficulty ended up just sitting down in front of a house not yet completely burned down, resigned to dying there, I think, because they remained motionless and passive as the flames began to lick them before transforming them into human torches and consuming them completely. Suddenly I saw two Germans who were tossing inflammable "ribbons" into the house across the way. Maybe there is some special name for this kind of "lighter," but I don't know what it is. They roared with laughter as they threw these fireworks, which hissed as they rose up and stuck to the highest stories before exploding in a column of fire that set the whole building ablaze as fast as lightening. Suddenly, a young woman looked out of an open window. [...] A few seconds later, she raised a little boy in her arms, kissed him, threw him from the third floor into empty space and jumped out after him.[26]

Finally, there is the following strong argument against the thesis of a short battle: If Stroop was not lying, and the two flags were taken down on "the second day of the operation," in other words, on the 20th, if they had been up no longer than the afternoon of the 19th and the 20th, then why did Himmler, who only found out about this indirectly, through Cracow, shout on the phone that they had to be taken down at once – and when would he have had the time to do so?

In short, there is no room for doubt. Half a dozen accounts from witnesses of all persuasions unaminously agree (except for one written afterward, with reason enough to lie) that the particularly hard-fought battle for the flags lasted for three days or almost four, from the afternoon of the 19th until the afternoon of the 22nd or the morning of the 23rd. In any case, this was the longest and fiercest battle of the uprising.[27]

---

26. Kaczynska, *Obok piekla*, pp. 68–69.
27. Another example of Stroop's imprecision, or rather of deliberate lying, concerns the number of deaths. In his daily teletype report for April 19, dated the 20th, Stroop says, "Losses: 12 men (6 SS and 6 Trawniki)." Stroop, *The Stroop Report*, daily report, April 20, 1943. But

Warsaw Ghetto

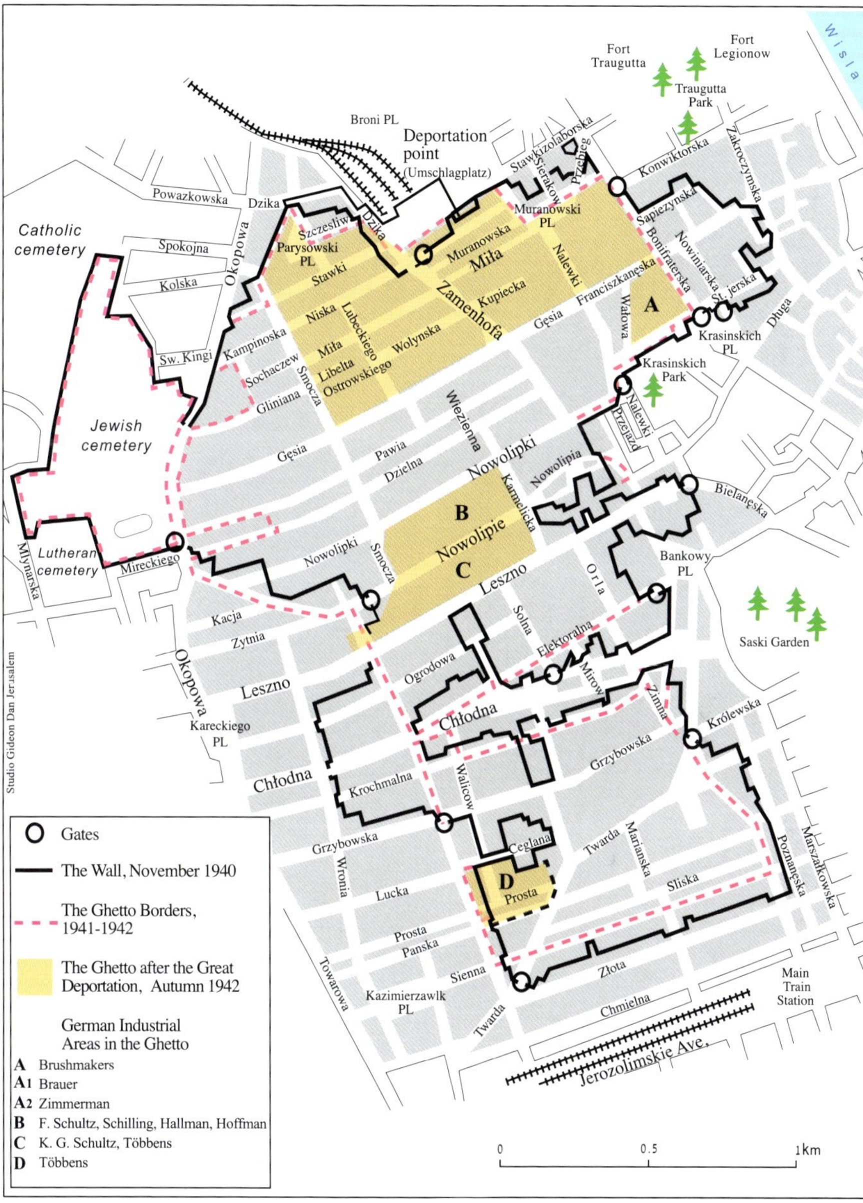

A street in the Warsaw Ghetto

Children caught by the Germans after smuggling food into the ghetto

A unique means for identifying communication liaisons between the ZZW and the AK consisted of two gold identity rings set with a red stone and engraved with Jewish symbols that had to be presented and explained. The ZZW ring was lost but the Polish underground's was kept by Henryk Iwanski, an underground commander, who told former partisan Chaya Lazar about it in 1960. Just prior to his death he asked that Chaya and Chaim Lazar bring the ring to Israel and exhibit it.

A star is incised upon the red stone – "A star rises from Jacob" (Num. 24:17). The number 7 is incised in the center of the star representing the seven arms of the menorah. On both sides of the ring are fruits, flowers, and plants that symbolize the seven species and the belief that the Jewish people will yet blossom and flourish and produce fruit.

The lion, whose shape is engraved on the inside of the ring, represents the strength of Judah – "Judah is a lion's whelp" (Gen. 49:9).

The lamb, whose shape is engraved on the inside of the ring, symbolizes the nation being led like a lamb to slaughter. (Personal communication from Chaya Lazar to the author.)

Members of the German engineering corps
taking Jews out of a bunker

Waffen-ss soldiers taking a Jewish fighter out of a bunker

Warsaw Ghetto Uprising, 19/4/1943

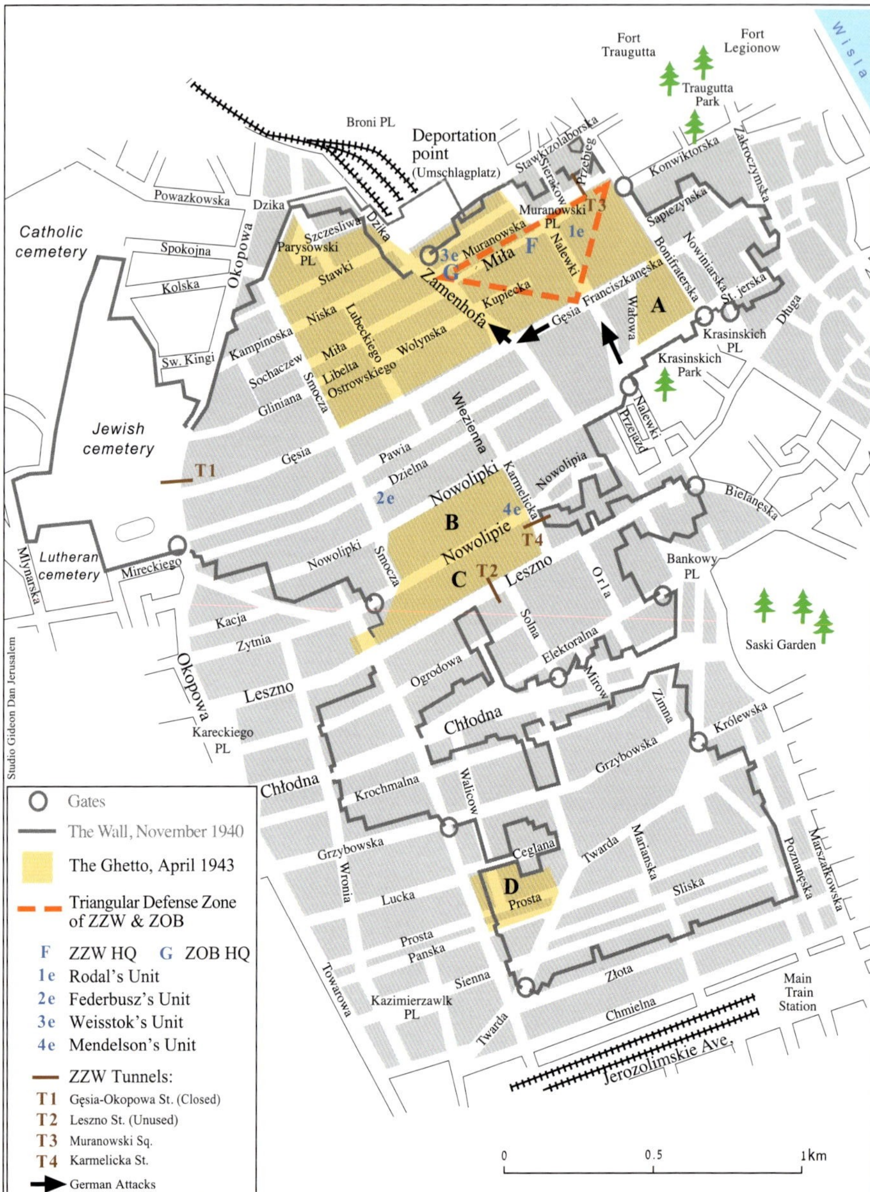

The Second Battle of Muranowski Square

Let's return to the Stroop report:

> [...] The resistance offered by the Jews and bandits could be broken only by the energetic and relentless day and night commitment of our assault units. On 23 April, the Reichsführer-SS promulgated his order, transmitted through the Higher SS and Police Leader East in Cracow, to complete the sweeping of the Warsaw ghetto with the greatest severity and unrelenting tenacity. I therefore decided to embark on the total destruction of the housing blocks belonging to the armament enterprises. One enterprise after another was systematically evacuated and destroyed by fire. [Incendiary devices had been used to eliminate rebels since the beginning; it was the systematic burning of the ghetto as a whole that began on the 23rd.] In almost every instance, the Jews then emerged from their hiding places and bunkers. It was not unusual for Jews to remain in the burning houses until the heat and their fear of being cremated forced them to jump from the upper floors. They did so after throwing mattresses and other upholstered items into the street. With broken bones, they still tried to crawl across the street into housing blocks that had not yet been set on fire or were only partly in flames [...].[28]

Once burned to the ground, the Muranowski area afforded shelter, because the buildings were made of reinforced concrete and their skeletons were solid. It is known with certainty that on the morning of the 26th, the ZZW once again took the ruined square and held it until the night of the 27th.

---

none of them are included in the final tally of those who died "for the Führer and the fatherland" – Stroop does not cite a single death on the 19th. Given the events of that day – the surprise double ambush of that morning, producing a retreat and the panic of the commanding officer, followed by, still that morning, the counterattack against the ambush positions, and that afternoon, the attack so full of "Teutonic fury" provoked by the flags – it is not credible that there was not a single death on the Nazi side. It is reasonable, however, to conclude that Stroop didn't care about the dead Slavic volunteers and therefore gave an inaccurate figure of the number of total losses.

28. Stroop, *The Stroop Report*, p. 9.

Here is a description by one of the Polish officers who took part in the battle:

> On April 26 [It is because of this date, confirmed by three other witnesses cited below, that I put the retaking of the square on the 25th or that night], a liaison agent of the ZZW unit led by Janek Pika informed us that Major Dawid Moryc Apfelbaum was wounded and that he requested immediate supplies of arms and ammunition. The Jewish combat units were once again the masters of 7 Muranowski Square and they had made the tunnel leading to number 6 functional again. The exit on the "Aryan" side had been checked out and the house occupied. Following these reports, the KB high command ordered our unit to enter the ghetto and join the fighting. Our objective was to drive the Germans away from the tunnel entrance to make it more secure. Once that was done, we were to retreat, carrying with us the wounded, and women and children.
>
> Our transport service was put on the alert, ready to receive the wounded and evacuated.
>
> The operation was commanded by Henryk Iwanski-"Bystry" and his aide Wladyslaw Zajdler-"Zarski" [the author of this report]. The covering unit was led by "Roch." Grabowsk funeral parlor vehicles were to move the arrivals to their hideaways.
>
> After organizing how the tasks of the various units were to be coordinated, the operation was scheduled to begin at 10 A.M. on the 27th.
>
> Tuesday, April 27.
>
> At 7 in the morning I was at Edward Zaremba's, 66 Krakowskie Przedmiescie, where I received the arms and ammunition. We rapidly loaded the packages into rickshaws and left for another safe house where we were to get the grenades and the rest of the weapons.
>
> At 10, we were at the tunnel entrance. Our support arrangements were going like clockwork. Kowalski and his six men were there to cover our entry and exit.
>
> The tunnel had been dug by the soldiers of Federbusz's unit. It

went under the street and came out in the basement of a house on the other side of the wall that separated the ghetto from the rest of the city and went through Muranowski Square. The entry was in the basement at number 7. It was difficult for the uninitiated to find one of the entrances.[29] The basement was a forest of bundles hiding the trap door, which in addition was also covered with bricks and sand. We went through one by one, protecting the weapons from the sand. There were 18 men in our unit. [Iwanski says 18 plus the two officers.] We were armed with automatic weapons and grenades.

The passage from the tunnel to the basement on the Jewish side was narrow and you had to wiggle through. Chaim Lopata and a few fighters were waiting for us at the exit. They were unshaven and dirty; they warmly embraced us, hugging us tightly [...].

A liaison agent came running with the news that tanks followed by Latvians were approaching Nalewki Street. A fighter wearing an SS uniform jacket and civilian pants guided our detachment.

We walked in trenches, passed through holes in the walls and over hot, still smoking scorched ruins.

Our guide moved through this jungle of iron rods, bricks and wires with the agility of a monkey, while we, loaded down with our weapons, grenades and ammunition, kept running into things at every step. Finally, we came to the inner courtyard of a large burned-out building. [...]

From somewhere in the ruins Dawid Apfelbaum emerged. After exchanging military salutes, "Bystry" gave his report. We stepped back a few paces. Apfelbaum painted a picture of the current situation. ZOB units were in charge on Niska Street. Right here, the ZZW units were fighting under joint command. [Was this a gallant effort by Apfelbaum to uphold Jewish unity in front of Polish colleagues, an overly positive memory on the part of Zarski, who is

29. A resident at number 6, A. Kaczynska, previously cited, says that the building's occupants did in fact know about it: "The concierge [...] told me to ask around to find out what was in my basement. [...] As I later found out, my father and my husband knew all about the entrance in our basement leading to the tunnel under Muranowska Street [...]." Kaczynska, *Obok piekla*, p. 74.

an excellent witness on other accounts, or a real, last-minute unity forged in the heat of battle? There is no other documentation that can resolve the question.]

Apfelbaum's unit occupied roof-top positions on Muranowska Street. Its machine gun and two automatic rifles covered our approaches from the SS, who were advancing in our direction. They were temporarily held back by the units led by Barlinski, Blum-Binsztok and Roman Weinsztok, which attacked by surprise. Our men knew the area and all the passages perfectly. They would appear in one place and then another, disorienting the enemy. A few bullets and a grenade thrown from behind them would stop the SS men in their tracks, discouraging them from advancing further.

Today we were to relieve the exhausted fighters so that they could get some rest, and evacuate the wounded.

Our unit was divided into two groups. "Bystry" took command of one, I the other. Each group was assigned liaison agents and Jewish fighters.

The two groups took up position amid the ruins of the burned-down buildings in Muranowski Square and on Nalewki Street.

Shortly after noon, the creaking of tank treads and the roar of motors told us that the Germans were advancing in our direction.

There were two tanks followed by SS infantry. Hiding in the ruins, we observed them attentively as they passed alongside us. They were watching the windows, and from time to time one of them would let loose a burst of automatic fire. My group, hidden in a doorway and a courtyard, was invisible to them. We let them pass by. I was not to attack until "Bystry" gave the signal.

We waited.

Suddenly, a grenade went off. That was the signal we were waiting for. I stood up and jumped out of the doorway, followed by the others. Another explosion. In the smoke I could see the Germans' silhouettes. I opened fire. Two short bursts and a Boche fell right next to me. "Stefan" and "Marek" were firing alongside me. I pulled the pin on a grenade and threw it into the building entrance where a few SS men had just run in.

Explosion! The sound of automatic weapons and grenades was joined by the characteristic rattle of long bursts from a heavy machine gun. The tank was beginning to sweep the street blindly.

After their initial surprise, the Germans regrouped and stepped up their fire. Enemy soldiers cut us off from "Bystry's" group. They were firing at us from the entranceways where they had taken shelter.

How could we get out of there?

A young Jewish boy named Jankiel came up to me and said, "Lieutenant, sir, we can get around them through the basements. I'll show you."

I left "Stefan" and a few others in position and went down with four boys, Jankiel in the lead, into the caves. We found ourselves in a neighboring building. In the entranceway I saw seven Germans, one of them wounded, sitting on the ground and leaning against the wall. They were close, some 20 meters away across a rubble-filled courtyard. We fired and the panicked Germans ran out into the street, where they were caught in the fire unleashed by "Stefan" and his men.

Our attack had attracted the tanks. We hid as best we could. Tank fire knocked down the few walls that were still standing. After a few rounds, the tanks withdrew.

After a few seconds I stood up. Two of my boys were lying in a sort of mutual embrace, killed by a tank shell. A third was wounded in the head and leg, unconscious. I heard a noise. I stood up again, ready to shoot. It was Jankiel, safe and sound. I sent him to get "Stefan" and gather our forces immediately.

The quiet before the storm.

"Stefan" quickly arrived with one part of our detachment. The others followed, carrying two wounded. We picked up the Germans' arms and ammunition.

I sent two wounded men with my report to Apfelbaum at Muranowski Square. A runner brought news from "Bystry"-Iwanski, telling me that he had been wounded and that his group suffered one death and three other causalities. He ordered me to take command,

and to keep the Germans from approaching the tunnel for as long as possible.

A moment later Apfelbaum appeared, one hand wrapped in a scarf and his head covered with a bloody bandage. The other soldiers from our unit were with him. Only eight of us were left.

Apfelbaum assigned two other units to me, headed by Roman Weinsztok and Lejzor Staniewicz, alias "Ryba." The "Ryba" unit had wiped out a group of Latvians during the first days of the uprising and thanks to that was very well armed. Our mission was to defend Muranowski Square.

We barely had the time to take up our positions when once again we heard the noise of motors and shooting. A tank and two armored cars, followed by SS soldiers, advanced slowly, sweeping both sides of the street with gunfire.

This time, we could not gain the advantage of surprise. The Nazis were being very careful, stopping to check the entranceways before moving on again.

We began to fire after they had already gotten fairly far from where we were. All we could do was fire off a few rounds in the direction of silhouettes we could barely see. The armored cars stopped and the German infantry occupied house after house, on both sides of the street, and under the cover of their vehicles kept up intense fire at our positions. We hardly shot back, in order to save ammunition.

A few fighters from Staniewicz's units went through underground passages and opened fire on the enemy from behind.

The fighting grew increasingly intense. Cannon fire destroyed our positions and we suffered casualties.

There was nothing we could do in that narrow street under constant heavy fire. The Germans moved slowly, but they were still advancing.

All of a sudden, a gray shadow stepped out of the burned and blackened walls. It ran a few meters, approached the tank, and threw a bottle. The fire spread quickly over the armor and into the interior. A second bottle and the flames grew, covering the tank entirely.

We stepped up our fire to cover the retreat of the Jewish hero who had risked his life to stop the iron monster. Unfortunately, he was killed by an SS bullet, falling near the blazing tank as the German crew leaped out and took cover in the rubble.

We had beaten back their attack.

The armored vehicles backed up. The Germans did not want to take any further risks, and they were also afraid that the ammunition in the burning tank would explode. Entrenched in ruined buildings, SS infantrymen were firing at us more vigorously than ever.

Our positions began to burn. The fires set by flamethrowers were driving us out of our hiding places.

Our worst losses came as we fell back to take up new positions. "Ryba"-Staniewicz was hit in the head and lost an eye. Both legs were broken. Also wounded were the brother of "Bystry" Waclaw Iwanski [who was to be evacuated and die the following day[30]], Dyjewski-"Dyl" and Lejewski-"Garbarz." I was wounded in the leg, and Apfelbaum had been hit again, this time in the chest. All of us had been wounded.

Realizing that the losses incurred in their attack were too heavy, and that they were not gaining ground, the Germans ceased firing at around 5 P.M. and the armored cars left.

We retreated to 7 Muranowski Square. The wounded left or were carried through the tunnel.

I went to speak to Apfelbaum, who was being treated by Wladka Cykop. "Why don't you come?" I asked. "I'm wounded, as you see," he replied, "but as long as my head still works I have to stay. These are my men and I can't abandon them."

He stayed. The next day, he died of loss of blood and exhaustion. In this battle, his closest associates and friends also died.[31]

---

30. Zajdler neglects to mention Henryk Iwanski's son, Roman, 16 years old, who was wounded and died a few hours after being evacuated. This incident is confirmed by several eyewitnesses. He does mention Roman in a longer work. See Wladyslaw Zarski-Zajdler, *Martyrologia ludnosci zydowskiej i pomoc spoleczenstwa polskiego*, Warsaw, 1968, p. 51.
31. Wladyslaw Zarski-Zajdler, "*Walki na placu Muranowskim w dniu* 27 IV 1943," ZIH Archives, no. 5790.

"Zarski" had only a partial view of the battle. All of the ZZW units had been concentrated around Muranowski Square, except for a platoon of the second company. His group had engaged the enemy on Nalewki Street, running parallel to Bonifraterska Street, which was in turn defended by the units under the command of Pika, Weinsztok, Bialoskora, Federbusz and Blum-Binsztok.

The rest of the W regiment platoon was fighting at the corner of Mila Street and Muranowski Square. Number 7 was defended by Rodal's unit; Apfelbaum's platoon had made an advanced post of rubble in front of number 11. The battle raged until nightfall, but the Germans were not able to reach Muranowski Square.[32]

Following is Bednarczyk's description of these events:

> Soon we received a report [Bednarczyk was in the ghetto but did not take part in either of the battles of Muranowski Square] saying that German units were approaching [...]. [T]he Germans advanced very cautiously, protected and supported by tanks. At their head was a company of Latvians. The united forces of the ZZW and the OW-KB, commanded by Apfelbaum and Rodal, were able to trap them. They let the Latvians enter Muranowski Square and once these troops were surrounded, they began to wipe them out, firing from three sides at once. This unit was quickly destroyed and the Germans withdrew, with their tank, for about an hour to regroup their forces. The fighters seized many dozens of excellent weapons from them, and immediately gave them out to the volunteers who accompanied them. An hour later, they were assaulted by German elite troops, who were protected by tanks and armored vehicles and supported by the heavy guns and automatic weapons of the infantry. This time the Germans advanced on a broad front. They tried

32. The battle of April 27 is cited in the situation report of April 28 issued by the ZZK (Jewish Coordination Committee, comprised of the Bund and the ZKN, which itself was a coalition of Zionist organizations): "In the area around Muranowski Square, a combat unit launched an attack against the Germans. German columns were seen firing on the ghetto defenders." The ZZW is not mentioned. We must repeat that it is not cited in any of the ZKK's daily reports. See "*Meldunki sytuacyjne dzienne z powstania w getcie*," no. 1, 19 IV 1943, no. 3, 20.

to penetrate Muranowski Square from the side, via Bonifraterska Street, and from behind, up Franciszkanska and Nalewki Streets. The desperate fighting on these streets went on for many hours. Both sides took the heaviest losses near the intersection of Bonifraterska Street and Muranowski Square. The ZZW was no longer fighting in tightly defined units. Various fighting units came into being, merging sections, companies and platoons, led at any given moment by the bravest among their men.

The units commanded by Janek Pika, Weinsztok, Bialoskora, Federbusz and Blum-Binsztok fought on the right flank of Bonifraterska Street. The other end of Franciszkanska Street, on the Nalewki Street side, and the position that blocked the approach to Muranowski Square toward Nalewki Street, were defended by units under Eliasz Albersztein, a Polish army warrant officer who had recently been promoted to Second Lieutenant. The middle of Bonifraterska Street was defended by the units under Zlotogora, "Ryba"-Staniewicz, Berman, Lipszyc, Sniadowicz, Mendelson, Taube Pinkus, Likiernik, Luft and Barlinski; closer to the corner there was "Zarski"-Zajdler's OW-KB group; and at the intersection itself, in a collapsed building, "Garbarz"-Lejewski's unit. On Muranowski Square, Rodal's unit fought at number 7, and at number 11, in the corner created by two walls and a sort of outcropping formed by the ruins of a building, there was a platoon led by the overall commanding officer, Captain Apfelbaum; at the end of the square, on the Nalewki Street side, Frenkiel's unit.

Weisstok's powerful unit was in charge of the defense of the opposite side of the square, by Niska and Muranowska streets. The building at the Mila Street intersection was occupied by an OW-KB unit headed by "Bystry"-Iwanski equipped with a heavy machine gun on the roof. Their job was to cover the whole square and Nalewki Street with their firepower. Also inside this building, deeply entrenched, was Chaim Lopata's unit. Weisstok and Rodal's units had light machine guns. During the fighting, the automatic rifles of Frenkiel and Apfelbaum's groups supported the units fighting on Bonifraterska Street. The Germans suffered a sharp reversal during

> the course of the fighting. They were not able to get to 7 Muranowski Square despite artillery and tank support. In the fighting at the corner of the square, they even lost a tank to the Molotov cocktail thrown by a Jewish boy, a ZZW soldier.
>
> During the battle, units changed positions and came to each other's rescue in rhythm with the unfolding of events. For example, the units on Muranowski Square took part in the fighting on Bonifraterska Street. Finally the Germans disengaged, as was their habit.[33]

The surviving Poles (of the 18 or 20 men, 10 died) and some of the ZZW fighters, 34 apparently, got out through the tunnel. Lieutenant Rodal died soon after. Captain Mendelson (he had just been promoted; although wounded, he refused to be evacuated until ordered to do so by Apfelbaum), Sergeant Lejewski and Iwanski himself lived, all three of them suffering from serious long-term disabilities. (Mendelson was the only ZZW officer to survive the war; Walewski, a non-commissioned group leader, also survived.)

Iwanski describes the same events in the following way:

> April 26, seriously wounded, Apfelbaum sent a request for stepped-up military aid. He was almost out of ammunition and grenades. On April 27 at 10 A.M., I, my second-in-command and 18 of my men went through the tunnel at 6 Muranowski Square and emerged into the ghetto at number 7. After distributing the weapons we had brought especially for this purpose, I divided my unit into two groups. I took position along with nine of my men in the burned-out buildings facing Nalewki Street, on the right side, and Wladyslaw Zajdler on the left. Very soon two tanks appeared, followed by a big unit of fascist Latvians in the pay of the Germans. There were several hundred of them, with submachine guns and grenades. I let the tanks go by, then threw a grenade. This was the agreed-upon signal for the fighting to start. We and Apfelbaum's soldiers opened

33. Bednarczyk, *Zycie codzienne warszawskiego getta*, pp. 104–106.

> fire from all sides. The lead tank was destroyed by a Molotov cocktail thrown by Jankiel, a 12-year-old Jewish boy who died in this battle. The second tank started to retreat after being set ablaze by the soldiers under Edelman (ZOB), who fought courageously at the head of his "brushmakers" unit. [Edelman's participation in this battle has not been confirmed by any other eyewitness account.] The fascists retreated but soon counterattacked in even greater force, even using an airplane to bomb our positions. In this battle – the biggest during the uprising – almost all the ZZW officers and many soldiers died. Ten men in my unit died, including my son Roman and my brother Waclaw, and almost all the rest were wounded, myself among them. When we ran out of ammunition we had to retreat through the tunnel. We took dozens of wounded Jewish fighters with us (those who were not wounded didn't want to leave the ghetto under fire; it was only with great difficulty that we were able to take with us Apfelbaum's aide "Kalmyk"-Mendelson, who, despite being seriously wounded, did not want to abandon his post and his comrades-in-arms), as well as a large number of sick people and children. Outside, on the "Aryan" side, an escort unit led by "Sep"-Kowalski was waiting for us, along with half of a KB platoon from the Nalecz company. All the escapees lay down in the bottom of funeral vans (we had installed wooden structures so that those on the bottom would not be smothered by those on top of them) and were covered with canvas on which metal funeral wreaths were placed. A hearse with funeral wreaths would not attract attention; they were commonplace. The most seriously wounded were taken to safe houses in the city, most of them to my apartment, and the lightly wounded and sick were transported out of Warsaw.[34]

The second battle of Muranowski Square was also described by Stroop, but in his own way:

> April 27, 1943 [...] At 1600 hours, a special battle unit of 320 officers

34. Iwanski, "*Czy mozna bylo ratowac ludzi...?*"

> and men was sent into action to cleanse a large block of houses on both sides of the so-called Niska Street in the northeastern part of the former Jewish quarter. [As can be seen on the map, Niska Street runs into Muranowski Square and its southern side is the north side of Muranowska Street. This figure given for the number of troops involved is extremely large and unusual – at that point the Germans had been fighting in groups of a few dozen for many days and Stroop usually does not indicate anything but the number of groups, for example 24 on the morning of the 27th and the previous days. The importance of this event is brought out by the fact that Stroop says he organized a special battle group, reports their numbers and specifies their geographical objective, details that are unique in these reports. The creation of a special battle group that afternoon suggests that the regular units ran into serious problems earlier in the day.] [...] As usual, they remained until the end in the bunkers they had constructed underground or in attics. They fired until the last moment and jumped into the street below – sometimes from the fourth story – only when the flames left them no other escape. [...] The exterior appearance of the Jews who are now being apprehended shows that the turn has come for those Jews who directed the resistance.[35]

Thus Stroop, the three Polish officers and the Jewish officer all agree on one thing: On April 27, Muranowski Square was the object of a particularly intense battle, and the ZZW forces were resupplied through the tunnel, receiving grenades, ammunition and automatic weapons from a group of 18 (or 20) Polish soldiers. This was an especially bloody battle. At nightfall, the Germans withdrew, without having succeeded in breaking the resistance. The Polish survivors, the Polish and Jewish wounded and a few civilians left through the tunnel. During the night, the surviving Jewish fighters withdrew to the industrial zone.

In addition to the battle of Muranowski Square and the para-

35. Stroop, *The Stroop Report*, daily report, April 27, 1943.

graph about the "special battle unit," there is a related, secondary question concerning April 27. Here is what Stroop says about it:

> An anonymous letter disclosed that large numbers of Jews were to be found in a block of buildings adjoining but outside the northeastern part of the Jewish quarter. A special assault unit, commanded by First Lieutenant of the Protective Police Diehl, was sent into action against this building. The assault party discovered a gang of 120 men, heavily armed with pistols, rifles, hand grenades, and light machine guns [...]. The rest could not be captured or destroyed because of approaching darkness. The buildings, however, were immediately surrounded, so escape is not possible. The purge will continue tomorrow. Also taken into custody were 17 Poles, including two Polish Police [...].[36]

Stroop's mention of "a block of buildings adjoining but outside the northeastern part of the Jewish quarter" would seem to indicate 6 Muranowska Street. The ZZW had rented an apartment several months earlier on the fourth floor of this building. Kaczynska recounts the same events on a more modest scale:

> The Germans brought up an armored car, surrounded our house and began to hunt for Jews in every apartment, checking everyone's papers. The Aryan men were loaded into trucks and taken to an unknown destination. My husband was among them. The women and children were taken out into the street and lined up against the ghetto wall. Then they caught Jews who were trying to hide in the apartments. They were taken into the courtyard and every one of them killed. About a hundred people.[37]

Why did Stroop exaggerate the importance of this battle? On this occasion he requested that Diehl be awarded the highest military

36. Stroop, ibid.
37. Kaczynska, *Obok piekla*, p. 73.

honor. Is this why he magnified this skirmish? Asked about this at his trial, he replied, "The 120 Jewish fighters are mentioned separately because they appeared not in the ghetto but outside. This was not a more important battle than the others. But nevertheless we were worried that the uprising would spread beyond the ghetto walls into Warsaw as a whole."[38]

THE PARTISANS

Starting on April 23 for the ZOB, and April 28 for the ZZW, the units hid in bunkers, coming out only when forced to or to launch hit and run operations.

The ZZW fighters who did not want to leave through the tunnel remained to fight until the end. They decided to evacuate Muranowski Square (the tunnel was anyway no longer usable because, as we have just seen, the Germans had occupied 6 Muranowska Street) and withdraw to the Nowolipki-Smocza area, the location of the quarters of the second company and, above all, the last functional tunnel at 5 Karmelicka Street (leading to the Evangelical hospital at 4 Karmelicka Street), through which they could get ammunition and help.

Iwanski recounts the following:

> After that, and until the end of June, our patrols remained in touch with those who continued to fight amid the rubble, the "*gruzowcy*" [*gruzy* means "ruins"], entering the ghetto to bring them ammunition, grenades, food and bandages, and bring people out, always a number equal to the number of our men, because each could carry only one person at a time. We went through the sewers dragging the wounded in a specially-sewn bag that had openings for the legs and a handle near the head. The amount of room in the sewers was very variable and often the men had to hunch over and continue for quite a way in that position; and at the same time, they were

38. Cited in Borwicz, *L'insurrection du ghetto de Varsovie*, pp. 221–22.

> walking in sewage and had to keep the heads of the wounded as high as possible [...].
>
> There were no longer major battles against the Germans, but occasionally our patrols skirmished with the "scavengers" who were carefully combing the ghetto. The evacuated wounded were brought to my apartment, where they were given first aid and washed. We burned their tattered clothing.
>
> One day [May 3, according to Datner – see below], my wife Wiktoria passed out. In one of the bags was our second son, Zbigniew. He had been wounded and died while they were carrying him. Thus we lost our two sons, and I my two brothers, because Edward was killed during the same expedition as Zbigniew.[39]

There were very few ZZW survivors. The battle of the 27th had been very costly; in particular, most of the officers (and almost all of the veterans of the 1939 fighting) died that day: Zylberberg, Barlinski, Blum-Binsztok, Sniadowicz, Pinkus [Taube], Federbusz, Lipszyc, Staniewicz, Dermatolski, Makower, Goldberg, Bialoskora and still others. Captain Apfelbaum, promoted to major after his death, died from his wounds on the 28th.

The survivors were brought ammunition via the Kamelicka Street tunnel on April 30[40] and May 3. Datner recounts:

> By order of Major Henryk Iwanski-"Bystry," around May 3, 1943, a KB-AK battle unit made up of about 15 people entered the ghetto through the manhole on Zimna Street, coming out at [...] 4 Karmelicka Street. They were led by "Tomasz" [...], a municipal water department employee.
>
> Their mission was to resupply the groups still fighting with bandages and medications, food and ammunition, and take the most

39. Iwanski, "*Czy mozna bylo ratowac ludzi...?*"
40. "The units [...] of the ZZW regrouped near the tunnel, still in operation, at 5 Karmelicka Street. During the night of April 30, I entered the ghetto through the Evangelical church with an OW-KB patrol carrying ammunition, which hooked up with them." Bednarczyk, *Zycie codzienne warszawskiego getta*, p. 107.

> seriously wounded out of the ghetto. Their orders were carried out; 15 wounded were evacuated under extremely difficult conditions. There was a firefight with the Germans even as they were lowering the wounded into the sewers. During the exchange of fire in which the men of "Bystry," among others, took part, the ZZW members who made up the escort, two Jews and the son of "Bystry," Zbigniew Iwanski, 18 years old, all three of them already wounded, were hit again. They died in the sewers a few minutes later. Two KB members were also wounded, Stanislaw "Zbik"-Gladkowski and Jan "Kot"-Cieplikowski.[41]

The Germans attacked the sector, which was a theater of combat from May 4–7. The last of the survivors moved on once again, northward toward Niska and Muranowska streets. That same day, the Germans found the ZOB bunker,[42] and the next day, they attacked it from all sides and destroyed it. Almost all the ZOB fighters, including their commander, Anielewicz, committed suicide. A few found their way out through an unguarded exit.

There is a cruel irony regarding the fratricidal struggles of the past and future: Of the two organizations, Stroop only knew about the ZZW, and he wrote in his report:

> The entire area of the former Jewish Ghetto was searched today by assault sweep detachments for bunkers and Jews. As was reported several days ago, subhumanity – bandits and terrorists – remains in bunkers, which the fires have caused to become unbearably hot. These creatures know that their choice is either to remain in hiding as long as possible or to come to the surface and try to wound the men of the Waffen-SS, Police and Wehrmacht [...].
>
> The discovery of the bunker of the so-called inner party leadership [this phrase, used twice, remains incomprehensible] reported

41. Szymon Datner, "*Wspolna walka*," *Tygodnik Demokratyczny*, no. 17 (1968).
42. "The location of the bunker used by the so-called inner party leadership is now known. It will be forced open tomorrow." Stroop, *The Stroop Report*, daily report, May 7, 1943.

> in yesterday's teletype message was further pursued today. We succeeded in opening the bunker of the party leadership and seizing about 60 heavily armed bandits. The deputy head of the Jewish military organization, the ZWZ[43] [this is a twofold error on Stroop's part: the initials are ZZW, not ZWZ, and the bunker did not belong to the ZZW but to the ZOB command] and his so-called chief of staff were caught and liquidated. About 200 Jews were sheltered in this bunker; 60 of them were apprehended and 140 destroyed due to the strong impact of smoke candles and heavy explosives laid in several places. One Jew that we removed reported that countless Jews had been killed by the smoke candles. [...] We have statements that 3,000 to 4,000 Jews still remain in the subterranean holes, sewers and bunkers. The undersigned is determined not to terminate the grand operation until the last Jew has been destroyed.
>
> A total of 1,091 Jews were apprehended in the bunkers today; about 280 Jews were shot in battle; countless Jews were destroyed in 43 demolished bunkers. The total number of Jews apprehended has risen to 49,712. Buildings which have not yet been destroyed by fire were set on fire today. In the process, it was discovered that isolated Jews were still hiding somewhere within walls or staircases. [...][44]

THE RUINS

The remaining ZZW and ZOB units were cut off into small groups. The surviving soldiers of the two organizations hid and fled; now there were nothing but occasional firefights.

Stroop wrote on May 15:

> [...] The reconnaissance detachments patrolling the Ghetto last night reported only sporadic encounters with Jews. [During the previous phases, the Germans withdrew at nightfall. The sending in of night hunter commando units began in early May.] In contrast

43. The ZWZ was the initial Polish resistance organization created in 1939.
44. Stroop, ibid., daily report, May 8, 1943.

> to preceding nights, only six to seven Jews were shot. The assault sweep detachments dispatched today during the day also had only minor success. 29 new bunkers were discovered, but some of them no longer had occupants. Altogether, 87 Jews were apprehended today and an additional 67 bandits and Jews shot in battle. In a skirmish that developed around noon, the bandits again resisted, using Molotov cocktails, pistols and homemade hand grenades. The gang was destroyed, but subsequently one member of the Order Police was shot through the right hip.
>
> A special commando unit once more searched the last building complex which had been left standing intact in the Ghetto, and subsequently destroyed it. In the evening, the chapel, mortuary and all the other buildings at the Jewish cemetery were blown up or destroyed by fire.
>
> The total number of Jews apprehended has risen to 55,885.[45]

On May 16, he declared the resistance over:

> [...] Progress report of the grand operation on 16 May 1943. Start of operation: 1000 hours.
>
> 180 Jews, bandits, and subhumans were destroyed. [This tautological description should be taken as a discreet expression of jubilation.] The Jewish quarter of Warsaw is no more! The grand operation terminated at 2015 hours when the Warsaw synagogue was blown up.
>
> To the Commander of Police Battalion III/2 [...] were transferred all necessary measures to be taken concerning the restricted areas that have been established.
>
> The total number of Jews apprehended and destroyed, according to the record, is 56,065.
>
> We had no losses.
>
> I will submit my final report to the conference of SS and Police Leaders on 18 May 1943.[46]

---

45. Ibid.
46. Stroop, ibid., daily report, May 16, 1943.

A few weeks later, Stroop was awarded the highest military distinction, the Iron Cross first class.

In the burned-out ruins now being leveled, some people held out and fought for several more months. Of that period, all that remains are the account of Walewski[47] and Leon Najberg's diary (which we have already mentioned – see footnote 183), written between October 1943 and May 1944. Najberg, who emerged from the rubble of the ghetto at the end of September, hid on the "Aryan" side, where he had what he described as "ideal conditions" for writing. After the war he gave his diary to the Central Commission for Jewish History[48] and moved to Israel. His diary was published in 1993 in a private edition by the Warsaw Institute of Jewish History.[49] Citations from Najberg's diary are followed by the notation "(N.)", and Walewski's accounts by "(W.)."

> June 2. Last night, we learned from the fighters of the "Pika" group who were at Muranowski Square (this seems to have been a *Unterwelt* group ["underworld" – we have previously discussed the ZZW's recruitment of Jan Pika and the porters and smugglers] that fought courageously) that they had been "found out" that day by the Germans and had waged a pitched battle in which many of that group's fighters were killed. The survivors joined the group led by "Mojche the Bolshevik" (I didn't know who he was) [that makes two of us – MA] which was fighting at 13/11 Bonifraterska Street (N.).

The wiping out of the Pika group seems to have marked the end of the organized resistance. The survivors fought only when discovered or to protect their flight.

---

47. Walewski, "*Protokol*," respectively pp. 553, 549–50, 555, 549, 553, as noted with "(W.)."..
48. This commission was the forerunner of the Jewish Institute of History. See Borwicz, *L'insurrection du ghetto de Varsovie*, p. 250.
49. Najberg, *Ostatni powstancy getta*, respectively pp. 94, 130, 135, 139, 88, 113, 131, 132, 151, 85, 92, 106, 120–21, 109, 116, 127–28, 130, 136, 142, 147–48, 151–52, 157–58, 159–60, 161, as noted with "(N.)."

> June 3. [...] At 10 A.M., the Germans succeeded in penetrating through the building at 38 Swietojerska Street into ours at 4 Walowa Street (which we called the "hotel," since about 150 Jews were hiding there). The Ukrainians and Wehrmacht soldiers came up to the fourth floor, whistling the "Horst Wessel Song." In the burned-out rooms, they found sleeping pallets, abandoned backpacks and disguised firing holes. [...] Our group managed to withdraw to 34 Swietojerska Street, taking a large number of Jews with us. But about 15 families stayed behind in the burned-out rooms. They spread out on different floors and hid themselves as best they could. The Germans opened up with a flame thrower, yelling "Alle Jude heraus!" No one came out. Suddenly they noticed a passage leading to 34 Swietojerska Street (the building in which we found refuge) and without the slightest inkling began to move toward us. Our boys were waiting for them, holding their breath, arms at the ready. When the torturers came close enough, we opened fire and killed three of them. The other three who followed retreated while firing at us. Our success was temporary but magnificent. A half-hour later, a unit [...] of about 150 soldiers began to encircle us. We defended ourselves by firing one shot at a time and once in a while throwing grenades into the courtyard of the building at 4 Walowa Street. German sappers got into the building's basement and blew the front off the building. Now they had a clear line of fire from below and far away. They began to shoot at us from all directions; a rain of bullets and metal fell on us. Czarnoczapek and Szerman were wounded but our group remained calm. After that, the unfolding of events was very rapid. The Germans gained access to the "hotel" by using ladders; since we were almost out of ammunition we decided to retreat. We fled through holes in the walls we had prepared in advance and headed toward Franciszkanska Street. The Germans were keeping watch there too, but we were able to disperse into the "free-fire" zone. When we regrouped again that night, we realized that Pierocki had fallen in combat. The Germans took about 70 people out of the building at 4 Walowa Street (N.).

Najberg's motley group hid in rooms left suspended in the upper stories of burned-out buildings. This was an ideal location from which to watch and listen.

A month later, the relentless hunt was still underway:

> Saturday, July 3. [...] We fell back to Gesia, where the Germans welcomed us with retaining fire. Kanalowna fell. Lolek [Lewinson] gave the order to retreat to 24 Zamenhof Street to make our last stand. We took up our positions.
>
> A few minutes later, we could hear the sound of boots on the cobblestones and the murderers entered the courtyard firing in every direction. Our boys let them approach. Mosze Halbersztadt threw a grenade, turning two of them into a bloody mass of flesh. A firefight broke out. We were running out of ammunition. We faced certain defeat. The boys decided either to leave or to die where they were. Mosze Halbersztadt, Lolek and Trinker quietly approached the entryway and threw grenades we had taken from dead Germans or found in the ghetto. The Germans panicked and fled. We had just enough time to disperse onto Pawia Street and from there through 13 Zamenhof Street to Gesia Street. But we were not all destined to survive. Lolek, Mosze Halbersztadt, Trinker, Rozenberg and Lipski hid in the courtyard at 13 Gesia Street. The Germans trapped them there. The boys decided to fight and when their ammunition ran out they died. The courtyard at 13 Zamenhof Street is their common grave (N.).
>
> July 7. [...] We were surprised by a German night patrol (the Germans had wrapped their boots in cotton). All of a sudden we heard "Hände hoch!" and a few shots fired in the air. We were standing in Indian file (to pass bricks from hand to hand). Zemsz, who was closest to the Germans, fired off a number of rounds in their direction and was killed. Everyone else had time to retreat to the back of the basement. It had two exits. We went through the second and came out on Nalewki Street. Under the entryway, we saw the body of Henpeck Billauer, who belonged to our patrol. [...] Of our group of seven people [...] only three survived (N.).

In late July, the Germans began to systematically demolish

the burned-out buildings where the ghetto used to stand. In this way they also hoped to destroy, once and for all, the last pockets of resistance, the last Jewish fighters, the last of the Mohicans of the Warsaw ghetto (N.).

Water

While awaiting the complete leveling of the former ghetto, one of the first methods of extermination adopted by the Germans was thirst.

May 23. Today, for the first time, Polish workers from the Water Department came under German escort and cut off the mains that brought water to the brushmakers' area. Henpeck Zemsz got us out of this hopeless situation when, with the help of several men, he improvised a wrench and opened a major pipe, the one bringing water to the second courtyard at 38 Swietojerska Street. [...] A few days afterward, the Germans ordered a Water Department team to completely cut off the water supply to this area.

We began to draw water from the artesian wells behind the bunkers. [...] The complications of getting in and out of the bunkers made this even more difficult. One of the wells was in a bunker discovered by the Germans at 28 Swietojerska Street. It was in the basement right under the building's main toilets. The entrance to the bunker was under a toilet [...] fastened to the wall with disguised hinges. After moving the toilet bowl you could go through the hole and down a ladder into the cellar. We got our water supplies there for several days. One day we noticed the water had a funny color. The people hiding nearby told us not to use it because the Germans had come that day and probably poisoned it.

After cutting off the water mains under the brushmakers' area, the Germans adopted a new technique after every operation, which consisted of poisoning the water in the bunkers they had found and blowing up the artesian wells (N.).

June 15 [...]. For several days now there has been no more water in the "free-fire zone." But it rained hard and we decided to use the rainwater. Up until then we had used it to shower but now we had to drink it. We brought some plywood from Grynbaum's bunker and above our hideout built a little roof with a sheet metal tube fastened to it [...] the other end of the tube led to the balcony situated next to our hiding place. On it we placed a number of receptacles meant to hold rain water (N.).

July 3 [...]. Luckily, we have some real experts among our ranks. Henpeck Zemsz and a group of workers are digging a tunnel below the water main running under the pavement (N.).

July 5 [...]. Inside the burned-out buildings, in luxury apartments with all the amenities [...] and in the burned-down Werterfassung company warehouses in our courtyard, there are water heaters. [...] It seems that there are many dozens of boilers that are just blackened and still full of water, which won't run out of an open faucet because there is no longer enough water pressure for that. Using a nail, Henpeck Zemsz made holes in the boiler so that the water could run into various receptacles. [...] After eyeballing the volume of our pail, Zemsz [...] made holes at the right height so that we could get enough water to meet our vital needs (N.).

At that point [August 23], after the Germans took away pieces of the boilers on 23/25 Nalewki Street and shot up the others to empty them, our water supply situation became catastrophic (N.).

Traps

The manhunt included tracking down Jews and using all sorts of snares and traps.

In late June our living conditions got even worse, because the Germans began to patrol at night. [Night patrols, at first only sporadic, had begun two months earlier.] This enriched our lives with a certain emotion. When someone left our hideaways at night, no one knew if he would come back. Out in the streets we tried to take the patrols by surprise and frighten them so that they wouldn't dare come into the ghetto at night any more. During the day we reinforced our sentry posts and set up lookouts in places near the streets around our

> hideout, or in other words, Nalewki, Gesia and Zamenhof Streets. We wanted to know what time the German patrols came at night, their itinerary and their numbers. Up until now, the sound of the "Scavengers' Hymn" was our signal that their "work day" was over. Now conditions had changed and this forced us to carry out reconnaissance and figure out their new tactics. We had noticed that the patrols were made up of three to five soldiers [...], and that they came between 9 P.M. and midnight. Their new tactic consisted of [...] spreading flour or chalk on the most used paths so that the tracks would allow them to follow the Jews to their hiding places. They also used other methods. For example, near the bunkers they had already discovered they would pile up burned sticks of wood or bricks so that they could see if people were still coming to these places. This meant we were forced to step up our vigilance at night and be even more careful (N.).
>
> We went into a small one-story house near a large empty lot. It had been miraculously spared as the fire raged all around it. [...] During the day it served me as an excellent observation post. I could see the Germans go by, police chasing Jews and Ukrainians rampaging all over. It turned out that the Germans had deliberately saved this house to trap Jews in it. The Jews no longer had any hiding places and would go in there to take shelter. Since they didn't know about the hideout behind the wooden partition wall, they hid in the back bedrooms and the attic. The Germans came by several times a day just to "harvest" the Jews found there. (W.)

"Cockroaches"

The most disgusting method of extermination was the systematic use of stool pigeons, nicknamed "cockroaches."

> [...] The Germans then used another subterfuge. Immediately after finding a bunker, they would shoot some of the Jews in front of the others. Once the execution was over, a German officer [...] would proclaim an amnesty for anyone who would tell them where Jews were hiding.

Driven by fear and completely terrorized, more than one person broke and led the Germans to the bunkers they knew about. A new epidemic was ravaging the ghetto – an outbreak of "cockroaches." The Germans tolerated them as long as they furnished new victims but as soon as a "cockroach" ran out of bunkers to snitch on, they would be shot on the spot. The life expectancy of a "cockroach" averaged only a few days. (w.)

> Sunday May 16. [...] It was a peaceful afternoon. The murderers didn't come until around 1 P.M. and they discovered the bunker (called the "General") at 38 Swietojerska Street. The Germans made holes in the walls and poured in phosgene gas to drive the people out. After getting their prisoners ready to be executed (carrying out body searches and stealing their personal belongings), they began to try to force them to reveal where Jews were hiding. Out of the group of 60 people they chose Moniek Kirszenbaum, 18 years old, whose leg was completely consumed by gangrene and who looked more like a corpse than a living man. They demanded that he show them the locations of bunkers where the Jews were hiding. Moniek firmly told them that he didn't know of any. That is what the Germans were waiting for; they set upon him with their leather and lead-wire whips. Moniek gritted his teeth and remained heroically stubborn so as not to betray his brothers. But the Germans had a method for everything... An SS man put a revolver bullet through his hand, threatening him, "*Wenn du zeigst nicht Judenbunker, schiesse ich dir tot.*" But Moniek, writhing in pain, shouted at them, insolently, "Murderers! I'll never betray them. You can kill me!"
>
> This was too much for the furious bandits, used to getting what they wanted without encountering resistance. They began to beat him with their rifle buts, the blood poured out of his wounded hand, and since these tortures did not break Moniek's courage, they used a Browning. This time the bullet in his leg knocked him down. Moniek passed out. Then the three bandits used their whips... They beat him atrociously.
>
> The unfortunate victim, who knew that Leonek's bunker on 2

Walowa Street had been discovered, gave his torturers this address, thinking that there would be no one left alive there. But the murderers pulled out 12 people who had taken refuge there the night before. [...] And then the executioners finished off Moniek (N.).

May 26. [...] From time to time, Ajzenberg cried out, "Zemsz, save me!" After carefully examining Ajzenberg, the doctor said it was impossible to treat him in conditions such as ours. Klojnski finished off Ajzenberg. This was the only way, brutal as it was, to keep him from talking about the bunkers and giving us away without wanting to (N.).

There were some shacks there [on a small square at 101 Zelazna Street] with some 60 Jews and Jewesses. The SS took Lolek inside and ordered that he be served breakfast in the kitchen. Lolek looked around the shack and saw people from various bunkers and groups, and figured out that from each group of people to be shot, the bandits had chosen one to make him or her talk. In this shack there was a canteen with cakes and sweets (N.).

When we got back to the Bonifraterska Street area, we were told that some "cockroaches" were locked up in the ruins of one of our bunkers where Brauer's shop had stood. [...] These "cockroaches" turned out to be three men, one of them accompanied by his small eight-year-old daughter. Because of the presence of the girl, we left him under guard in the bunker. The other two we took with us.

The court martial took place in the ruins of the burned-out building. Eyewitnesses declared that they had seen them lead the Germans to the "Moment" bunker. The accused acknowledged having betrayed many other bunkers. I ordered that the accused be brought to the grounds of the Brauer shop to be given the death penalty and that their bodies should be thrown into the still-smoking bunker. (W.)

Wednesday, June 21. At 5 A.M., our sentry spotted groups of bandits marching down Gesia Street Indian file, taking two Jewish "cockroaches" with them [...]. Suddenly they all halted in front of the place where a building had been destroyed in 1939 – on 3 Gesia Street. Voices could be heard speaking Yiddish and calling on people to come out of the bunker. Once again they used the old ruse, shouting, "Jews, come out, the war is over!" But no one came out. Then the bandits began to move aside the rubble and dig holes into the ruins. This job took them four hours; they would not give up their hunt. At 10 A.M. they made a hole, and the bandits could be heard yelling happily, "Judenbunker!" (N.)

Sewers and Bunkers

The sewers were the only source of supplies and the only way out. From the first day of the *Grossaktion* until the last, their neutralization was a constant German objective.

With the aim of completely cutting off the Jews from the Polish quarter, they ordered the Water Department workers to build thick walls inside the sewers in certain sectors and make it impossible to go through them from the ghetto to the Polish side. To make any attempt to enter the sewers impossible inside the ghetto […], all the manholes there were destroyed and the sewer outlets were blocked with iron, pieces of sheet metal, bricks and rubble. (N.)

The last opening through which the Jews could still get to the Aryan side was the sewers. Hundreds of people fled into the sewers, thinking that they would be safe there. But instead of safety, death awaited them there. At that point the sewers were already partially flooded and a great many of those who descended into them drowned. Other people who could not find their way among the passages, and didn't know where the outlets were, died of hunger and exhaustion. […] Corpses piled up in the narrow sewer corridors. It was common to see children crawling alongside oozing bodies and to hear the screams of people who had lost their minds. (W.)

One night in late June, around midnight, [the smugglers] came through the sewers from the Polish quarter to the brushmakers' area […]. They went through the sewers to Wybrzeze Kosciuszkowskie, then took the storm sewer that goes under Starowka Street and Franciszkanska Street to the destroyed manhole on Franciszkanska next to the wall surrounding the ghetto on Bonifraterska Street. The smugglers cleared the way and came out. Our group, under a heavily-armed escort, carried Szymek Kac, his wife, his mother and his child and old Niemcewicz who was then hiding in the bunker at number 11 [in the "free-fire zone" on 11 Walowa Street]. That day the smugglers didn't want to take anyone else and Szymek Kac promised to see what he could do to save the other people in our group. (N.)

On July 2, the group of smugglers […] came back. We were to clear the manhole on Franciszkanska Street for them. The Germans had dynamited it and blocked it up with sheet metal and iron. The smugglers had told us previously […] that they would come at 2 A.M. Our group took up positions at the outlets of Swietojerska, Bonifraterska, Franciszkanska and Walowa streets to protect us from German night patrols. Under this cover we began to unblock the manhole. […] This time, the smugglers stayed until four in the morning. In addition to food, they brought us candles, matches, batteries and newspapers. In exchange they were given many sacks of old clothes that we had gathered up for them in discovered bunkers. (N.)

[…] The smugglers demanded 15 thousand zlotys per person […]. We didn't even dare think about it because we didn't have enough money to get us all out, and anyone who did have that kind of money would not leave without the rest because we were all bound together by the blood shed in battle. (N.)

Nevertheless, our groups hiding in the ruins above ground came out to fight hit-and-run battles. Little by little they fell, one after another. […] In July 1943, through various stages, we succeeded in getting out of the ghetto through the sewers. (W.)

July 14. Once again the smugglers came to see us, headed by Szladkowski, announcing that this time they could only take five people (for a previously agreed-upon price). After discussion, we decided to send Klojnski, Felek Rozenberg and Lejzor Szerszen. Szerszen refused to leave the group, declaring that he looked too obviously Jewish. Mietek Lizawer was chosen to replace him. Preparations for leaving for the "other side" were now underway. The men shaved with dull razors; Abram Starowiejski served as the barber and cut the hair of the chosen few. Then they began to pick out appropriate clothing to look as much like the "Aryans" as possible. For an hour we felt as if they were preparing for a costume party, as they borrowed an appropriate item of clothing from each of our wardrobes. We carefully "picked out" […] the cleanest shirts, ties, head gear, shoes. Klojnski dressed in blue work clothes, carrying a screwdriver and a battered old helmet with the intention of trying to pass as a worker from the "other side." When everything was ready, and after the verdict of the jury, or in other words, those who stayed behind, the "delegation" left in the direction of the manhole where the smugglers were waiting for them. (N.)

August 10. […] Last night Lewinson left for the Polish quarter. […] We began to feverishly prepare for our exit to the "other side" by letting the sun shine on us during the day (when conditions would allow it) to hide the paleness of our faces, and picking off the lice that covered us. (N.)

August 18. […] The smugglers arrived at midnight, with Szladkowski and Lewinson in the lead. Just after they came out of the manhole we had to hide because we could hear the footsteps of a German patrol on Bonifraterska Street. The smugglers brought tomato, fruit and lard. […]

A brief conversation with Lewinson dampened our enthusiasm about going over to the Aryan side. Lewinson told us it was suicide and that we could continue to live in our present conditions. […] After leaving the ghetto, Lolek [Lewinson] took refuge in the home of a relative, an "Aryan" who lived on Poznanska Street. Two days later, someone in the building ratted to the authorities and a Jewish family who were hiding there were arrested and shot along with their "Aryan" protectors. The Germans confiscated all the property found in the apartment. This new situation forced Lolek to leave the apartment where these friends had welcomed him, and after that he spent his nights on the banks of the Vistula, hiding in the rushes. All of his friends whom he went to see reassured him and even invited him to share their meals, but to be put up in someone's apartment for the night was simply a dream. During the long days Lolek looked for a shelter where we could hide for at least one day after we came out of the sewers. But unfortunately, he couldn't find one. [...] It was unthinkable to go around the Polish quarter without papers and it was even more difficult to survive without money on the "Aryan" side than in the former ghetto. His week in the "Aryan" quarter had brought nothing but one nightmarish disillusionment after another.

[...] The smugglers [...] agreed not to make us pay to be taken out. This time it was Lolek who refused to go, saying that we would fall into the Germans' hands as soon as we emerged on the "Aryan" side.

After a brief conclave (some people held that if we had to die it might as well be with all the other Jews), we decided to go back to our hideout. Szladkowski promised us he would continue to look for a place for us to hide. The smugglers promised to bring us some food. They left the ghetto at dawn and we, feeling completely crushed, Lewinson in tears, went back to our hideout. (N.)

Late August. [...] The smugglers still have not come back. Lolek Lewinson and someone else decided to go to the Polish quarter to buy some food, taking the same sewers because they knew the way. [...] We decided to clear the manhole. It turned out to be obstructed by rubble for dozens of meters. That night, with Mojsze Trajger's comrades, we cleared it out, and when our work was finished we covered it up with a hand cart, as the Germans had done. Overnight once again the exit was covered several meters deep in a pile of rubble, timbers, iron and sheet metal. There was no longer any question of accessing the sewers through that manhole. (N.)

Saturday, September 25. Reinforced German patrols prowl the ghetto all night. We've lost all hope of getting food because the manhole through which the smugglers came has been covered with iron by the Germans [...] and is under constant observation by night patrols.

[...] Of our group of 45 people, only four are still alive. (N.)

Sunday, September 26. The day of decision-making has come. It has been pouring with rain since this morning [...]. At noon, a decision was reached: We're going. A "shower" in the rain, some

> lice hunting and picking through the tatters that passed for our clothes took several hours. Dusk came slowly; the rain continued to fall, sometimes harder, sometimes less. Last-minute preparations and a last check: ladder, rope, weapons. Last decisions: a division of labor, order of march, and the last of the Jewish Mohicans arose from the bottom of their graves for their last action. Each of us tried to look "Aryan," but we looked like caricatures heading for a costume party. (N.)

The little group left the ruins of the ghetto by climbing the walls between two patrol rounds.

> When we got to Franciszkanska Street, passersby greeted us by saying, "These Jews are clever! " We heard others say, "The rats have fled the ghetto again." But no one dared come near us. Maybe they were afraid of the guns in our hands.
>
> [...] For the moment, we are saved. Tomorrow, I am to make contact with Stefan Müller of the AL [People's Army] so that he can help us join the partisans.
>
> It is a night of black storms but those who survive until tomorrow will live until the dawn...(N.)

Both Walewski and Najberg survived the war, and then moved to Israel. Walewski died in 1971 and Najberg is still alive.

CHAPTER 9

AGENDAS AND OBFUSCATIONS

A KETTLE

Freud tells this joke: A. borrows a copper kettle from B. A. gives it back, but B. sues him, accusing him of having made the big hole that now makes the kettle unusable. A. defends himself along the following lines: "First, I never borrowed a kettle from B.; second, it already had a hole in it when he lent it to me; third, I gave it back in perfect shape."[1]

The Warsaw ghetto uprising is the best-known and studied event in the history of rebellion during the Holocaust; its anniversary is a holiday in Israel and is celebrated in Paris and other international cities. It has been the subject of hundreds of books and thousands of articles. A museum and a research center are dedicated exclusively to the Warsaw ghetto uprising. One Internet search engine reports 12,650 mentions of this event. Yet, in this ocean of information, the ZZW and its fighters are treated like that famous kettle. Usually nothing at all is said about it. Often, we're told that there was a ZZW but that practically nothing is known about it. Sometimes we learn that they had a large quantity of arms but didn't use them much. More rarely, that they did fight, but only on the first day, and after that they fled. A witness or historian can

---

1. Sigmund Freud, *Jokes and Their Relation to the Unconscious* (London: Routledge and Kegan Paul, 1963 [1905]).

write one thing and then contradict himself in the next book or even within the same work.

Here we will cite three major firsthand participants and two leading historians.

Adolf Berman was the representative of all the Zionist movements to the Polish resistance authorities, a member of Zegota Council and the Jewish Coordinating Committee, chairman of the Association of Jews in postwar Poland, and later a politician in Israel. He left extensive personal archives. In a penetrating analysis written in January 1943, revised and published 15 years later, he said of the ZZW: "There was a rumor about the existence of a 'Revisionist' group (a far-right Zionist organization founded by Jabotinsky supporters) but it never manifested itself through any activity whatsoever."[2]

Marek Edelman was deputy commander-in-chief of the ZOB and led its forces in one of the three ghetto districts. He is venerated as a national hero in Poland, where he still lives, as well as abroad, and has been involved in the writing of many books. In an account published in 2000,[3] he makes a number of statements in succession: there's no point talking about the ZZW because they were fascist; at any rate there is nothing to say about them, they didn't do anything, they only had one building, they had neither a political council nor a military command; they were a bunch of porters, smugglers and thieves; they stayed locked up in their house, let off a few rounds and then fled the same day; they were founded long after September 1942 and even after January 1943; the ZOB never met with them but in fact there were meetings between the ZZW and the ZOB; the ZZW not only had plenty of weapons but far more than the ZOB; they were composed of no more than three groups of ten individuals each; all they wanted to do was to run away and the proof is that they dug tunnels for this purpose; nothing is known about them because no one had any contact with

2. Berman, "*O ruchu oporu w getcie warszawkim. Refleksje.*"
3. Edelman cited in Grupinska, *Ciągle po kole*, pp. 273–75.

them, and when there was contact they came to meetings carrying guns; they were criminals and not Polish army soldiers because there were no Jewish soldiers in the Polish army; and the whole thing was simply made up.

Icchak Cukierman was also a deputy to the ZOB commander-in-chief and leading member of the two political committees that headed the organization. He represented the ZOB to the Polish civilian and military authorities. He has been a living symbol of heroism for the Ghetto Fighters' Kibbutz, and has been questioned, filmed and feted; his memoirs were published in Hebrew in 1990 and were translated into Polish in 2000. Cukierman asks a rhetorical question:

> What did the ZOB fighters do? [...] They went from one base to another and they fought. What did the Revisionist fighters do? They also rose up in a very important battle, raised flags, which had a strong impact [...] but after fighting briefly they left the ghetto through their tunnel [...].
>
> There is a German proclamation [...] according to which the Revisionists had some Jewish fighters and partisans who died.
>
> Since then there has been the *suspicion* [my emphasis – MA] that their Polish guide betrayed them. He told them to stop and rest, and while they were doing so he warned the Germans. This information has *made us even more strongly convinced* that the Revisionists remained in contact with members of the Endecja [the most anti-Semitic political trend in Poland]. After the war, allegedly "humanitarian" and "liberal" AK forces began to make themselves known. To this day I don't know how much of all this is true.[4] [...] I asked him [a certain Pawal] to write a report on the fighting waged

4. Nowhere in Cukierman's book is there any argument to support the assertion that the ZZW entertained a relationship with the Endecja; in Edelman's memoirs a different extremist organization is mentioned, without any further proof; Bronek Jaworski writes of "suspicious contacts between Polish reactionary extremist groups, which could only be a bad omen." This passage with little information, only vague and undocumented suspicions, ending in the confirmation of the most serious conviction, is typical of the accusations made against the ZZW. See Jaworski, "*Informacje Bronka Jaworskiego.*"

> by the Revisionists. He drew on two documents that I was already familiar with. One had been [...] written at the request of two Gestapo agents [...]. The description of the work of the ZZW in this report includes activities carried out by the ZOB! [5]

Here we have the Gestapo robbing the ZOB to pay the ZZW...

Shmuel Krakowski was archives director of the Jewish Institute of History in Warsaw and later director of the Yad Vashem archives in Jerusalem. Israel Gutman was a member of the ZOB and took part in the uprising; he subsequently became head of the Institute for Contemporary Jewry at Hebrew University and director of the Holocaust Research Center at Yad Vashem. In a joint book, they write:

> We know of no contacts between the Jewish organized underground and any of the headquarters of the Polish underground during the early phases of the occupation and in the period immediately following the establishment of the ghetto. Whatever contacts did take place [no contacts?] were sporadic, and occurred between individuals and groups sharing social or political ties that had been established before the war. Thus [...] there were veteran Revisionist Zionists who managed to communicate with former Polish army officers who seem to have been active in the Polish underground.[6]
>
> The members of the ZZW managed to secure support from two groups affiliated with the AK-KB and PLAN but which have no independent status and no competence to negotiate on behalf of AK. According to testimonies of Major Iwanski, he, his family and a few of his subordinates and an associate were strongly involved in supplying weapons and cooperation with the ZZW and they took an active part in the uprising of the ghetto. This claim is not confirmed by Jewish or first-hand sources, but it is known that the ZZW was equipped with more heavy arms than the ZOB, and that

5. Zuckerman, *A Surplus of Memory*, pp. 412–13.
6. Gutman and Krakowski, *Unequal Victims*, p. 148.

> the ZZW managed to establish contacts with cells of the Polish underground. On the other hand another Polish army officer involved in the connection with the ZZW testified that he was interested in profit rather than other motives, and in this case it was more a business deal [there is no supporting reference here] than an act of help motivated only by humanitarian or ideological principles. On the other hand, Iwanski's approach and a group of Polish underground activists seems to have been an expression of personal deep involvement and a desire to help the Jews in their struggle.[7]

All these assertions border on the nightmarish and resemble the story of the kettle. "They" had no contact; the contacts they did have were sporadic, except that some were not sporadic; but in this case it is a matter of contacts between groups of people with personal and political links dating back to before the war; the Polish groups that helped them weren't supposed to because that wasn't authorized; this was above all a business deal, which is bad, even if some people were paid in blood, and because they were so good at "managing," the ZZW was better armed than the ZOB even though it didn't exist.

"THE POLISH CONSPIRACY"

In contrast to this phantom, protean image, we have said that the ZZW was militarily the strongest organization that took part in the ghetto uprising, that it was the only group to have waged strategic battles of position, which were protracted and fierce, and that they raised two flags, the Jewish and the Polish banners, deliberately provoking the "Teutonic rage" that was rained down upon them. Our account is basically taken from Polish sources.

But in the literature on the Warsaw ghetto uprising, when it comes to the ZZW, the general silence is often broken only by comments such as, "These claims are by Polish eyewitnesses (or

7. Gutman and Krakowski, ibid., p. 163.

writers) and have not been confirmed by Jewish sources." In the course of a conversation with a very great and celebrated historian, he remarked to me that the time has certainly come to tell the truth about the ZZW, but that we should be wary of the Polish conspiracy. Edelman says these accounts of the ZZW's work were made up and that in fact it was negligible because "all they did was fire off a few rounds and then they fled." And Cukierman admits as much (as we'll see shortly).

By way of an epilogue, we will examine successively the likelihood of a "Polish conspiracy" and the testimony of several people whom, if such a plot were to have existed, could not have been part of it.

Among Polish firsthand accounts we have emphasized those of Iwanski, Bednarczyk, Zarski, Ketling and Mendelson. Iwanski describes the participation of a Polish unit under his command in the second battle of Muranowski Square. Could he have fabricated it? His account is completely confirmed by those of Bednarczyk, Zarski and Mendelson, but since all four of them were members of allied resistance organizations they could have constituted the plot's core conspirators. A strong argument in favor of Iwanski's honesty is recognition of his military activities and the aid he provided the Jews that came not only from General Petrykowski – which might be considered suspect since he was the head of the military organization to which certain members of this "gang of four" belonged – but also from the Communist military authorities of that period who had no propensity to vaunt the exploits of the AK whose former members they were violently persecuting.

Nevertheless, there is a variant on the thesis of a Polish conspiracy that would extend its reach into Communist circles and even consider them the initiators of the said plot. In this vein, Cukierman comments:

> After the war, a group of Poles belonging to the AK came forward to claim that the Revisionists had been in contact with them. The first person to construct a whole theory on this subject immediately

> after the war was Bernard Mark, an eminent journalist but a very bad historian. [...] When writing of the Communists who were ZOB members, he could not deny that of the 22 combat units only four were made up of Communists. How could he accept that? Thus he created a whole line of thought according to which there were two [Communist] currents, one around the ZOB and the second organized by the Revisionists.[8]

Thus the implication in this version is that Mark, following the orders of his superiors, invented the complex history of the ZZW to exaggerate the importance of the Communists in the armed resistance. This explanation would make sense only if Mark emphasized the participation and role of the Communists within the ZZW. But that is not the case at all.

> The difference between the ZOB and the ZZW resided principally in the fact that the ZOB was an anti-Fascist organization whose membership was largely composed of socialist workers, whereas the ZZW limited itself to armed self-defense activities and its members, bourgeois youth, were ex-Polish army officers and non-coms as well as members of the rightist organization Betar. Later, certain groups of leftist porters and smugglers joined the ZZW, led by Janek Pika, "Crooked Nose," Pawel Rudy and Chaim Federbusz.[9]

Neither here nor elsewhere does he say a word about any Communists in the ZZW. Furthermore, the adjectives "bourgeois," "rightist" and "leftist" are hardly terms of endearment coming from the pen of a Stalinist writing in "people's" Poland.

In any case, Mark's participation in such a nationalist and patriotic plot would have been paradoxical, since he was a Jewish Communist and a Stalinist, and was clearly determined not to glorify the AK, an enemy organization persecuted by the regime,

8. Zuckerman, *A Surplus of Memory*, pp. 410–11.
9. Mark, *Powstanie w getcie warszawskim*, p. 9.

to which all the witnesses cited belonged. It would be simpler to suppose that as director of the Jewish Institute of History Mark was flooded with firsthand accounts, which, furthermore, were quite fresh at that time. He gave the ZZW due mention because it would have been impossible for him to do otherwise, but he did so without any particular enthusiasm for it, as can be seen in the quote from him above. To highlight the factors that distinguished him from other "conspirators," suffice it to say that after the war he glorified the role of the PPR (Communist Party) and the GL (People's Guard), a Communist resistance organization that in fact barely existed at the time of the ghetto events, to the detriment of the nationalist resistance. So much for the Communist variation of the Polish conspiracy thesis.

Barring the theory of an explicit conspiracy – which is ruled out by the concurring firsthand descriptions of the ZZW's role by nationalists and Communists alike, even though they were mortal enemies – could patriotic sentiments alone have modulated these accounts? With regard to some details, such as the role of the Polish "blue" police, certainly. But could this be said for the most essential elements?

The Yad Vashem Research Center is also above suspicion of being partial to the Polish nationalist resistance, and Iwanski was recognized as a Righteous Gentile by an Israeli commission headed by a Supreme Court judge on the basis of a report considering both sides of the question submitted by the Jewish Institute of History (see appendix 1):

> The Iwanski family [...] in aiding numerous Jews during the occupation and providing military aid to the resistance movement in the Warsaw ghetto [...]. He was a member of the ZZW and later the AK. [...] The Iwanskis were particularly active during the ghetto uprising in April 1943. The brothers Henryk and Waclaw, as well as Henryk's son, Roman, fought alongside the ZZW members in the battles against the Germans at Muranowski Square. There on April 27 Waclaw was killed; Henryk and his son Roman were also seri-

ously wounded there. Roman died of his wounds soon after. Wictoria and Maria also [...].[10]

Bednarczyk confirms almost all of Iwanski's affirmations.[11] Bednarczyk's daily presence in the ghetto, and his role as coordinator of aid to the Jews on behalf of the Polish underground organizations, make him an especially important source of information on the organization and activities of the ZZW. His function, in turn, has been attested to by the AK authorities, and his merit by the three military medals he was awarded. The thrust of his relation has been confirmed by two Jews. One is Berman, who describes conditions in the ghetto and explains the lack of resistance during the genocide of the summer of 1942. The other is Mendelson, in regard to the ZZW. It is true that the latter, the only surviving ZZW officer, remained in Poland and was in touch with Iwanski and Bednarczyk. Zajdler confirms and fills in Iwanksi's description of the April 27 battle of Muranowski Square, but, then, he too remained in Warsaw until after the war. There are other eyewitness accounts as well: a police officer, a fire department officer and a sanitation department official all speak of the ZZW and Bednarczyk's leading role, as well as his daily participation in the ZZW's clandestine work in the ghetto (on Bednarczyk's credibility, see appendix 2).

The only conceivable motive tying together these "conspirators" would be patriotism – the Polish resistance, and, on that score, Poland itself has been accused of remaining passive during the ghetto genocide and in particular of having given the ZOB very little assistance. It is clear that the leadership of the AK, which constituted the only organized resistance at that point, was dubious about the Jewish will to wage armed resistance, and feared that any fighting might spread to the other side of the wall, which would have been counter to their strategy of twofold resistance against both

10. Michal Grynberg, *Ksiega sprawiedliwych* (Warsaw: Państwowe Wydawnictwo Naukowe, 1993), pp. 194–95.

11. There is a minor divergence between the two concerning the identity of one of the five founders of the ZZW in the fall of 1939, which we have already pointed out.

the Germans and the Soviets when the right time came. For these patriotic purposes, the ZZW presented the twofold advantage of being an organization closely linked to the Polish resistance and very much aided by it. In this sense, to magnify the activity of the ZZW and the help it received would have been both a patriotic act and a source of glory for those who were its members. If there is any distortion in these accounts, it is due to this Polish patriotic fervor that we have pointed out all along.

For the moment, let us leave aside the testimony of the Poles and "assimilated Jews" and review the other sources, those from the "other camp," on two essential points, the arms involved and the two main battles.

Ringelblum, an outstanding and universally respected historian who took up the mission of preserving the memory of a disappearing community for posterity by creating a major historical monument, Oneg Shabbat, confirmed that the ZZW were equipped with automatic weapons and heavy armament; what's more, they boasted a serious level of military organization. Further, Ringelblum was a Marxist who cared little for the ZZW, whose members he labeled "Italian-style fascists." In passages cited previously (see chapter 7), he describes his visits to the ZOB and the ZZW headquarters respectively.

In this account there is a noteworthy contrast between the clandestinity and amateurish quality of the ZOB, on the one hand, and the military and professional qualities of the ZZW on the other, with its dozens of automatic weapons and rifles, dozens of soldiers, simultaneously intense and smoothly-functioning activities, and its atmosphere of a "real army headquarters." Since the accuracy of Ringelblum's scrupulous observations is unassailable, Cukierman, deputy-commander of the ZOB and later its commander-in-chief, writes in his memoirs, from which we have excerpted extensively, that the contradiction between Ringelblum and the "ZOBist" historians can be explained simply by a sort of Potemkin Village.[12] Did

12. "On the occasion of Ringelblum's visit, they [the Revisionists] staged the call-up of their armed units," Zuckerman, *A Surplus of Memory*, p. 227.

the ZZW, when it learned that the historian was about to make a one-day visit, hire some military-looking extras, put together some prop weapons and ammunition, and stage the orders going out, the reports coming in, the arms deal negotiations? This explanation is as audacious as it is ridiculous; no other pro-ZOB historian has dared to cite or comment on this paragraph from Ringelblum's book, even though it has been translated into many languages.

A far different evaluation, in quantitative terms in this case, is provided by the previously cited Krakowski, who attributes practically all the automatic weapons and heavy armament in the ghetto to the ZZW.[13] (See appendix 4.)

Edelman, the ZOB deputy commander, reluctantly acknowledges that the ZZW was better armed than the ZOB. Let us return to Edelman's words, quoted in the preface: "...plenty of weapons. Compared to us, they had a lot more."[14]

With regard to the two battles of Muranowski Square, we have an unexpected "ally" in the person of SS General Stroop. About the battle that began on April 19, he wrote, "The Jewish and Polish flags were hoisted on top of a concrete building in a call to battle against us."[15] (Also see appendix 3.) He confirms the ferocity of this battle, its importance and the fact that it lasted three days. About the second battle, on April 27, Stroop says that he was forced to improvise a "special battle unit" to put an end to the resistance.[16] These are indisputable confirmations, furnished despite Stroop's

---

13. "It cannot be excluded that the ZZW was better armed [...]. It is very likely that all the ZZW sub-units were armed with approximately 20 machine guns and eight automatic rifles, a large number of grenades and Molotov cocktails, and handguns." Krakowski, *The War of the Doomed*, p. 178.
14. Grupinska, *Ciągle po kole*, p. 275.
15. Stroop, *The Stroop Report*, opposite p. 5; "This was a Revisionist operation at Muranowska.[...] There was a white and blue banner. Maybe they raised the Polish flag [white and red]. In any case, there was certainly no red flag." See Zuckerman, *A Surplus of Memory*, p. 370. Cukierman himself "gives back" the two flags to the ZZW, one of them unconditionally, the other with a maybe. "Those who try to ascribe the banners to the ZOB are greatly wronging the ZZW and committing an historical error." Ibid., p. 412.
16. Stroop, *The Stroop Report*, daily report, April 27, 1943.

constant efforts to brag about his own efficiency and the essential weakness of "subhumans."

Thus the case has been heard: Polish conspiracy or not, all concerned – the scrupulous Ringelblum, the ignoble Stroop, the surviving ZOB leaders Edelman and Cukierman, the Communist eyewitnesses Walewski and Jaworski, and others all concur, each in their own way, on certain points:

– That the ZZW was (relatively) well armed.
– That it raised the two flags and defended them against the "Teutonic rage" thus provoked for three days.
– That it waged the two most hard-fought battles of the uprising.

LIES AND THEIR REASONS

Throughout this book, I have used quotations from protagonists in this tragedy and other eyewitnesses. Now it is time to recapitulate the contradictions between them and even within their accounts. Then we will ask ourselves who has lied and determine the degree of their deception. Then, in the only speculative part of this book, we will examine the reasons behind the lies.

That the ZZW was relatively well armed, and that its main theater of operations was Muranowski Square, has been attested to by one and all. The contradiction concerns the use made of these arms, especially at Muranowski Square. Edelman, Cukierman and Gutman write that after a very brief battle, the ZZW left through a tunnel, abandoning the ghetto in general and Muranowski Square in particular once and for all. The survivors, and especially Iwanski, in the letter addressed to Cukierman with which chapter 2 begins, recount that the last and most violent battle of the uprising took place on April 27, eight days after the initial fighting. Who is lying? I am certain that it is not Iwanski. First of all, it is hard to imagine a man fabricating the loss of his son and his brother. Further, his assertions have been confirmed by many of his comrades-in-arms, officially recognized by the medals awarded him by the Polish army under a Communist regime with little sympathy for the nationalist resistance, and also recognized by the considerations given in the background report when he was named one of the Righteous Among the Nations by a Yad Vashem commission (see the set of documents concerning Iwanski in appendix 1). Finally, as we have just seen, the duration and the magnitude of the battle waged by the ZZW for the two flags raised at Muranowski Square, and the importance of the second battle have been basically described by the ghetto's chief executioner, Stroop, in his teletype communiqués, the report addressed to Himmler and his testimony during his two trials.

I won't repeat what has been said about the innumerable contradictions concerning the dates, the names of the leaders or who carried out exactly what, all of which has little relevance for our present purposes. Stroop lied to maximize his own image by minimizing his losses and the efficacy of the Jewish resistance. The Polish Communists lied throughout their reign by exaggerating the part played in the resistance by their own organizations, the ghetto uprising in particular, at a time when they were practically nonexistent. The nationalist resistance lied in exaggerating its military aid to the Jews, which in reality was minor if we take into account its resources in men and arms kept in reserve for the final battle in which they were supposed to simultaneously liberate Poland from the Germans and protect it from the Russians.

But the Jews? There has been a collective lie by omission. The incredible cloak of silence with which the historical literature has covered the ZZW for more than a half-century seems to me to have no rational explanation. Rather than an explanation, I'll try to provide some personal reflections that are necessarily schematic and incomplete.

Since before the war, Jewish political life in Poland was characterized by profound antagonism. The majority of Polish Jews considered themselves Jews living in Poland rather than Polish. There were numerous powerful religious movements, which all had in common, among other things, a militant anti-Zionism platform. The Zionist movement, although split into diverse and mutually antagonistic currents, had a common commitment not only to the basic Zionist project but to the creation of a New Jew. They shared this utopianism with the two ideologies then on the rise in Europe that also wanted to create the new man: communism and the two variants of fascism, the Italian and German models. Another driving idea on the continent at that time was pacifism, a powerful consequence of the slaughter of World War One and a basic constituent element of left-wing thinking. The Bund, a highly organized movement that often won majority support among the Jews in various elections, was proletarian, exclusively Jewish and yet internationalist. Its project was a Jewish proletariat that would safeguard its own culture and language while at the same time displaying greater solidarity not so much with the Jewish bourgeoisie as with other proletariats and the Polish working class represented by the Polish Socialist Party in particular.

In contrast to leftist Zionism and the Bund, the Revisionist-Zionist trend was neither leftist nor pacifist. On the contrary, it borrowed from Poland the cult of the rebirth of the fatherland through war, a faith developed by more than a century of armed uprisings that had finally, against all reasonable expectations, brought about the very recent resurrection of Polish national independence.

Thus the Revisionist-Zionist trend brought together all the necessary elements for its own demonization. It advocated an immediate mass departure for Palestine, without any process of selection or preparation of the New Jew. It was anti-religious, or rather a-religious. It was neither anti-bourgeois nor leftist. It was militaristic, proclaiming that armed struggle alone could liberate Palestine, just as it had liberated Poland. It had close relations with the rightist and somewhat fascistic Polish government, which was in favor of the departure of the Jews. Its association with a bourgeois group of assimilated officers who were more Polish than Jewish, opposed to ideologies but in favor of polished boots and ignorant of Yiddish, did not make it any more attractive to the religious currents or to the Bundists or even less to the pacifist and leftist Zionists.

This context explains why unity of action was rejected even in the midst of a desperate situation, for the reasons that served as both a pretext and the truth: because the ZZW maintained close contact with Polish rightist elements that were or had been anti-Semitic, because its soldiers carried out their military preparations with a certain ostentation as a matter of principle, because when they executed German and Jewish Gestapo agents they deliberately did it at the wrong time, and because the ZZW recruited on the sole basis of previous military training, physical fitness and courage, deliberately seeking an apoliticalism that the left always found extremely suspect if not downright diabolical. Thus we can better understand why on the eve of the insurrection the reasonable Ringelblum could calmly claim that the ZZW was a fascist force.

Leftist Jews, protagonists and eyewitnesses alike all suffer from the same contradiction: how can they claim that these people, so close and yet so foreign and such enemies, were basically bastards, but admit that they behaved well during the final battle? It is far easier to go back and forth between denials and confirmations, even if they are mutually exclusive.

In the period immediately following the war, historians were hampered by ideological affinities as well as a sense of loyalty to the dead and their quarrels. Further, their work was influenced by the political situation at that time. The Polish regime drew much of its legitimacy from claims about the Communist resistance to the Nazis, and since for a long time there was very little such resistance, Orwellian lies were necessary. Wartime documents were grossly falsified and those concerning the non-Communist Polish resistance – and, incidentally, its Jewish component – were made inaccessible. In Israel, the struggle between the ruling leftist parties and the Revisionist party was also ideologically ferocious, although obviously without physical terror.

It was against this background that the first books and articles were written. Since historians are professionals, these materials contain no clumsy lies; rather they are characterized on the whole by silence or deliberately perverse doubt, often with the excuse that "we have no documentation" or "this has not been confirmed by Jewish sources." Once the myth was constructed, it was adopted by innumerable writers who cited the original sources.[17]

Poland is no longer Communist and all the archives there are now open. The ideological struggle between the Marxists and Revisionist Zionists in Israel has died down, at least to the degree that both have enjoyed the ideological legitimacy that comes with political power. Those who took part in the ghetto events are almost all dead.

Out of respect for the Warsaw ghetto uprising, the time has come to complete its history. As imperfect and provisional as this book may be, it is an attempt to break the silence.

17. The linguistic barriers don't help. Almost all of the contemporaneous source material is in Polish, both the AK and ZZW archives, and Polish historians are suspected of wanting to defend their country's honor. Among Jewish historians in Israel and the United States, only the oldest and thus most "personally involved" historians read Polish.

APPENDIX 1

DOCUMENTS CONCERNING IWANSKI

Attestation by the Security Corps General Command:

We the undersigned confirm that citizen Henryk Iwanski, alias "BYSTRY," actively participated in the struggle against the German occupier and carried out his duties as commanding officer of the "W" unit.

He was promoted to the rank of major by order of the Security Corps General Command (number 15 of 9. IV. 1944).

Former commander of the Security Corps General Andrzej "Tarnawa"-Petrykowski. Former chief of staff, Security Corps General Command Former commander of the Security Corps, General Edward "Wilk"-Biernacki.

Veracity of the signatures of [...] confirmed [...] Historical Verification Section of the Security Corps [...]

From Archives of the Jewish Institute of History (ZIH), 5792.

* * *

Chancellery of the State Council:

The Chancellery of the State Council certifies that citizen Iwanski Henryk, alias "BYSTRY," commanded a partisan unit which he led in providing armed support to the Warsaw Ghetto fighters. Among other operations, during the battles in the Ghetto he and his unit evacuated many wounded Jewish fighters.

He supplied arms and medicine to the fighters in the struggle and helped them liquidate Gestapo agents inside the Ghetto.

In recognition of these acts, by decision of the State Council, Citizen Henryk Iwanski-"Bystry" was awarded the Silver Cross of the Order of Virtuti Militari.

From Archives of the Jewish Institute of History (ZIH), 5792.

* * *

Attestation:

I the undersigned, Mendelson Kalmen, son of Abram and Adela, née Lewinson, born in Warsaw November 28, 1902, a Polish citizen of Jewish origin, journalist by trade, state the following:

During the Nazi occupation I was given the name of Madanowski Kazimierz by citizen Iwanski Henryk, alias "BYSTRY," who, starting in October 1939, headed a special unit whose mission was to protect the lives and health of Polish citizens of Jewish origin both inside and outside the Warsaw Ghetto and help them in every way possible.

He grabbed my wife, my daughter and me out of the hands of the Nazi butchers and hid us in his home on the "Aryan" side, at 56a Zlota Street in Warsaw, where he fed us at his own expense, clothed us and gave us medical care, and not only us but a whole group of my Jewish brothers and sisters who were totally penniless. In his apartment every one of us was fed, served, clean and rested, and he and his wife Wiktoria treated us all like cherished family members. For this reason, I extend to him and his wife Wiktoria my warmest sincere and human thanks, and I commend him to my Jewish brothers and sisters.

I make this attestation as a ZZW officer who along with other Jewish fighters from the Ghetto benefited from the apartment of Major Iwanski Henryk-"Bystry," who, because of the wounds he received during the course of providing armed support to the Jews, is presently unable to work, finding himself in financial straits, with a wife ill with tuberculosis who is also unable to work.

Madanowski Kazimierz-Mendelson Kalmen, former ZZW officer

Certified by the State Notarization Service 2/12/1959.
From Archives of the Jewish Institute of History (ZIH), 5792.

* * *

Attestation by the Jewish Institute of History:

The Jewish Institute of History hereby attests that citizen Iwanski Henryk, alias "Bystry," currently a retired major, residing at 15 Spacerowa Street in Kolonia Blota, near Warsaw, formerly a leader of the Polish underground, played an active and self-sacrificing role in helping the Jewish population during the Nazi occupation, specifically:

1. Starting in October 1939, he organized groups and units to provide aid to the ghetto, furnishing food supplies and transporting people to the east.
2. During the period from August 1942 to April 1943, he organized the escape from the ghetto of many groups of Jews, moving them to apartments and other hideouts including hospitals, churches, cemeteries and places out of town, got them papers and provided them with food and protection.
3. In his capacity as the commander of a combat group of the Polish underground/KB, he organized and worked with Jewish fighting groups in the ghetto, organized the shipment of arms and ammunition to the ghetto and the production of grenades, organized and carried out death sentences against traitors, blackmailers and Gestapo spies, and trained Jewish combat units.
4. Personally, along with his wife, he hid in his apartment, saved from death and fed Jews he had gotten out of the ghetto.
5. He organized the transport of Jews to Polish partisan units.
6. In all of his work he actively opposed anti-Semitic propaganda.

Citizen Iwanski's aid to the persecuted Jewish population was unselfish, motivated only by his ideological and moral convictions. His relations with the people he protected and his subordinates were warm and infused with a profound understanding of their tragedy.

The above attestation is based on documents in the ZIH Archives and the testimony of people Henryk Iwanski saved who now live in this country and abroad, especially Israel. All these facts have been confirmed by Major Henryk Iwanski's military superiors during the Occupation.

Director of the ZIH. Professor Bernard Mark.

From Archives of the Jewish Institute of History (ZIH), 5792.

* * *

Attestation:

Major Iwanski Henryk alias "Bystry"
Iwanska Wiktoria alias "Janka"
Iwanski Waclaw
Iwanska Maria

The Iwanski family performed meritorious service in helping many Jews during the occupation as well as providing military aid to the resistance in the Warsaw ghetto.

In his youth Henryk Iwanski fought during the Silesia uprising. In September 1939, during the siege of Warsaw, he played an active role in the fighting to defend the city. Certain documents indicate that Iwanski was wanted by the Germans after they entered the capital. It was then that Iwanski took the name "Bystry." During the occupation, H. Iwanski was a member first of the ZWZ and then the AK. Here is an excerpt from his memoirs: "One day in November 1939, four […] Jewish Polish Army officers came to my house […]: Lieutenant Dawid Moryc Apfelbaum, Second Lieutenant Henryk Lipszyc, the lawyer Bialoskora and Kalmen Mendelson. 'Captain Iwanski,' the ex-lieutenant said to me, 'we don't want to go to the Oflag as the Germans have ordered us. Help us organize the Jewish youth [...]. We cannot remain passive in the face of a wave of humiliations and persecution.'"

This was the start of Iwanksi's active help to the ghetto resistance and aid for the people who managed to get out from behind the wall. The Iwanskis were especially active during the ghetto uprising in April 1943. Henryk, his brother Waclaw and his son Roman took part in the fighting against the Germans at Muranowski Square alongside the members of the Zydowski Zwiazek Wojskowy (ZZW). Waclaw was killed there on April 27 and Henryk and his son Roman were seriously wounded. Roman died of his wounds shortly after.

Wiktoria and Maria Iwanska also selflessly threw themselves into aiding the struggle in the ghetto by supplying arms, ammunition and surgical supplies. In their apartments they took care of rescued fighters who had been gotten out of the ghetto after the defeat of the uprising. One of them, Kalmen Mendelson (Kazimierz Madanowski), remembers: "My unit and that of 'Bystry' had suffered serious losses, dead and wounded. More than 20 of my Jewish brothers were gotten out of the ghetto and taken to the 'Bystry' apartment, where they were faithfully attended to by his wife. Many of us owe them our lives [...]. As a Jew, citizen and soldier, I never met anyone, before or after, who did as much for my fellow Jews [...], people from the ghetto and from outside, as he and his wife would have done for even one person [...] and for a group of Jews, even though they lost so many of their family members."

From the AZIH [ZIH archives], "Testimonials" file, file number 5792, 1615.

Cited in M. Grynberg, op. cit., pp. 194–95.

* * *

I the undersigned, Celmajster Jozef, son of Jan and Dwoira Wolsdorf, born on December 17 1901 in Warsaw, doctor, Polish citizen of Jewish nationality, declare the following:

The name Niemirski Jozef I have used for many years was

given to me by Iwanski Henryk, alias "BYSTRY," who from 1940–44 commanded special units for the aid of the Jews during the Nazi occupation of Poland, protecting their lives and health and providing material and military aid and moral support. He snatched my wife, my children and me from the hands of the Nazi torturers and hid us in his home, his apartment on the Aryan side of Warsaw at 56a Zlota Street. There he fed us and a large group of Jews, clothed us and treated us as if we were his own children with warmth and affection. He brought several people [...] including myself into the struggle to fight the Nazis and help the unfortunate people of the ghetto by getting them out of there and taking them either to his own apartment or other people's homes where they found rest, medical care and every other kind of aid. I thank him and his wife Wiktoria from the bottom of my heart and I commend them to the Jews and the Jewish people for whom they did everything they could [...], Wicktoria even caught tuberculosis from a Jewish woman who died in her arms (the Jewish woman was named Rojza Nauman, she was 35 and lived at 42 Muranowska Street in February, 1943), and he was wounded while evacuating wounded Jewish fighters from the ghetto through the sewers to the Aryan side. Among those who died in this operation was their son. Even though I don't usually talk much about the very noble work he and his wife did, here I am writing the plain truth. I swear to this by signing this declaration. I add that he is ill now and unable to work because of the serious wounds he received in the ghetto and that his wife is in the same situation because of her tuberculosis and that their financial situation is very difficult.

From Jozef Celmajster, Oswiadczenie (Declaration) 02/12/1959, Jabotinsky, W (8) R 6.

APPENDIX 2

DOCUMENTS CONCERNING TADEUSZ BEDNARCZYK[1]

Tadeusz Bednarczyk, born in 1913, was employed by the Treasury Department for the mainly Jewish quarter of Warsaw that was to become the ghetto in 1940. He was the only Pole to have an unlimited pass from the day the ghetto was created until April 1943. His last visit to the ghetto took place on the night of April 30–May 1, 1943, during a ZZW munitions delivery.

In January 1940, he was named head of the department for national minorities and aid to the Jews of the OW (a military organization founded in the fall of 1939 by General Sikorski). In 1942, when the armed Polish resistance was unified under the aegis of the AK (Armia Krajowa, Home Army), Bednarczyk was made responsible for Jewish affairs in Warsaw, not only for the OW but the AK as a whole.

Because of his official duties and his resistance work, he is the most complete Polish source of information about the ghetto. His book, *Zycie codzienne warszawskiego getta...* (*Daily Life in the Warsaw Ghetto*), published in Warsaw in 1995 and never translated from the Polish original, reiterates and fills in his previous eyewitness accounts and writing, but this time in the context of a situation in which there was freedom of expression, which was far from

1. The declarations quoted here are from the appendix to Bednarczyk's book *Zycie codzienne warszawskiego getta.*

being true before the fall of the Communist regime. In addition to being a highly factual and well-documented history of the ghetto, which we have mined deeply for this present work, Bednarczyk's book contains a sharp polemic against Jewish historians on the subject of the humanitarian and military aid provided by Poles. Bednarczyk goes much too far in the course of this polemic and ends up in open anti-Semitism.

* * *

Attestation:

I the undersigned, Ludwik Muzyczka, using the name "Benedykt" in Poland during the Nazi occupation, presently residing in Cracow, at 14 Sowinski Street, apt. no. 1, formerly department chief of the former general staff of the ZWZ-AK from April 1940 to October 4, 1944, formerly head of the Korpus Bezpieczenstwa [KB, Security Core] in the name of the head of the ZWK-AK [...] hereby declare the following:

I personally met Tadeusz Bednarczyk, alias "Bednarz," in the beginning of 1942. Andrzej Petrykowski, alias "Tarnawa," who was at that time the commander in chief of the ZW-KB, introduced him to me as having been his assistant in charge of aid to the Jews since 1940, and later, as the representative of the KB general command for clandestine contacts with engineer Adam Czerniakow (at that time chairman of the Warsaw Jewish Council) and authorized to set up various forms of aid to the Jews, and to plan and help to form underground Jewish military cells to fight the Nazi occupiers.

Tadeusz Bednarczyk's mission was to plan, organize and oversee aid to the Jews. From the beginning, he received unstinting support, in terms of organization, material and personnel from the KB general command, and later, through me, starting in the second half of 1941, from the commander in chief of the Home Army [AK]. This aid consisted of evacuating members of the Jewish intelligentsia from the ghetto, helping evacuated people establish a "legal" cover, furnishing food and medications to the ghetto poor, finding work and the means to survive for those Jews who had none, ferreting out and suppressing Jewish Gestapo agents, etc.

At the urging of Tadeusz Bednarczyk and thanks to his direct help and work with other members of the underground, Jewish clandestine military cells were organized in the ghetto. Later they gave rise to the Zydowski Zwiazek Wojskowy (ZZW). Tadeusz Bednarczyk himself took a hand in training the officers of that organization's combat units, and set up a system for bringing in arms and material.

In January 1943, Tadeusz Bednarczyk personally took part in the fighting in the ghetto and in May of that year he took responsibility for providing military cover for the operations to aid the ghetto fighters organized by the KB-AK unit of Major "Bystry"-Iwanski. After the ghetto uprising was crushed, he continued to help the Jews who were hiding out.

Tadeusz Bednarczyk participated in the Warsaw Uprising, in the beginning as deputy commander and then as the commander of the KB-AK company whose mission was to protect the uprising's leadership. During the second part of the uprising he was my special officer for the manufacture of arms. [...]

In light of his underground work, and the courage he demonstrated in the face of the enemy, Tadeusz Bednarczyk was twice awarded the War Cross and once the National Order of Merit in gold with Swords. At the end of the Warsaw Uprising, he was promoted to the rank of captain. [...]

Written in Cracow, May 4, 1967

* * *

Attestation:

I the undersigned, Kazimierz Madanowski (formerly Kalmen Mendelson), residing at 12 Dabrowski Square, apt. 125, declare and state the following:

I met colleague Tadeusz Bednarczyk, a retired commander, while he was using the names "Bednarz" and "Tadeusz" in Warsaw in the spring of 1940 through my commanding officer Moryc Apfelbaum at the time when various Jewish resistance groups were reunified to found the Zydowski Zwiazek Wojskowy [ZZW, Jewish Military Union]. "Bednarz," then a lieutenant, was the co-initiator and co-founder of a number of Jewish resistance military circles which a few months later were to form the ZZW's Second Company. My special independent platoon (whose task was to get members of the intelligentsia and scientists out of the ghetto) stayed in constant contact with that company. At that time, colleague Bednarczyk was head of the Jewish affairs committee of the OW-KB command and its representative for matters pertaining to the Warsaw ghetto and collaboration with chairman Adam Czerniakow. He also continued to serve as deputy to Andrzej "Tarnawa"-Petrykowski, in charge of aid to the Jews in Poland.

Because of his tasks, and thanks to his unlimited pass to enter the ghetto as an employee of the Treasury Department, he took part in and led the operations to aid the ghetto (including economic and medical aid) and was responsible for the organization, training and arming of the ZZW throughout the period of the ghetto's existence, until May 1943. To this end, he set up a network of safe houses and organized transportation to move weapons and people. He also arranged hideouts for those evacuated from the ghetto (such as those of the first and fourth companies of firemen on Nalewki and Chlodna streets, or provided accommodation for them in the homes of his own subordinates: Stefan Woszczyk at 2A Nalewki Street, in the courthouse buildings on Leszno Street, in the ZOM company of Teodor Niewiadomski, in the police cells run by Tadeusz Zmudzinski and others). Colleague Bednarczyk contributed a great deal to the allocation of arms to the ZZW by the OW-KB command, helped move them into the ghetto, and got many people out of the ghetto and provided them with hideouts. Quite often, he himself transported the weapons and took people out. He was in the ghetto during the four days of battle in January 1943, directing the movement of the ZZW Second Company's units. In April and May 1943, he organized the supply of arms and ammunition, and took care of providing protective cover for the military aid operations carried out by OW-KB soldiers within the ghetto.

On the occasion of the 25th anniversary of the launching of the Warsaw ghetto uprising, I would like to hereby emphasize and recall his neglected merits in regard to the persecuted Jewish people, and, in my capacity as former deputy commander of the ZZW and comrade-in-arms in the common struggle against the Nazi occupier, send him my thanks.

"Captain Kalmen Mendelson-Madanowski, alias 'Kalmyk'"
Warsaw, April 1968

* * *

Attestation:

I the undersigned, Karol Szwarc, born in 1901, residing in Warsaw on 77 Zlota Street, apt. 29, in full awareness of my responsibility before the law in case of perjury, hereby declare the following:

I have known citizen Tadeusz Bednarczyk since before the war. During the Nazi occupation, both of us belonged to the same underground organization founded by General Sikorski, the OW-KB. As part of organizing the Jewish resistance movement in the ghetto, T. Bednarczyk facilitated a meeting on January 20, 1940, between members of a number of clandestine organizations, which took place in my chambers as a lower court judge in the courthouse on Leszno Street. That day, in the presence of engineer Adam Czerniakow, chairman of the Judenrat, decisions were made concerning the tasks of the ZZW and Polish aid to that organization as well as to the ghetto. On that occasion, the OW-KB named T. Bednarczyk, an expert in Polish-Jewish relations, as its representative for ghetto affairs, in charge of aid to the ghetto and relations with A. Czerniakow. At that time T. Bednarczyk worked as an employee of the Treasury Department in the ghetto, first on 12 Leszno Street then in the courthouse buildings. We were in frequent contact; we worked together to aid the ghetto, and he was the chief organizer of this work. His pass to come and go in the ghetto as a tax official facilitated his work. The underground authorities assigned both of us the responsibility of keeping an eye on the general morale of the people around us, as well as their attitude toward the Germans and the Jews. T. Bednarczyk's work at the Treasury Department was just a cover – and a very good one at that – for his clandestine work. The salary he received then was the same as before the war, and it was not a sufficient source of income. Actually, at that time, as now, he owned a small workshop. Thanks to his pass, T. Bednarczyk came to the ghetto every day to oversee aid operations. Everyone knows how much he threw himself into this work. As someone fascinated by history, and an economist by profession, he presented and published his analyses and impressions on the subject of the ghetto in dozens of articles and two books, put out by Iskry and KAW publishers.

During the Occupation, T. Bednarczyk carried out his mission of humanitarian aid to the Jews flawlessly, often risking his own life to do so. Both as a tax official and an underground activist, his behavior attested to a friendly attitude toward the Jews. Many Jews, common acquaintances, such as for example professor Plockier, the industrialist Elper and the lawyer Kisiel, among others, have expressed their thanks to him, the first two publicly during major meetings. I am proud to have worked with citizen T. Bednarczyk in aiding the Jews.

Karol Szwarc, retired lawyer
Warsaw, 19/4/1983

APPENDIX 3

THE STROOP REPORT ON THE LIQUIDATION OF THE WARSAW GHETTO IN 1943

The document entitled the "Stroop report" is composed of three distinct parts: the first is a narrative introduction, the second consists of daily reports sent to Krüger, and the third is a set of photographs. It is written in Gothic German and bound in black leather. Three copies of it were made.

The text we have used for our work is an official translation in Polish from the German original (see bibliography). For obvious reasons, we have translated only the second part (which goes from page 143–199 in the Polish text, i.e., the daily reports). We have translated the heading only once, for the first telegram. For the other telegrams, the omission of the heading has been indicated with bracketed ellipses.

* * *

Copy

Teletype Message
From: SS and Police Leader in the Warsaw District
Warsaw, 20 April 1943
[…]
Re: Ghetto operation
To: Higher SS and Police Leader East
Cracow

Progress report of the Ghetto operation on 19 April 1943:

Sealing of the Ghetto at 0300 hours. At 0600 hours, the Waffen-SS was sent into action to sweep the remnant Ghetto. Waffen-SS strength was at 16 officers and 850 men. Immediately after the units assembled, a heavy and organized surprise attack by the Jews and bandits began. The tank assigned to this operation and both heavy armored cars were pelted with Molotov cocktails (incendiary bottles). The tank was set on fire twice. During the surprise attack, our units were directed not to engage the enemy. Our losses in the first attack: 12 men (6 SS privates and 6 Trawniki men). At 0800 hours, our units went into action for the second time, under the command of the undersigned. Despite a second, less forceful attack upon us, we succeeded in our plan to sweep the blocks of buildings during this engagement. The enemy was forced to retreat from the roofs and other equipped strongholds that were located above ground level to basements or bunkers and sewers. About 200 Jews were apprehended during the sweep. Assault troops were subsequently sent against known bunkers with orders to bring out the occupants and destroy the bunkers. About 380 Jews were apprehended. The presence of Jews was detected in the sewer network. The sewers were flooded to render presence impossible. Around 1730 hours, very strong resistance, including machine-gun fire, was encountered from one group of houses. A special battle unit subdued the enemy and forced its way into the houses without apprehending the enemy. The Jews and criminals offered resistance from one stronghold after another and escaped at the last moment across attics or through subterranean passages. Around 2030 hours, the barricade surrounding the Ghetto was reinforced. All units withdrew from the Ghetto and were dismissed to their quarters. Barricades were reinforced by 250 men of the Waffen-SS.

The operation continued on 20 April 1943.

Units at my disposal:

SS Panzer Grenadier Reserve Battalion 6 officers / 400 men

SS Cavalry Reserve Division	10 officers / 450 men
Order Police (Orpo)	6 officers / 165 men
Security Police (SD)	2 officers / 48 men
Trawnikimen	1 officer / 150 men
Wehrmacht	
1 10-cm howitzer	1 officer / 7 men
1 flamethrower	1 man
Engineers	2 officers / 16 men
Medical unit	1 officer / 1 man
3 2.28-cm anti-aircraft guns	2 officers / 24 men
1 French tank of the Waffen-SS	
2 heavy armored cars of the Waffen-SS	
Total:	31 officers / 1,262 men

I transferred command of today's operation to Police Major Sternhagel, subject to my further instructions as necessary.

At 0700 hours, 9 assault units drawn from mixed formations were sent into action, each with a strength of 1 officer and 36 men, to conduct an intensive sweep and search of the remnant Ghetto. The search, whose first goal shall be reached by 1100 hours, is still in progress. Meanwhile, it has been established that there are several pockets of resistance in the uninhabited part of the Ghetto, the part which is still restricted, containing several armament plants and the like. Due to the resistance, a tank that had been parked nearby could not be mobilized. Two assault units had to bear down on these pockets of resistance to clear a path for the tank crew. This operation records 2 wounded (Waffen-SS) men.

The enemy is much more cautious than he was yesterday, since he is obviously now aware that heavy weapons have been allocated.

I propose to thoroughly sweep the remnant Ghetto and then go on to purge the uninhabited but still restricted Ghetto. Meanwhile, it has been established that this part of the Ghetto, and even the armament plants themselves, contain 10 to 12 bunkers. The operation is being made more difficult by these Ghetto enterprises, whose machines and tools must be protected against bombardment and fire.

Further report will follow tonight.

SS and Police Leader in the Warsaw District

(signed) Stroop

SS Major General and Major General of the Police

* * *

[...]

Warsaw, 20 April 1943

[...]

Re: Ghetto operation

To: Higher SS and Police Leader East, SS General and General of the Police Krueger-or deputy

Cracow

Further to the teletype message of 20 April 1943, Ref. No. I ab/St/Gr. 1607, re: Ghetto operation, I report the following:

The pockets of resistance identified in the uninhabited but still restricted Ghetto were crushed by a battle unit of Wehrmacht Engineers and flamethrowers. In this engagement, the Wehrmacht sustained one casualty, shot through the lungs. Nine assault parties advanced as far as the northern border of the Ghetto. Nine bunkers were located, their resistant occupants crushed, the bunkers blown up. Enemy losses in this engagement are indeterminable. Activity by the 9 assault parties yielded 505 Jews; those able to work among them were secured for transfer to Poniatowo. At about 1500 hours, I succeeded in having the block of buildings that housed the Army Quartermaster's office cleared; it supposedly quartered 4,000 Jews. The German administrator was asked to request the Jewish workers leave the block voluntarily. Only 28 Jews honored this request. I thereupon decided to evacuate the block by force or to blow it up. The anti-aircraft unit assigned to this operation (consisting of three 2-cm guns) sustained 2 deaths.

The 10-cm howitzer dislodged the gangs from their strong fortifications and, to the best of our knowledge, inflicted losses on them. The operation had to be halted because of darkness. On 21 April 1943, a new attack will be launched against this pocket of resistance, which will be sealed off overnight to the greatest extent possible.

During today's operation we captured, apart from the Jews previously reported, considerable stores of incendiary bottles, hand grenades, ammunition, military tunics, and other equipment.

Losses: 2 dead (Wehrmacht).

7 wounded (6 Waffen-SS men, 1 Trawniki man).

There was one instance of bandits having planted land mines.

I prevailed on the firms W.C. Toebbens, Schultz & Co., and Hoffmann to be ready for evacuation with their entire personnel on 21 April 1943 at 0600 hours so that we can at last see our way toward purging the Ghetto. The trustee for Toebbens pledged to lead the 4,000 to 5,000 Jews on a voluntary basis to the designated assembly point for the move. If a voluntary departure proves impossible, as in the Army Quartermaster's case, I will also purge this part of the Ghetto by force.

I acknowledge receipt of the orders with full authority, communicated to me today by telephone by the General.

Next report on 21 April 1943 at noon.

SS and Police Leader [...]

* * *

[...]

Warsaw, 21 April 1943

[...]

Progress report of the Ghetto operation on 21 April 1943. Further to the report made by telephone today at 1400 hours, I report as follows:

Forces at my disposal were the same as on 20 April 1943.

Start of operation: 0700 hours. The blockade of the entire

Ghetto, which commenced at the start of the operation on 19 April 1943, continues without change.

Since the partial operation in the eastern part of the Ghetto in the Army Quartermaster's building complex had to be halted yesterday due to darkness, a battle unit reinforced by Engineers and heavy armor returned to action at the designated time. Sweeping the huge building complex revealed a large number of bunkers and subterranean passages. Approximately 60 Jews were apprehended. Despite all efforts, no more of the 700 to 800 Jews located in this block could be apprehended. They kept withdrawing through subterranean passages, moving from one hiding place to the next, firing from time to time. I decided to blow up the passages that were known to us and then to burn down the entire block. Only when the fire grew to considerable proportions did screaming Jews come into view. They were immediately removed. We had no losses in this operation. Precautions were taken to ensure that the resultant conflagration remains localized.

The main body of forces was committed to the cleansing of the uninhabited but still restricted Ghetto, proceeding south to north. Before this operation started, 5,200 Jews were apprehended who had been employed by the former Ruko enterprises [Commission for Armament]. They were transported under armed guard to the railroad freight yard that was designated for transshipment. Three search commandos were formed and assigned special assault troops, with orders to attack or blow up identified bunkers. After one-half of the designated area had been swept, the operation had to be halted due to darkness.

Continued on 22 April 1943 at 0700 hours.

Besides the Jews who were to be transferred, 150 Jews or bandits were disposed of in battle. About 80 bandits were destroyed by being blown up inside their bunkers. The enemy fought today with the same weapons used yesterday, especially with homemade explosives. Samples were retained by the SS and Police Leader. For the first time we identified members of the Jewish women's fighting organization (He-halutz movement). Captured were rifles, pistols, hand grenades, explosives, horses, and parts of SS uniforms.

Our losses: 2 Order Police, 2 SS Privates, 1 Trawniki man lightly wounded.

SS and Police Leader [...]

* * *

[...]

Warsaw, 22 April 1943

[...]

Re: Ghetto operation; supplement to first teletype of 21 April 1943

[...]

During the night, the fires we had started earlier forced the Jews to appear in front of the housing blocks to escape from the flames in any way they could. Until then, they had remained hidden in attics, cellars and other hideouts despite our search operations. Masses of burning Jews – entire families – jumped from windows or tried to lower themselves using tied-together bed sheets, etc. Measures had been taken to liquidate them as well as the other Jews immediately. Throughout the night, there was shooting once again from the buildings which had ostensibly been cleared. No losses occurred along the barricades.

5,300 Jews were apprehending for transfer and transported onward.

SS and Police Leader [...]

* * *

[...]

Warsaw, 22 April 1943

[...]

Progress report of the Ghetto operation on 22 April 1943 up to 1200 hours.

One battle unit was again dispatched to invade the largely burned-out or still burning housing blocks in order to apprehend remaining Jews. Because the men of the Waffen-SS were again fired upon from one block of buildings, this block, too, was set on fire. The result was that a considerable number of bandits were frightened out of their hiding places and shot while trying to escape. We apprehended an additional 180 Jews in the courtyards of buildings. The main body of our forces proceeded with the cleansing of the unsearched Ghetto buildings, starting from the line where the operation had ended yesterday. This operation is still in progress. Local resistance, as on previous days, was broken and the bunkers that were discovered blown up. Unfortunately, it is impossible to prevent some Jews and bandits from taking refuge in the sewers below the Ghetto, where they are difficult to apprehend, since they disrupted the flooding operation. The city administration is not in a position to remedy this inconvenience. Neither the use of smoke candles nor mixing creosote into the water had the desired results. Liaison with the Wehrmacht has been excellent.

SS and Police Leader [...]

* * *

[...]

Warsaw, 22 April 1943

[...]

Progress report of the Ghetto operation on 22 April 1943. Report on operation until 1200 hours already submitted today by earlier teletype message.

I continue with the following report:

The already-mentioned search by assault units of the remaining blocks of buildings met partial resistance. It had the following results: 1,100 Jews apprehended for transfer, 203 Jews and bandits shot, 15 bunkers blown up. 80 incendiary bottles and other booty were captured.

Units at my disposal: same as reported by teletype message on 20 April 1943, Journal No. 516/43 secret.

Our losses: SS Second Lieutenant Dehmke of the SS-Cavalry

Reserve Division dead; enemy hit a hand grenade he was carrying. One Sergeant of the Police shot through the lung.

When the Engineers blew up the bunkers, considerable numbers of Jews and bandits were buried under the ruins. On a number of occasions, fires had to be set to smoke out the gangs.

It must be further reported that since yesterday, some of our formations have been repeatedly shot at from outside the Ghetto – i.e., from the Aryan part. Assault units immediately entered the area in question and in one case succeeded in apprehending 35 Polish bandits, Communists, who were liquidated at once. At executions, which became necessary today, bandits repeatedly collapsed shouting, "Long live Poland!" and "Long live Moscow!"

The operation will be continued on 23 April 1943 at 0700 hours.

SS and Police Leader [...]

* * *

[...]

Warsaw, 23 April 1943

[...]

Progress report of the Ghetto operation on 23 April 1943. Start of operation: 0700 hours.

The entire former Ghetto was divided into 24 districts for today's sweep. One reinforced assault search party was dispatched to each district with special orders. The assault search parties were given until 1600 hours to carry out these orders.

Results of this operation: 600 Jews and bandits routed out and apprehended, and about 200 Jews and bandits shot. 48 bunkers, some of them most artful, were demolished. Besides money and valuables, several gas masks were captured.

Notice had been given to all units that the operation would be terminated today. By this morning, this information was already known to the Jews. For this reason, assault search parties were again dispatched after a pause of 1 to 1½ hours. The result, as usual, was that we established the presence of Jews and bandits in various blocks. The blockade detail was even shot at from one building complex. A special battle unit was dispatched, and all the buildings were set on fire to smoke out the bandits. The Jews and bandits stood fast until the last moment and then concentrated their gunfire on our units. Even carbines were fired. A number of bandits firing from balconies were hit and came crashing down.

Today also, the so-called headquarters of the PPR14 was discovered unoccupied and destroyed. On this fifth day of operations, the leading terrorists and activists have been taken, those who had managed to evade every takeover or transfer until now.

An ethnic German reported that once again Jews had escaped through the sewers to the Aryan part of the city. Informers reported that several Jews were hiding in a house. A special motorized assault search party invading the building was able to capture 3 Jews, including 2 Jewesses. During this operation, our truck was pelted with an incendiary bottle and an explosive; 2 members of the Order Police were wounded and put out of action.

The operation is being made more difficult by the cunning ways in which the Jews and bandits behave. For example, we discovered that the wagons used to collect the scattered corpses were also carting live Jews to the Jewish cemetery, thus enabling them to escape outside the Ghetto. The continuous search of these wagons will close off this escape route.

At the conclusion of today's operations, around 2200 hours, it was discovered that once again 30 bandits had moved over to a so-called armament enterprise to find refuge. Because the Wehrmacht stores goods of great value in this plant, the request was made to clear it by noon on 24 April, so that this labyrinth of houses can be attacked tomorrow.

Today 3,500 Jews were apprehended for transfer from the enterprises. Until today, a total of 19,450 Jews were apprehended for transfer or already transported onward; 2,500 of these Jews are still to be loaded. The next train departs on 24 April 1943.

Our strength: the same as on 22 April 1943, less 150 Trawniki men. These have been reassigned to the Commander of the Order Police as reinforcements for another mission.

Our losses: 2 Polish Police (SB) wounded, 1 Trawniki man wounded.

Operations to be continued on 24 April 1943 at 1000 hours. This time was chosen to make the Jews who are remaining in the Ghetto believe that the operation had definitely ended today.

SS and Police Leader [...]

* * *

[...]

Warsaw, 24 April 1943

[...]

Progress report of the Ghetto operation on 24 April 1943. Start of operation: 1000 hours.

In contrast to previous days, the 24 assault search parties, which were again dispatched today, did not start their sweep of the Ghetto from one flank only but proceeded simultaneously from all sides. Since the operation did not start until 1000 hours, the remaining Jews apparently believed that the matter had ended yesterday. Today's search operation was therefore especially successful. But our success is also due to the fact that the non-commissioned officers and men have become accustomed to the underhand fighting and tricks of the Jews and bandits, and have acquired great skill in tracking down the innumerable bunkers. Today, toward evening, after the return of the assault parties, a particular block of houses in the northeastern part of the former Ghetto was taken on. This labyrinth of buildings housed a so-called armament firm where military goods supposedly worth millions were manufactured and stored. On 23 April 1943, about 2100 hours, I notified the Wehrmacht of my intention and requested that they remove their goods by 1200 hours. Since the Wehrmacht did not start to move until 1000 hours, I had to extend the time limit to 1800 hours. At 1815 hours, the buildings were sealed off. An assault search party forced its entry and discovered that a large number of Jews were present. Since some of the Jews resisted, I ordered that the buildings be burnt down. Only after the street and courtyards were ablaze did the Jews come out of the housing blocks. Many were on fire, and they tried to save themselves by jumping from windows or balconies into the street below, where they had previously flung beds, blankets and other articles. Again and again, one could observe that the Jews and bandits, notwithstanding the gigantic conflagration, preferred to go back into the fire rather than fall into our hands. The Jews continued to shoot almost until the end of the operation. Toward the end of the day, a unit of engineers had to make their way under machine-gun protection into a specially reinforced concrete building.

End of today's operation: 25 April 1943 at 0145 hours.

Today, 1,660 Jews were collected for transfer; 1,814 were pulled out of bunkers, circa 330 shot. Countless Jews burned to death or perished in blown-up bunkers. 26 bunkers were blown up and an uncounted quantity of paper money, especially dollars, gathered.

Our forces: same as on the preceding day, minus 50 Waffen-SS men.

Our losses: 2 SS Privates and 1 Trawniki man wounded.

Altogether, a total of 25,500 Jews who lived in the former Jewish quarter have been apprehended in the current operation. Since there are only vague estimates as to the strength of the Jews, I assume that only very small numbers of Jews and bandits still remain within the Ghetto.

Operation to be continued on 25 April 1943 at 1300 hours.

I confirm receipt of teletype messages Nos. 1222 and 1223 of 24 April 1943. As far as can be foreseen, the current grand operation will last until the second day of Easter [26 April 1943].

Posters were affixed on the outside walls of the Ghetto today announcing that anyone entering the former Ghetto without valid papers will be shot.

SS and Police Leader [...]

* * *

[...]

Warsaw, 25 April 1943

[...]

Progress report of the Ghetto operation on 25 April 1943. Start of operation: 1300 hours.

Today, 7 assault sweep detachments were formed. Strength: 1 officer and 70 men; each was assigned to a specific block of houses.

Order: "Renewed sweep of all buildings; discovery of bunkers and their demolition; apprehension of any Jews. Wherever they offer resistance or bunkers are beyond reach, the buildings are to be burned down."

In addition to the activity of these 7 assault sweep detachments, a special operation was mounted against a covey of bandits located outside the former Ghetto walls, which was housing Poles only.

Today's operation ended for almost all assault units with gigantic fires, which induced the Jews to leave their hiding places and refuges. A total of 1,690 Jews were apprehended alive. According to Jewish accounts, these definitely included parachutists who had been dropped and bandits who had been supplied with weapons from an unknown source. A total of 274 Jews was shot. As on previous days, uncounted Jews were buried under the rubble of demolished bunkers and burned to death, as we discover all the time. In my opinion, today's booty of Jews encompassed a very large part of the bandits and the lowest elements of the Ghetto. Because darkness set in, we did not proceed with immediate liquidation. I will try to obtain a train for T II [Treblinka] tomorrow. Otherwise, the liquidation will be carried out tomorrow. There was armed resistance again today. In one bunker, 3 pistols and explosives were captured. Further, considerable amounts of paper money, foreign currency, gold coins, and jewelry were secured today. The Jews still have considerable wealth at their disposal. During last night, a glare of fires hovered over the former Ghetto; this evening one can see a gigantic sea of flames. Since large numbers of Jews continue to be discovered during each systematic and regular sweep, the operation will be continued on 26 April 1943, starting at 1000 hours.

As of today, a total of 27,464 Jews of the former Warsaw Jewish Ghetto have been apprehended.

Our forces: same as on the previous day.

Our losses: 3 members of the Waffen-SS and 1 member of the Security Police wounded.

Total losses to this date:

Waffen-SS	27 wounded
Order Police	9 wounded
Security Police	4 wounded
Wehrmacht	1 wounded
Trawniki men	9 wounded
	50 wounded

and 5 dead, consisting of:

Waffen-SS	2 dead
Wehrmacht	2 dead
Trawniki men	1 dead
	5 dead

SS and Police Leader [...]

* * *

[...]

Warsaw, 26 April 1943

[...]

Grand operation in the Ghetto; supplemental report

1) The operation on 25 April 1943 was ended at 2200 hours.

2) General consequences of its implementation:

The Poles living in Warsaw are deeply impressed by the toughness of our intervention in the former Jewish quarter. It is evident from the reported course of events that a general pacification, notwithstanding small incidents, has occurred since the beginning of the current operation, especially within the city of Warsaw. We draw the conclusion that the bandits and saboteurs had been living in the former Jewish quarter and have been destroyed.

In this connection, it will be of interest that an illegal ammunition cache exploded in a burning building in the very district in which we are doing work.

SS and Police Leader [...]

* * *

[...]

Warsaw, 26 April 1943

[...]

Start of operation: 1000 hours.

The entire former Jewish quarter was swept again today by the same assault search details assigned to the same districts. My aim was to have the leaders return to familiar streets and blocks of houses and courtyards so they could penetrate further into the maze of bunkers and subterranean passages. The assault search details, almost without exception, reported resistance, which was overcome completely when gunfire was returned or the bunkers were blown up. It is more and more evident that the turn has come for the toughest and most resilient Jews and bandits. Several bunkers have been forced open whose inhabitants had not gone above ground level during the entire operation. In a number of cases, the occupants of the bunkers were barely in a condition to crawl to the surface after the bunkers had been blown up. The captured Jews reported that many bunker inhabitants had gone mad from the heat, smoke and explosions.

Various Jews who had maintained a close liaison and collaborated with the Polish terrorists were arrested. 29 Jews were arrested outside the former Jewish quarter.

During today's operation, several blocks of houses were burned down. It is the only method and method of last resort to force this rabble and subhumanity to the surface.

We again captured weapons, including incendiary bottles and explosives, and large amounts of cash and foreign currency.

Today I again directed several so-called armament and defense enterprises to immediately transfer their inventories. Jews have found refuge in these blocks of houses under the protection of helping arm the German Wehrmacht and Police. The buildings have to be swept. One case provided a familiar picture: a supposedly giant enterprise had practically no inventory, nothing of value. One enterprise was immediately closed and the Jews transferred.

Results of today's operation: 30 Jews transferred; 1,330 Jews removed from bunkers and immediately destroyed; 362 Jews shot dead in battle. Total apprehended today: 1,722 Jews. This brings the total figure of Jews apprehended to 29,186. Further, countless Jews have undoubtedly perished in 13 demolished bunkers and in the fires.

At present, none of the apprehended Jews are still in Warsaw. The prescribed transport to T II has been carried out.

Our forces: same as on the previous day.

Our losses: none.

End of today's operations at 2145 hours. To be continued on 27 April 1943 at 0900 hours.

SS and Police Leader [...]

* * *

[...]

Warsaw, 27 April 1943

[...]

Progress report of the Ghetto operation on 27 April 1943. Start of operation: 0900 hours.

For the operation scheduled today, 24 assault units were formed. These were to act as they did several days last week as small assault sweep detachments, to search the former Jewish Ghetto. The assault sweep detachments removed 780 Jews from bunkers and shot 115 resistant Jews. Conclusion of operation at 1500 hours. Several assault units had to stay in action, since they had uncovered new bunkers.

At 1600 hours, a special battle unit of 320 officers and men was sent into action to cleanse a large block of houses on both sides of the so-called Niska Street in the northeastern part of the former Jewish quarter. After the search, the entire block was sealed off and set on fire. A considerable number of Jews were apprehended during this operation. As usual, they remained to the last in the bunkers they had constructed underground or in attics. They fired to the last moment and jumped to the street below – sometimes from the fourth story – only when the flames left no other escape. First, they threw down beds, mattresses, etc.

Today, a total of 2,560 Jews were apprehended in the former Jewish quarter and 547 of them shot. An undetermined number of Jews perished, as usual, in the fires or when the bunkers were blown up. The number of Jews apprehended to date in the current operation in the former Jewish quarter totals 31,746.

An anonymous letter disclosed that large numbers of Jews were to be found in a block of buildings adjoining, but outside, the northeastern part of the Jewish quarter. A special assault unit, commanded by First Lieutenant of the Protective Police Diehl, was sent into action against this building. The assault party discovered a gang of 120 men, heavily armed with pistols, rifles, hand grenades, and light machine guns, who offered resistance. The unit succeeded in liquidating 24 bandits in battle; 52 bandits were apprehended. The rest could not be captured or destroyed because of approaching darkness. The buildings, however, were immediately surrounded, so escape is not possible. The purge will continue tomorrow. Also taken into custody were 17 Poles, including 2 Polish Police, who should have known of the whereabouts of this gang. Captured during this operation were 3 rifles; 12 pistols, some of heavy caliber; 100 Polish oval hand grenades; 27 German steel helmets; parts of German uniforms and coats, some even including the ribbon of the Eastern front medal; reserve magazines for light machine guns; 300 rounds of ammunition; etc. The leader of the assault unit had an extremely difficult task with bandits disguised in German uniforms. He nonetheless pushed ahead with great energy. Polish terrorists were identified with certainty among the bandits who were apprehended or killed. We even succeeded in apprehending and liquidating one of the founder-leaders of the Jewish-Polish defense formation.

The external appearance of the Jews who are now being apprehended shows that the turn has come for those Jews who directed the resistance. Jumping from burning windows and balconies, they reviled Germany and the Fuehrer and cursed the German Army.

SS men who descended into the sewers discovered that a large number of Jewish corpses were being washed away.

Our forces:

From 0700 to 1900 hours	288 German Police 200 Trawniki men 140 Polish Police

Blockade forces

From 1900 to 0700 hours	288 German Police 250 Waffen-SS 140 Polish Police
Strength of assault forces	3 officers / 115 German Police 4 officers / 400 Waffen-SS 1 officer / 6 Technical Emergency Corps 2 officers / 21 Engineers

Our losses: 3 wounded, including 2 Waffen-SS men and 1 Trawniki man.

End of operations at 2300 hours.

To be continued on 28 April 1943 at 1000 hours.

SS and Police Leader [...]

* * *

[...]

Warsaw, 28 April 1943

[...]

Progress report of the Ghetto operation on 28 April 1943. Start of operation: 1000 hours.

Today, 10 assault units were dispatched to sweep the entire Ghetto. Proceeding with thoroughness and tenacity, these assault units again located a large number of bunkers. We have now established that the Jews had prepared these bunkers for resistance as early as the middle of last year. A total of 335 Jews were forcibly removed from these bunkers. Besides these undertakings, we tackled the stronghold of the Jewish military organization, which is situated at the edge of the Ghetto. We succeeded today in shooting 10 bandits in addition to those caught yesterday, in apprehending 9, and in capturing more weapons, ammunition and military equipment.

In the afternoon, a battle detail was once more dispatched against a block of buildings that had already been swept; the block was set on fire in the course of this undertaking. As on previous days, the powerful fire and massive smoke forced masses of Jews out into the open. Elsewhere, an Engineer officer assigned by the Wehrmacht worked tenaciously to open a bunker that had been prepared last October and was equipped with running water, toilet, electricity and other conveniences. 274 of the most influential and richest Jews were removed.

Today, strenuous armed resistance was again encountered and overcome at various locations. It is now clearer than ever that due to the extended duration of the operation, the real terrorists and activists are being struck.

Today's results: 1,655 Jews apprehended for transfer, including 110 killed in battle.

Further, many Jews burned to death in the fires, and an indeterminable number of Jews were destroyed when several bunkers were demolished.

Today's success raises the total number of Jews apprehended

or destroyed to 33,401. This figure does not include the Jews who burned to death or were destroyed in the bunkers.

Our forces: same as on the previous day.

Our losses: 1 Police and 2 Waffen-SS wounded.

End of operations at 2200 hours. To be continued on 29 April 1943 at 1000 hours.

SS and Police Leader [...]

* * *

[...]

Warsaw, 29 April 1943

[...]

Progress report of the grand operation on 29 April 1943. Start of operation: 1000 hours.

As on the previous day, assault sweep detachments were charged with the search of the newly separated blocks of buildings. A larger battle detail was dispatched to purge a block of houses (the former Hallmann enterprise) and destroy it by fire. Altogether, 36 new bunkers were located; 2,359 Jews were apprehended from these and other hideouts and from burning buildings. Of these, 106 were killed in battle.

Once again captured were 2 rifles, 10 pistols, 10 kilograms of explosives, and various types of ammunition.

When a large bunker was blown up, the entire building collapsed and the bandits perished without exception. In the ensuing blaze, loud detonations and jets of fire showed that large stores of ammunitions and explosives must have been present. Several sewer shafts were blown up. Two exits discovered outside the Ghetto were also demolished or walled up to make them useless.

Statements made by various bunker crews revealed that these Jews have not been outside for the last 10 days and that they are running short on food, etc., due to the extended duration of the grand operation. The Jews also explained that Jewish or perhaps Polish bandits wearing black masks show up at night to wall up the bunkers from outside. They urge those inside not to give any signs of life if they wish to continue living in the Ghetto. The evacuation of several armament enterprises is proceeding at a slow pace. In some cases, it would appear to be almost intentional. Thus, I discovered today, Thursday, that there has been no move by one firm (Schultz & Co.) to comply with my orders to start immediate evacuation, which I had issued during my visit there on Easter Monday, three days ago.

Our forces: same as on the previous day.

Our losses: none.

End of operations at 2100 hours. The grand operation will be continued on 30 April 1943 at 0900 hours.

Total number of Jews apprehended or destroyed: 35,760.

SS and Police Leader [...]

* * *

[...]

Warsaw, 30 April 1943

[...]

Progress report of the grand operation on 30 April 1943. Start of operation: 0900 hours.

Today, assault sweep detachments continued the sweep. Although huge blocks of buildings are now completely burned out, the Jews continue to remain in bunkers located 2 to 3 meters below ground. Often we are able to find these bunkers only when an apprehended Jew tips us off. During the last few days, repeated testimony from Jews has established that armed Jews emerge at night from some hideout or bunker and threaten to shoot Jews who attract attention in any way. It was incontrovertibly established that several bunkers were sealed from the outside by these bandits to underline their orders. Today, a total of 30 bunkers was located, emptied and blown up. Again, a large number of bandits and subhumans were apprehended. Besides the sweep operations conducted by smaller assault detachments, 2 larger battle details were dispatched to sweep and destroy by fire various contiguous housing blocks.

A total of 1,599 Jews were apprehended today, including 179 killed in battle. The total number of Jews apprehended to date thus rises to 37,359. Today, 3,855 Jews were loaded for shipment. The proportion of armed Jews has risen considerably among those apprehended during the last few days. Today, weapons and especially parts of German uniforms were again captured from the Jews. The results of today's undertaking in Fort Traugutta were negative. Any subterranean exits located were occupied or blown up. A cannon had to be brought up to join in the combat against one of the buildings today.

Our combat forces:

Police	5 officers / 133 men
Security Police	3 officers / 36 men
Waffen-ss	6 officers / 432 men
Engineers	2 officers / 40 men
Staff	3 officers / 7 men

Blockade forces:

Waffen-ss	3 officers / 310 men
German Police	2 officers / 89 men
Trawniki	200 men
In addition, Polish Police	

Our losses: 1 wounded (Protective Police).

End of today's grand operation at 2100 hours. To be continued on 1 May 1943 at 0900 hours.

ss and Police Leader [...]

* * *

[...]

Warsaw, 1 May 1943

[...]

Progress report of the grand operation on 1 May 1943. Start of operation: 0900 hours.

10 assault sweep detachments were sent into action; further a larger battle detail to sweep a housing block was dispatched with orders to destroy this block by fire. This block, too, contained a so-called armament enterprise that had not been completely evacuated, although there had been adequate time. It was encompassed in the execution of the mission.

Today's undertaking yielded a total of 1,026 Jews, of whom 245 were killed either in battle or while resisting. Moreover, a large number of outright bandits and ringleaders were caught. In one case, a Jew who had already been processed for deportation fired 3 shots at a First Lieutenant of Police; however, the bullets missed their mark. All the Jews apprehended today were removed from the bunkers by force. There was not a single case of voluntary surrender when the bunkers were opened. A large number of the Jews were apprehended in the sewer network. We continued to systematically blow up or plug the sewer exits.

In one case, the Engineers laid a concentrated charge and had to move to an adjacent opening to attend to some other matter. In the meantime, a Jew emerged from the sewer, removed the fuse, and stole the explosives. At a later stage in the pursuit of this part of the undertaking, we succeeded in catching the Jew with the explosives.

To establish the nightly movement of Jews, I assigned, for the first time, 5 reconnaissance details of 1 officer and 9 men each for night duty at irregular intervals.

It is a fact, generally speaking, that extraordinary diligence and energy are demanded of the troops to uncover the Jews who still are in the so-called bunkers, caves and sewer network. We anticipate that the remaining inhabitants of the former Ghetto will be apprehended shortly. The total figure of Jews apprehended to date has now risen to 38,385. Not included are the Jews who burned to death or perished in the bunkers. One assault unit discovered that an indeterminable number of corpses were floating in a sewer main below the Ghetto.

Outside the Ghetto, in the immediate vicinity of the city of

Warsaw, the Gendarmerie has shot 150 Jews since the start of the grand operation; there is proof that these Jews had escaped from Warsaw.

Pistols and explosives were again captured.

Our combat forces:

German Police	4 officers / 102 men
Waffen-SS	7 officers / 350 men
Engineers (Wehrmacht)	2 officers / 38 men
Technical Emergency Corps	1 officer / 6 men
Security Police	2 officers / 1 man

Blockade forces:

Waffen-SS	300 men
German Police	1 officer / 71 men
Trawniki	250 men

Our losses: 1 member of the Order Police, wounded yesterday, succumbed to his injuries.

End of today's grand operation at 2200 hours. To be continued on 2 May 1943 at 1000 hours.

SS and Police Leader [...]

* * *

[...]

Warsaw, 2 May 1943

[...]

Progress report of the grand operation on 2 May 1943. Start of operation: 1000 hours.

Sweep of the entire territory of the former Ghetto was conducted by 9 assault detachments; a larger detachment was further detailed to purge and/or destroy a housing block grouped around the 2 armament works, Transavia and Wisniewski. To locate new bunkers, the assault detachments took along as guides Jews who had been apprehended the day before. The assault sweep detachments removed 944 Jews from bunkers during the course of this undertaking; an additional 235 Jews were shot. When the aforementioned housing block was destroyed, 120 Jews were apprehended and countless Jews destroyed when they jumped from burning attics to the inner courtyards. Many other Jews perished in the flames or were destroyed when bunkers and sewer entrances were blown up. Two armament concerns were deprived of their Jews and the plant managers requested complete evacuation within a brief span of time.

Altogether, 1,852 Jews were apprehended today. The total number of Jews apprehended thereby rises to 40,237.

27 bunkers were located, forcibly opened, and destroyed; arms and ammunition were captured. There were a total of 7 casualties, consisting of 4 Order Police and 3 Polish Police. These occurred when the outer barricade came under fire and when Jews attacked while breaking out through a sewer entrance outside the former Jewish quarter. The Waffen-SS reconnaissance detachments assigned during the night met some armed resistance from Jews who ventured out of manholes and bunkers under the protection of darkness. We suffered no losses. A considerable number of Jews, on the other hand, were killed or wounded.

OUR FORCES:

Sent into action

German Police	3 officers / 98 men
Technical Emergency Corps	1 officer / 6 men
Security Police	3 officers / 12 men
Engineers	2 officers / 37 men
SS Grenadiers	11 officers / 409 men
SS Cavalry	3 officers / 7 men

Blockade forces

German Police	2 officers / 9 men
SS Grenadiers	1 officer / 300 men
Trawniki	200 men

Our losses: 4 Order Police and 3 Polish Police wounded

The Higher SS and Police Leader East, SS General and General of the Police Krueger, attended today's grand operation.

End of operations at 2030 hours. To be continued on 3 May 1943 at 0900 hours.

SS and Police Leader [...]

* * *

[...]

Warsaw, 3 May 1943

[...]

Progress report of the grand operation on 3 May 1943. Start of operation: 0900 hours.

Today's sweep of the former Jewish Ghetto, during which 19 new bunkers were discovered, had the following results:

Apprehended in bunkers 1,392 Jews

Shot 95 Jews

Transferred from former armament enterprises 177 Jews

Total number of Jews apprehended to date 41,806 Jews

In most cases, the Jews offered resistance, weapon in hand, before leaving the bunkers. This accounts for 2 of our men being listed as wounded. Some of the Jews and bandits fired pistols from both hands.

Since it was established in several instances today that Jewesses had concealed pistols in their underpants, all Jews and bandits are requested, from today on, to strip completely and be searched.

Captured today were 1 German rifle, model 98; 2 pistols of .08 caliber and other calibers; and homemade hand grenades. Only after the burning of several smoke candles could the Jews be induced to leave their bunkers. According to testimony received yesterday and today, the Jews were summoned to build air-raid shelters during the second half of 1942. Under the camouflage of constructing air-raid shelters, the Jews then began to build the bunkers they now occupy in order to be able to make use of them during an operation against the Jews.

Some of the reconnaissance detachments detailed to the Ghetto were fired upon last night. One man was wounded. The reconnaissance detachments reported that groups of armed bandits marched through the former Ghetto.

Our forces: same as on the previous day.

Our losses: 3 SS Privates wounded.

End of today's undertaking at 2100 hours. To be continued on 4 May 1943 at 0900 hours.

Loaded for shipment were 3,019 Jews.

SS and Police Leader [...]

* * *

[...]

Warsaw, 4 May 1943

[...]

Progress report of the grand operation on 4 May 1943. Start of operation: 0900 hours.

An assault detachment, 1 officer and 60 men strong, reinforced by the Wehrmacht Engineers, was dispatched to clear out the bunkers. This assault detachment pulled 550 Jews from bunkers and shot 188 Jews in battle. Locating the bunkers becomes more and more difficult. Many bunkers can be discovered only when other Jews betray their location. If Jews are ordered to leave bunkers voluntarily, they almost never obey; they can be compelled to do so only by the use of smoke candles.

Our main forces were dispatched about 1100 hours to sweep, purge and destroy 2 large housing blocks of the former firms of Toebbens, Schultz & Co., and others. After these blocks were completely cordoned off, the Jews who were still in the buildings were first ordered to come forward voluntarily. 456 Jews were thereby apprehended for transfer. Only when the housing blocks were engulfed by fire and headed for destruction did a considerable number of Jews emerge, forced to flee the flames and smoke. Repeatedly, the Jews tried to pass through burning buildings. Countless Jews who had been visible on the roofs during the conflagration perished in the flames. Others came into view on the uppermost floors at the very last moment and could save themselves from being cremated alive only by jumping. Today, a total of 2,283 Jews were apprehended, of whom 204 were shot; countless Jews were destroyed in fires and in bunkers. The total amount of Jews apprehended to date has risen to 44,089.

According to testimony by the Jews, part of the leadership of the so-called party was apprehended today. One member of the leadership of the gang will be used tomorrow to clear out other fortified bunkers and their armed inhabitants. During the evacuation of the armament plant, it was again established that trifles like used furniture and other requisitioned items were carted away in place of the so-called valuable military equipment. Appropriate countermeasures were taken at once.

Reconnaissance detachments patrolling the former Jewish quarter during the night reported renewed movement by Jews in the burned-out ruins of streets and courtyards. The reconnaissance detachments wrapped rags and other material around their footgear at night to enable them to take the Jews by surprise. 30 Jews were shot in skirmishes with the reconnaissance detachments.

Captured today were 1 carbine, 3 pistols and ammunition. During the blaze, a large amount of stored ammunition exploded.

OUR FORCES:

Sent into action

German Police	4 officers / 101 men
Technical Emergency Corps	1 officer / 6 men
Security Police	2 officers / 14 men
Engineers	2 officers / 41 men
Waffen-SS	11 officers / 407 men

Blockade forces

	DAY	NIGHT
German Police	2 officers / 87 men	1 officer / 11 men

Waffen-ss	25 men	1 officer / 300 men
Trawniki	200 men	
Polish Police	1 officer / 180 men	1 officer / 180 men

Our losses: none.

End of operations at 2330 hours. To be continued on 5 May 1943 at 1000 hours.

ss and Police Leader [...]

* * *

[...]

Warsaw, 5 May 1943

[...]

Progress report of the grand operation on 5 May 1943. Start of operation: 1000 hours.

At first glance, it appeared as if the assault detachments committed to today's grand operation would have less success. However, by the end of today's undertaking, a great many more bunkers had been located due to betrayal by Jews and the tracking ability of the men. 40 of these bunkers were destroyed. As far as possible, the Jews found in these bunkers were apprehended (1,070 altogether). The assault sweep detachments shot about 126 Jews. Today, the Jews again offered resistance in various places before they were caught. In several cases, the entrance hatches to the bunkers were forcibly kept closed or bolted from the inside so that only a strong explosive charge could force an opening and the bunker occupants be destroyed. Once again, weapons and ammunition were captured, including one .08-caliber pistol. 2,850 Jews were apprehended for transshipment at a still existent enterprise in the so-called Prosta. Because this figure was included in the total reported earlier, only 1,070 are to be added, raising the total number to 45,159.

Our forces: same as on the previous day.

Our losses: 1 SS Private and 1 Order Police wounded. Total losses to date: 8 dead, 55 wounded.

End of operations at 2200 hours. To be continued on 6 May 1943 at 0930 hours.

SS and Police Leader [...]

* * *

[...]

Warsaw, 6 May 1943

[...]

Progress report of the grand operation on 6 May 1943. Start of operation: 0930 hours.

Today, we especially swept housing blocks that were destroyed by fire on 4 May. Although it was scarcely expected that any living beings would still be encountered, a large number of bunkers were discovered where intense heat had developed. A total of 1,553 Jews were apprehended in these bunkers and in bunkers discovered in other sections of the Ghetto. 356 Jews were shot while resisting during a skirmish. In this skirmish, Jews fired from .08-caliber and other caliber pistols and threw Polish oval hand grenades. One SS Sergeant was wounded. Altogether, 47 bunkers were destroyed.

Two men serving on the blockade were wounded. Apparently, Jews who had broken out of the Ghetto were now returning with the intention of assisting or liberating the Ghetto Jews by force. One Jew who had escaped from Lublin was apprehended just outside the Ghetto walls. He was armed with one .08-caliber pistol, ample reserve ammunition, and 2 Polish oval hand grenades. So far, it could not be reliably ascertained whether the so-called Jewish party leadership (PPR) has been apprehended or destroyed. The bandits' trail is known. It is to be hoped that tomorrow's undertaking will succeed in clearing out this so-called party leadership. Security posts of the surrounding barricade were moved farther into the Aryan section to more effectively intercept the Jews and bandits who are pushing toward the Ghetto. Prosta, the former mini-Ghetto, was searched today by assault sweep detachments. Jews who had stayed behind were apprehended. The firm of Toebbens was charged with evacuating the mini-Ghetto by noon on 10 May 1943. The so-called library, located outside the Ghetto, was placed at their disposal for temporary storage of raw materials, etc.

The total number of Jews apprehended so far has risen to 47,068. The Polish Police, spurred by the cash rewards, are making a great effort to deliver to headquarters any Jews found in the city. The undersigned is receiving anonymous letters that draw attention to the presence of Jews in the Aryan part of the city. One anonymous letter concerned a comparison between Katyn and the grand operation in the Ghetto.

OUR FORCES:

Sent into action

German Police	4 officers / 101 men
Technical Emergency Corps	1 officer / 6 men
Security Police	2 officers / 14 men
Engineers (Wehrmacht)	3 officers / 72 men
Waffen-SS	10 officers / 500 men

Blockade forces

	DAY	NIGHT
German Police	2 officers / 87 men	1 officer / 11 men
Waffen-SS	25 men	1 officer / 300 men
Trawniki	200 men	
Polish Police	1 officer / 180 men	1 officer / 180 men

Our losses: 1 Order Police dead; 1 Order Police wounded; 1 SS Sergeant less seriously wounded

End of operations at 2100 hours. To be continued on 7 May 1943 at 0930 hours.

SS and Police Leader [...]

* * *

[...]

Warsaw, 7 May 1943

[...]

Progress report of the grand operation on 7 May 1943. Start of operation: 1000 hours.

The assault sweep detachments sent into action today were able to record the following results: 49 bunkers located. A number of Jews were apprehended. A larger but unknown number of Jews who refused to leave the bunkers and offered armed resistance perished when the bunkers were blown up. Altogether, 1,019 Jews were apprehended alive today; 255 were shot. The total number of Jews apprehended so far has risen to 48,342.

Today, armed resistance was again encountered in several instances, whereby 1 SS Private was wounded. Four pistols of various calibers and ammunition were captured.

The location of the bunker used by the so-called inner party leadership is now known. It will be forced open tomorrow.

The Jews testify that they emerge at night to obtain fresh air, since an uninterrupted stay in the bunkers due to the long duration of the operation is becoming unbearable. On average, the assault detachments shoot between 30 and 50 Jews each night. It must be assumed from the testimony that a considerable number of Jews still remain underground in the Ghetto. Today, a concrete building that could not be destroyed by fire was blown up. In the process, we established that the blowing up of houses is a protracted matter and requires enormous quantities of explosives. Setting fires still remains the best and only method for destroying the Jews.

Our forces: same as on the previous day.

Our losses: 1 Waffen-SS man wounded.

End of operations at 2100 hours. To be continued on 8 May 1943 at 1000 hours.

SS and Police Leader [...]

* * *

[...]

Warsaw, 8 May 1943

[...]

Progress report of the grand operation on 8 May 1943. Start of operation: 1000 hours.

The entire area of the former Jewish Ghetto was searched today by assault sweep detachments for bunkers and Jews. As reported several days ago, subhumanity – bandits and terrorists – [sic] remain in bunkers, which the fires have caused to become unbearably hot. These creatures know that their choice is either to remain in hiding as long as possible or to come to the surface and try to wound or kill the men of the Waffen-SS, Police and Wehrmacht, who keep the pressure on them.

The discovery of the bunker of the so-called inner party leadership reported in yesterday's teletype message was further pursued today. We succeeded in opening the bunker of the party leadership and seizing about 60 heavily armed bandits. The deputy head of the Jewish military organization ZWZ and his so-called chief of staff were caught and liquidated. About 200 Jews were sheltered in this bunker; 60 of them were apprehended and 140 destroyed due to the strong impact of smoke candles and heavy explosives laid in several places. Jews that we removed reported that countless Jews had been killed by the smoke candles. If the battle against the Jews and bandits was difficult for the first 6 days, it must now be stated that the Jews and Jewesses who bore the responsibility in those days are finally being apprehended. Every time a bunker is opened, the Jews inside offer resistance by using the weapons at their disposal, be they light machine guns, pistols or hand grenades. Again today, a large number of Jewesses were apprehended who carried loaded pistols, their safety catches released, in their underpants.

We have statements that 3,000 to 4,000 Jews still remain in subterranean holes, sewers and bunkers. The undersigned is determined not to terminate the grand operation until the last Jew has been destroyed.

A total of 1,091 Jews were apprehended in the bunkers today; about 280 Jews were shot in battle; countless Jews were destroyed in 43 demolished bunkers. The total number of Jews apprehended has risen to 49,712. Buildings which had not yet been destroyed by fire were set on fire today. In the process, it was discovered that isolated Jews were still hiding somewhere within the walls or staircases.

OUR FORCES:

Sent into action

German Police	4 officers / 101 men
Technical Emergency Corps	1 officer / 6 men
Security Police	2 officers / 14 men
Engineers (Wehrmacht)	3 officers / 69 men
Waffen-SS	13 officers / 527 men

Blockade forces

	DAY	NIGHT
German Police	1 officer / 87 men	1 officer / 36 men
Waffen-SS	1 officer / 300 men	
Trawniki	160 men	
Polish Police	1 officer / 160 men	1 officer / 160 men

Our losses: 2 Waffen-SS dead; 2 Waffen-SS and 1 Engineer wounded.

An Order Police wounded on 7 May 1943 today succumbed to his injuries.

15 to 20 pistols of various calibers were captured, along with considerable stores of ammunition for pistols and rifles, and a number of handmade hand grenades made in the former armament plants.

End of operations at 2130 hours. To be continued on 9 May 1943 at 1000 hours.

ss and Police Leader [...]

* * *

[...]

Warsaw, 9 May 1943

[...]

Progress report of the grand operation on 9 May 1943. Start of operation: 1000 hours.

Today's grand operation produced the following results: the assault sweep detachments found 42 bunkers. 1,037 Jews and bandits were pulled alive from these bunkers. 319 Jews and bandits were shot in battle, and countless numbers were destroyed when bunkers were blown up. The housing block surrounding the former Transavia enterprise was destroyed by fire and in the process Jews were again caught, despite the many sweeps.

Again, pistols and hand grenades were captured.

OUR FORCES:

Sent into action

German Police	4 officers / 103 men
Security Police	2 officers / 12 men
Engineers (Wehrmacht)	3 officers / 67 men
Waffen-ss	13 officers / 547 men

Blockade forces

	DAY	NIGHT
German Police	1 officer / 87 men	1 officer / 36 men
Waffen-ss	1 officer / 300 men	
Trawniki	160 men	
Polish Police	1 officer / 160 men	1 officer / 160 men

Our losses: none

The total number of Jews apprehended to date has risen to 51,313. 254 Jews and bandits were shot outside the former Jewish Ghetto.

End of operations at 2100 hours. To be continued on 10 May 1943 at 1000 hours.

SS and Police Leader [...]

* * *

[...]

Warsaw, 10 May 1943

[...]

Progress report of the grand operation on 10 May 1943. Start of operation: 1000 hours.

Assault search detachments were again dispatched today to sweep the area of the former Jewish quarter. As on previous days, a large number of Jews were unexpectedly pulled from the bunkers. Jewish resistance continued undiminished today. Unlike on previous days, members of the main Jewish fighting group who have not been destroyed, and appear to be still present, retreated into the ruins which are eminently accessible to them to direct their fire and inflict casualties on our commandos.

Today, a total of 1,183 Jews were apprehended alive. 187 Jews and bandits were shot. Again, an indeterminable number of Jews and bandits were destroyed in blown-up bunkers. The total number of Jews apprehended so far has risen to 52,683.

Today at 0900 hours, a truck drove up to a manhole in the so-called Prosta. A passenger of this truck exploded 2 hand grenades, the signal for the bandits who were waiting to climb out of the manhole. The Jews and bandits – they always include Polish bandits – were armed with carbines, small arms and 1 machine gun. They climbed into the truck and drove off in an unknown direction. The last man of this gang, who stood sentry in the sewer and was charged with closing the sewer lid, was caught. He provided this information. He explained that most members of the gang, which was subdivided into several fighting groups, had either been killed in battle or had committed suicide because of the futility of continuing the fight. The search for the truck has been fruitless so far.

The bandits further testified that the Prosta has become the refuge for the remaining Jews because the former Ghetto has become too hot for them. For this reason, I have resolved to give the Prosta the same treatment as the Ghetto and destroy this miniature Ghetto.

Today, small arms and ammunition again were captured. Yesterday, the Security Police succeeded in raiding a workshop outside the Ghetto which was manufacturing between 10,000 and 11,000 explosives and other ammunition.

Our forces: same as on the previous day.

Our losses: 3 SS Privates wounded.

The Engineer detachment was reinforced due to good relations with the Wehrmacht. At the same time, a large amount of explosives was placed at our disposal.

End of operations at 2200 hours. To be continued on 11 May 1943 at 0930 hours.

SS and Police Leader [...]

* * *

[...]

Warsaw, 11 May 1943

[...]

Progress report of the grand operation on 11 May 1943. Start of operation: 0930 hours.

The reconnaissance detachments sent into action last night again reported that Jews must still be in some of the bunkers, since they were observed in the ruined streets. The reconnaissance detachments shot 12 Jews. On the basis of these reports, assault sweep detachments were once again dispatched today. The sweep netted a total of 47 bunkers, which were raided and destroyed. Today, Jews who had settled into the shells of buildings whose roofs were not totally destroyed were again apprehended. The Jews and bandits are frequenting these new hiding places because it is becoming unbearable to remain in the bunkers. One bunker containing 12 rooms equipped with plumbing, running water and separate bath facilities for men and women was discovered. Large amounts of food were apprehended or secured to make it more difficult for Jews to resupply themselves.

A total of 931 Jews and bandits were apprehended. 53 bandits were shot. More perished when bunkers were blown up and a housing block was destroyed by fire. The total number of Jews apprehended to date has risen to 53,667. Several pistols, hand grenades and ammunition were captured.

The sewers could not be systematically fumigated again, since there was a shortage of smoke candles. OFK has agreed to procure a new supply of smoke candles.

OUR FORCES:

Sent into action

German Police	6 officers / 126 men
Technical Emergency Corps	1 officer / 6 men
Security Police	2 officers / 14 men
Engineers (Wehrmacht)	4 officers / 76 men
Waffen-SS	12 officers / 308 men

Blockade forces

	DAY	NIGHT
German Police		
Waffen-SS	1 officer / 12 men	1 officer / 86 men
Trawniki	160 men	1 officer / 300 men
Polish Police	1 officer / 160 men	1 officer / 160 men

Our losses: 1 SS Private wounded.

Total losses to date: 71 wounded, 12 dead.

End of today's operations at 2145 hours.

To be continued on 12 May 1943 at 0930 hours.

SS and Police Leader [...]

* * *

[...]

Warsaw, 12 May 1943

[...]

Progress report of the grand operation on 12 May 1943. Start of operation: 0930 hours.

The assault sweep detachments' search for further bunkers where Jews are hiding resulted in the discovery of 30 bunkers. 663 Jews were pulled from them and 133 were shot. The total number of Jews apprehended has risen to 54,463.

Further, the miniature Ghetto Prosta was completely sealed off today and destroyed by fire. A large number of Jews probably perished in the flames. Accurate information in this regard could not be obtained because the fire was still blazing when darkness fell. A concrete house in the Prosta from which Jews had been removed was blown up to render it useless as a future base for the bandits. The front of the house directly across the street was heavily damaged as a result. It is noteworthy that lacking any announcement from us, the Poles nonetheless immediately took appropriate measures to protect their windowpanes, etc., before the explosion.

Starting today, the transports of Jews leaving from here will be sent to T II.

OUR FORCES:

Sent into action

German Police	5 officers / 126 men
Technical Emergency Corps	1 officer / 6 men
Security Police	2 officers / 14 men
Engineers	4 officers / 74 men
Waffen-SS	12 officers / 508 men

Blockade forces

	DAY	NIGHT
German Police	1 officer / 112 men	1 officer / 86 men
Waffen-SS	1 officer / 300 men	

Trawniki	160 men	
Polish Police	1 officer / 160 men	1 officer / 160 men

Our losses: 1 SS Private wounded.

End of today's undertaking at 2100 hours. To be continued on 13 May 1943 at 1000 hours.

SS and Police Leader [...]

* * *

[...]

Warsaw, 13 May 1943

[...]

Progress report of the grand operation on 13 May 1943. Start of operation: 1000 hours.

During today's sweep of the large and small Ghetto (Prosta), 234 Jews were arrested. 155 Jews were shot in battle. Today, it became clear that the Jews and bandits now being caught belong to the so-called fighting groups. All of them are young men and women between 18 and 25 years of age. A real skirmish developed while one bunker was being cleared. The Jews not only fired .08-caliber pistols and Polish Vis-pistols but also threw Polish oval hand grenades at the men of the Waffen-SS. As soon as some of the inhabitants had been cleared from the bunker and were about to be searched, one of the females, as so often happens, put her hand under her skirt and, quick as lightning, pulled an oval hand grenade from her underpants, pulled the safety pin, threw the grenade into the group of men conducting the search, and herself jumped for cover quick as lightning. No casualties resulted thanks to the presence of mind shown by the men.

During the last two days, the few Jews and criminals remaining in the Ghetto made use of hideouts still found among the ruins and returned at night to bunkers known to them to eat and get provisions for the next day. It has recently become impossible to extract information about other bunkers from the captured Jews. The remaining occupants of the bunker involved in the skirmish were destroyed with heavy explosives. 327 Jews were apprehended today in a Wehrmacht enterprise. The Jews that are apprehended now are all sent to T II. The total number of Jews apprehended has risen to 55,179.

OUR FORCES:

Sent into action

German Police	4 officers / 182 men
Technical Emergency Corps	1 officer / 6 men
Security Police	2 officers / 14 men
Engineers	4 officers / 74 men
Waffen-SS	12 officers / 517 men

Blockade forces

	DAY	NIGHT
German Police	2 officers / 137 men	1 officer / 87 men
Waffen-SS	1 officer / 300 men	
Trawniki	270 men	
Polish Police	1 officer / 160 men	1 officer / 160 men

Our losses: 2 Waffen-SS dead; 3 Waffen-SS and 1 Police wounded.

Both Waffen-SS men lost their lives in an air-raid attack in the Ghetto.

33 bunkers were taken and destroyed. Booty: 6 pistols, 2 hand grenades and explosives.

End of today's undertaking at 2100 hours. To be continued on 14 May 1943 at 1000 hours.

I intend to conclude the grand operation on 16 May 1943 and to transfer the implementation of further measures to Police Battalion III/23. I will submit a detailed report with a pictorial appendix to the conference of SS and Police Leaders, pending no other orders.

SS and Police Leader [...]

* * *

[…]

Warsaw, 14 May 1943

[…]

Progress report of the grand operation on 14 May 1943. Start of operation: 1000 hours.

The assault sweep detachments went into action in their assigned areas with orders to open more residential bunkers and apprehend the Jews. In this way, a large number of Jews and bandits were apprehended again today. Above all, trails discovered during the night were followed with good results. The night assault detachments clashed several times with armed bandits, who fired small arms and a machine gun. Our side suffered 4 casualties – 3 Waffen-SS and 1 Order Police. Shots were repeatedly fired from the Aryan section against the surrounding barricade. The line of sentries returned relentless fire. About 30 bandits were shot in the skirmishes, and 9 Jews and bandits belonging to an armed gang were captured. One bunker was cleared during the night, the Jews captured, and some pistols, including 12mm-caliber weapons, seized. 2 rifles, 16 pistols, hand grenades, and incendiary grenades were captured in another bunker, occupied by about 100 people. Some of the bandits who resisted again wore various German Army uniforms, German steel helmets and boots. In addition to carbines, 60 rounds of German rifle ammunition were taken. One assault detachment got into a skirmish with a 10- to 14-member gang on the roofs of a housing block at the edge of the Ghetto (Aryan part). The bandits were exterminated with no losses on our side.

The captured bandits repeatedly testify that not all persons in the Ghetto have been apprehended. They confidently expect that the operation will soon be over and that they will then be able to continue living in the Ghetto. Several bandits expressed themselves along the line that all along, they could have killed the leader of the operation, the "General" as they call him, but refrained from violating orders so as not to risk an intensification of anti-Jewish measures.

Today, the Engineers again blew up several concrete houses where bandits continued to find refuge.

To drive the bandits out of the sewer network, 183 manholes were opened at 1500 hours and smoke candles were lowered at a predetermined hour to force the bandits to the surface. The bandits fled from what they thought was gas into the center of the former Jewish quarter, where they were pulled from the manholes.

I will decide about the termination of the operation after tomorrow's engagement.

SS Lieutenant-General of the Waffen-SS von Herff was in attendance during this afternoon's undertaking.

OUR FORCES:

Sent into action

German Police	4 officers / 184 men
Technical Emergency Corps	1 officer / 6 men
Security Police	2 officers / 16 men
Engineers	4 officers / 73 men
Waffen-SS	12 officers / 510 men

Blockade forces

	DAY	NIGHT
German Police	2 officers / 138 men	1 officer / 87 men
Waffen-SS	1 officer / 300 men	
Trawniki	270 men	
Polish Police	1 officer / 160 men	1 officer / 160 men

Our losses: 5 wounded, including 4 Waffen-SS and 1 Order Police.

A total of 398 Jews were apprehended today, another 154 Jews and bandits shot in battle. Thus, the total number of Jews apprehended has risen to 55,731.

Booty: rifles, pistols and ammunition; also, a number of incendiary bottles (Molotov cocktails).

End of operations at 2115 hours. To be continued on 15 May 1943 at 0900 hours.

SS and Police Leader [...]

* * *

[...]

Warsaw, 15 May 1943

[...]

Progress report of the grand operation on 15 May 1943. Start of operation: 0900 hours.

The reconnaissance detachments patrolling the Ghetto last night reported only sporadic encounters with Jews. In contrast to preceding nights, only 6 to 7 Jews were shot. The assault sweep detachments dispatched today also had only minor success. 29 new bunkers were discovered, but some of them no longer had occupants. Altogether, 87 Jews were apprehended today and an additional 67 Jews and bandits shot in battle. In a skirmish that developed around noon, the bandits again resisted, using Molotov cocktails, pistols and homemade hand grenades. The gang was destroyed, but subsequently 1 member of the Order Police was shot through the right hip.

A special commando unit once more searched the last building complex, which had been left standing intact in the Ghetto, and subsequently destroyed it. In the evening, the chapel, mortuary and all other buildings at the Jewish cemetery were blown up or destroyed by fire.

The total number of Jews apprehended has risen to 55,885.

OUR FORCES:

Sent into action

German Police	4 officers / 184 men
Technical Emergency Corps	1 officer / 6 men
Security Police	2 officers / 16 men
Engineers (Wehrmacht)	4 officers / 73 men

Waffen-SS		12 officers / 510 men

Blockade forces

	DAY	NIGHT
German Police	2 officers / 138 men	1 officer / 87 men
Waffen-SS	1 officer / 300 men	
Trawniki	270 men	
Polish Police	1 officer / 160 men	1 officer / 160 men

Our losses: 1 Order Police wounded.

Booty captured: 4 pistols of large calibers, 1 time bomb with fuse, 10 kilograms of explosives, and a large quantity of ammunition.

End of operations at 2130 hours. To be continued on 16 May 1943 at 1000 hours.

I will terminate the grand operation on 16 May 1943 at dusk, blowing up the synagogue, which we failed to accomplish today. I will commission Police Battalion III/23 to continue or complete any necessary measures.

SS and Police Leader [...]

* * *

[...]

Warsaw, 16 May 1943

[...]

Progress report of the grand operation on 16 May 1943. Start of operation: 1000 hours.

180 Jews, bandits, and subhumans were destroyed. The Jewish quarter of Warsaw is no more! The grand operation terminated at 2015 hours when the Warsaw synagogue was blown up.

To the Commander of Police Battalion III/23, who received a thorough induction, were transferred all necessary measures to be taken concerning the restricted areas that have been established.

The total number of Jews apprehended and destroyed, according to record, is 56,065.

We had no losses.

I will submit the final report to the conference of SS and Police Leaders on 18 May 1943.

SS and Police [...]

* * *

[...]

Warsaw, 24 May 1943

[...]

I reply to the above-referenced message as follows:

Re: Number 1

Of the total 56,065 Jews apprehended, about 7,000 were destroyed directly in the course of the grand operation in the former Jewish quarter. 6,929 Jews were destroyed via transport to T II, making the total number of Jews destroyed 13,929. In addition to this figure of 56,065, an estimated 5,000 to 6,000 Jews were destroyed in explosions or fires.

Re: Number 2

631 bunkers were destroyed.

Re: Number 3

7 Polish rifles, 1 USSR rifle, 1 German rifle, 59 pistols of various calibers

Several hundred hand grenades, including Polish and homemade ones

A few hundred incendiary bottles

Homemade explosives

Time bombs with fuses

Large quantities of explosives, ammunition for weapons of all calibers, including machine-gun ammunition

Regarding the capture of arms, it must be taken into account that in most cases, arms could not be taken because the Jews and bandits, before their own capture, would throw them into hideouts and holes that could not be located or found. The fumigation of the bunkers also made it impossible for our men to take arms.

Since we had to blow up the bunkers immediately, it was not feasible to take arms later on.

The hand grenades, explosives and incendiary bottles captured by us were immediately put to use against the bandits.

Further captured were: 1,240 used uniform jackets (some with medal ribbons – Iron Cross and East Medal)

600 pairs of used trousers

Equipment items and German steel helmets

108 horses, 4 still remaining in the former Ghetto (hearse)

Counted as of 23 May 1943:

4.4 million zloty; further uncounted, about 4 to 5 million zloty; a large amount of foreign currency, including $14,300 in paper bills and 9,200 gold dollars; also large amounts of jewelry (rings, necklaces, watches, etc.)

Re: Number 4

The former Ghetto has been completely destroyed, except for 8 buildings (police barracks, hospital, and accommodations designated for plant security). Only fire walls are left standing where no explosives were set. However, the ruins would yield enormous quantities of stone and scrap material for further utilization.

SS and Police Leader […]

APPENDIX 4

BALANCE OF FORCES DURING THE WARSAW GHETTO UPRISING

by Stefan Krakowski[1]

NAZI FORCES

[…] In the introduction to his report, Stroop indicates the following composition of the battle group formed to fight in the ghetto under his command:

Unit name	Average number of personnel used per day[2]
Combat group general staff	5/6
Waffen SS – SS Panzer Grenadier Battalion no. 3 – Cavalry Battalion No. 1	 4/440 5/381

1. Stefan Krakowski, *"Stosunek sil w powstaniu w getcie warszawskim," Biuletyn ZIH*, no. 62 (1967). We have translated the bulk of this article, pp. 26–41.
2. The numerator represents officers and the denominator ordinary soldiers. It cannot be denied that the small number of non-commissioned officers was included in the total number of officers. [*All the footnotes to this text are from the Polish original.*]

Order Police	
– SS Police Regiment no. 22	3/94
– SS Police Regiment no. 22 3rd battalion	3/134
– Technical Emergency Corps	1/6
– Polish Police	4/363
– Polish Fire Brigade (police)	0/166
Security Police	3/32
Wehrmacht	
– Light Anti-Aircraft Alarm Battery no. III/8	2/22
– Engineers Detail of the Railway Armored Trains	2/42
– Reserve Engineer Battalion no. 14	1/34
Foreign Ethnic Unit	
– Trawniki battalion	2/335

Stroop's report contains numerous inaccuracies. First of all, the term Stroop uses, "Durchschnitts-Tageseisatz" (translated as "average number of personnel used per day"), is completely inappropriate. Further, what Stroop meant by that term is not at all clear. In his daily reports, as a general rule, he gives considerably lower numbers with regards to the forces used. Only once, in his report of April 20th, 1943, does Stroop give a higher number than in the introduction, in this case reporting the deployment of 460 soldiers of the 1st SS Cavalry, i.e., 74 more than stated in the introduction. At any rate, Stroop's daily reports do not provide any basis for obtaining the average indicated in the introduction to his report.

It must be emphasized that this term, "average number of personnel used per day," is not employed out of any military considerations. Supposedly, one speaks of the units really used, even if they enter into battle in successive waves. It is also undeniable that the "average number of personnel used per day" indicated by Stroop is less than the real number. According to Stroop, this "average number of personnel used per day" came to 36 officers and 2,054 non-commissioned officers and regular soldiers. This total is 3,000 men less than the number supplied by the Armia Krajowa intelligence services. It cannot be denied that Stroop used the expression "average number of personnel used per day" deliberately in order to hide the real number of forces used, which explains why the fighting was so prolonged.

The Stroop report contains other inaccuracies as well. For example, among the units listed in the introduction, Stroop never mentions the introduction of the field artillery unit, whereas in his report for April 20th, he mentions the use of a 100-mm. howitzer. Thus, a field artillery unit must have taken part in the fighting because none of the units mentioned had 100-mm. howitzers. Nor does Stroop mention the use of aviation against the rebels, whereas a number of Polish and Jewish sources, including eyewitnesses, are unequivocal on this point. In his introduction, Stroop also fails to speak of the 3rd battalion of the 23rd regiment of the SS Police. He first mentions this unit in his report of May 13th, in which Stroop says he will keep this battalion in the ghetto to carry out further measures once the main forces of the battle group have been withdrawn. Nor does he say how long this battalion had been used in the ghetto fighting. It is known that the 23rd regiment was stationed in Cracow.[3] The third battalion of this regiment was probably dispatched to Warsaw to reinforce Stroop's battle group.

The use in combat of these units cited by Stroop is confirmed by his aid, Captain Kaleske. But the latter gives much higher figures regarding the units deployed. According to Kaleske, the strength of the two SS units (the 3rd SS Panzer Grenadier Battalion and the 1st Cavalry Battalion) amounted to about 1,000 men each.[4]

---

3. *Wojna Wyzwolencza Narodu Polskiego w latach 1939–1945* [The Polish people's liberation war during the years 1939–1945], no. 29.
4. Josef Wulf, *Das Dritte Reich und seine Vollstrecker* (Berlin: Grünewald, 1961), p. 73.

As we can see, the various sources concur on which units were used in the fighting. The disagreements concern the number of men, with the lowest figure, 2,090, given by Stroop. According to Captain Kaleske, there were that many soldiers in the two SS units alone. This would confirm the data furnished by the Armia Krajowa, which estimated the strength of Stroop's battle group to be 5,000 men. It must be emphasized that the Zydowska Organizacja Bojowa[5] [*the* ZOB] estimated that the Nazi battle group's forces numbered about 6,000.

Nevertheless, the documents cited shed very little light on the Nazi units' armament. In his first report Stroop mentions the use of a 100-mm. howitzer, flamethrowers, three 22.8-mm. anti-tank guns, a French tank and two heavy armored vehicles.[6] On the other hand, he does not mention the other material or the degree to which his group's men were armed with automatic weapons. After the war, in his response written in Mokotow prison in Warsaw to questions submitted by the historian Josef Kermisz, Stroop declared, "Like the other forces deployed in the fighting, the German units were equipped and armed in the same way as units at the front. [...] The tank grenadiers had armored vehicles and a few light French tanks, probably Renaults."[7]

[...] The figures for the SS Cavalry battalion were similar to those cited. But reserve training units, although organized on the same model as front units, were not always equipped with heavy armor, according to the information in an American manual.[8] The two SS battalions that took part in the fighting against the Warsaw Ghetto insurgents were units of this type.

The battalion of the 22nd regiment of SS Police and the battalion of the 23rd regiment of SS Police were also constituent elements of the Nazi battle group. These two regiments belonged to

---

5. AZHP, file number 20/XV-2, p.320.
6. *Stroop Report*, p. 21.
7. AZHP, file number 76/III/332.
8. *Handbook on German Military Forces* – War Department Technical Manual TM-E 30–451, Washington 1945, p. II-31.

the operational units (Truppenpolizei) that were in turn part of the Order Police (Ordnungspolizei). The Truppenpolizei operational battalions previously belonged to the militarized police (Kasernierte Polizei). Thus, for example, the 1st battalion of the 22nd regiment had been the 301st battalion previously stationed in Bochum and the 3rd battalion of that regiment, the 307th battalion stationed in Duisburg.[9] According to the information supplied in this manual, SS Police operational battalions, made up of former battalions of the militarized police, were meant for fighting in occupied territories. Except for the fact that they lacked heavy weaponry, these battalions were organized and equipped identically to army units. A battalion's strength was about 550 men and it comprised a general staff and four companies. Its armament consisted of automatic weapons, anti-aircraft guns and armored vehicles.[10] The armament of the Order Police operational battalions was similar to those of the territorial defense battalions (Sicherungsbataillone) and consists approximately of:[11]

rifles	337
pistols	100
submachine guns	127
automatic rifles	31
heavy machine guns	6

We have no data on the armament of the Polish police [*called the "blues" because of the color of the uniforms they wore*] nor on the "Trawniki" battalion at the time when the fighting in the ghetto broke out.

Undoubtedly the real number of Nazi troops used, and in this particular case the strength of the army and SS Police battalions,

9. *Zur Geschichte der Ordnungspolizei 1936–1945*, Teil I: Hans Joachim Neufeld, *Entstenhung und Organisation des Hauptamtes der Ordnungspolizei*, Teil II: Georg Tessin, *Die Staebe und Truppeneiheiten der Ordnungspolizei*, p. 29.
10. *Handbook on German Military Forces*, p. III-23.
11. Ibid., p. II-57.

was considerably higher than the average indicated by Stroop. [...] Further, if we do not take into account the armament of the smaller details nor the automatic weapons carried by the police and the "Trawniki" battalion, we obtain the minimum figures for the Stroop combat group, as indicated in the following recapitulative table:

Unit name	Rifles	Machine pistols	Automatic rifles	Heavy machine guns
3rd Genadiers battalion	274	45	30	6
1st Cavalry battalion	246	40	30	5
1st and 3rd battalions of the 22nd police regiment	134	50	12	2
Polish police	367	–	–	–
"Trawniki" Battalion	337	–	–	–
Total	1,358	135	69	13

To these figures must be added the 15 armored vehicles that the Nazis are known for certain to have had, i.e., the three Stroop speaks of in his first report on the fighting in the early morning of April 19th and the 12; other vehicles sent by the Wehrmacht; a certain number of anti-aircraft guns and field artillery; the flamethrowers and a large amount of explosives used by the sappers and the aircraft weapons. [...]

THE GHETTO FORCES

The preserved source material does not provide an adequate basis for us to establish the exact strength of the Jewish units. It is known that in the period before the outbreak of the uprising, the ZOB's forces underwent fairly rapid growth. It is also known that during the course of the uprising a large number of fighters from so-called "wildcat" groups joined in or subordinated themselves to the ZOB and ZZW combat groups. Nevertheless, we do not have data that would enable us to make even an approximate evaluation of the number of people who fought in the ranks of the ZOB or the ZZW during the uprising. A great number of important documents have disappeared. The accounts of surviving fighters and Polish Resistance members who worked with the ghetto are contradictory.

The list of fallen ZOB fighters drawn up by the Zydowski Komitet Narodowy [ZKN, *Jewish National Committee*] in November 1943 and sent to London[12] is one of the few preserved documents concerning the strength of the ZOB. This list includes 224 names, but its authors emphasize that it is incomplete. However, it is not known how many names are missing. It is likely that this figure is several times higher than the total number of names listed. At any rate, taking into account the number indicated in the ZKN list, and the fact that more than 60 ZOB soldiers either fought their way out of the ghetto or were sent out on a mission to the "Aryan" side, it can be assumed that the ZOB had more than 300 soldiers. But how many more?

Wladyslaw Bartoszewski writes that at the outbreak of the uprising the ZOB had about 2,000 fighters.[13] According to Jozef Kermisz, in April 1943 the ZOB must have counted about 3,000 people in its ranks.[14] In both cases, these figures probably refer not only to

12. AZHP, file number 202/XV-2.
13. Wladyslaw Bartoszewski, "*Wielki tydzien pozarow*" [The great week of fires], *Gazeta Ludowa*, no. 106 (1946).
14. Jozef Kermisz, *Powstanie w getcie warszawskim* [The Warsaw ghetto uprising] (Lodz, 1946).

armed ZOB members but also to sympathizers who worked with the ZOB, which lacked the weapons to arm them. Actually, it is incontestable that the ZOB did not have enough weapons to arm 2–3,000 people. Even according to the most optimistic calculations, it is hard to imagine that such a large quantity of weapons could have been gotten into the ghetto or manufactured there. The existing source materials confirm the acquisition of a far more modest quantity of arms. Consequently, the historian Waclaw Poteranski's estimate of about 3,000 fighters in the ZOB[15] seems equally unlikely. B. Mark's opinion that on the eve of the uprising the ZOB's forces amounted to some 750–800 soldiers[16] seems considerably more realistic. Nevertheless, even that figure is contested by certain surviving ZOB soldiers and especially the former commander in the brushmakers' quarter, Marek Edelman.[17] Thus this figure should be taken as the closest to the true maximum probable number of ZOB fighters at the beginning of the insurrection.

As for the ZZW's forces, opinions are even more divided than the case of the ZOB. B. Mark estimates that the ZZW had 400 soldiers in early April 1943.[18] According to one of the surviving AK documents, in January 1943 that organization numbered only 150 men.[19] Of course, it is very possible that it expanded to 400 soldiers at the time of the outbreak of the insurrection, but we lack documentation that could give any serious confirmation of such a figure. Here, too, this number must be considered the maximum probable number of ZZW fighters on the day the uprising began.

We also know that unorganized and "wildcat" groups took part in the fighting in the Warsaw ghetto. Various works and accounts cite combat groups of porters under the command of "Mojche the Bolshevik" and "Krzywonos" [*Crooked Nose*], an Orthodox

15. Waclaw Poteranski, "*Walka warszawskiege getta*" [The struggle of the Warsaw ghetto], *Kultura* (April 21, 1963), p. 6.
16. Mark, *Powstanie w getcie warszawskim* [The Warsaw ghetto uprising], 1963, p. 36.
17. Edelman contested this figure in a conversation with the author on June 29, 1965.
18. Mark, *op. cit.*, p. 27.
19. AZHP, file number 203/IX-12.

group led by the engineer Drejczyn, the group headed by the school teacher Eiaear Frydenson, groups of butchers, coachmen, smugglers and many groups associated with workshops or private bunkers.

We have no conclusive data to estimate the number of such groups. According to certain accounts, many thousands of ghetto inhabitants became members of these "wildcat" groups. Still, there can be no doubt that such groups were particularly poorly armed. Thus they could not have played a major role in the first part of the uprising, although they probably inflicted causalities upon the Germans when it came to the defense of private bunkers.

It is much more important, but even more difficult, to establish the quantity of arms in the hands of the ghetto at the time when the fighting began. The ghetto combat organizations used every means possible to procure weapons. They asked for support from Polish underground organizations. To this end the ZOB established contact with both the People's Guard and the Home Army. The ZZW received significant military supplies from the PLAN[20] and the Security Corps (KB).[21] The manufacture of arms within the ghetto was developed. The two military organizations and the "wildcat" groups organized arms purchases and smuggling themselves.

Unfortunately, there is no documentation that might make it possible to at least approximately estimate the quantity of arms sent by the PPR and the People's Guard to meet the needs of the ZOB. There could not have been frequent arms shipments. During the period of preparations for the ghetto uprising (winter 1942–spring 1943), the People's Guard had no surplus of arms. At that time, the GL partisan units had only the most minimal armament. Yet the PPR had a very understanding attitude toward the ZOB's needs. To help arm the ZOB, the PPR set up a number of clandestine places

20. A democratic underground organization led by Barcikowski. It comprised a few combat groups under the command of C. Ketling.
21. A military unit commanded by H. Iwanski fought under this name. Its task was to organize aid to the ghetto. Later this unit joined a bigger military organization with the same name, formed in November 1943.

where arms changed hands. It had been possible to get a certain number of handguns, grenades and a few rifles into the ghetto.[22] But given the present state of the research, it is difficult to attempt to make a more precise estimate of the quantity of arms shipped by the PPR and the GL.

There is also no documentation that would make it possible to establish the quantity of arms shipped by the PLAN and the KB. B. Mark mentions 60 grenades that the PLAN group carried into the ghetto through the Muranowska Street tunnel for the ZZW, and three boxes of grenades for the ZZW from the KB carried by Captain Iwanski's group through the tunnel running from the "Aryan" side to the ZZW bunker on Karmelicka Street.[23] These were not the only arms shipments to the ZZW from the PLAN and the KB.

The ZOB received consistent aid from the Home Army. In this case, there exists documentation indicating the quantities. The document "*Polskie sily zbrojne w II-giej wojnie swiatowej, Armia Krajowa*," vol. 3 [The Polish military forces during the Second World War, the home army, vol. 3] published by the Sikorski Historical Institute in London, reports the following quantities of arms for the ghetto:

- 90 pistols with clips and ammunition
- 500 defensive hand grenades
- 100 offensive hand grenades
- 15 kg of plastic explosives with fuses and detonators
- 1 automatic rifle
- 1 submachine gun
- materials for the making of Molotov cocktails
- diversion material, such as time bombs and delayed-action detonators.[24]

---

22. AZHP, file number 76/III/332, p. 131.
23. Mark, *Walka i zaglada warszawskiego ghetta* [Struggle and destruction of the Warsaw ghetto], Warsaw, 1959, p. 249.
24. "*Polskie sily zbrojne w II-giej wojnie swiatowej*," vol. 3: *Armia Krajowa* [The Polish military forces during the Second World War, vol. 3: the home army], p. 326.

These figures generally coincide with those given by Henryk Wolinski, head of the Jewish affairs department of the Home Army general staff,[25] and by Marek Edelman[26] and Cywia Lubetkin.[27]

Clandestine arms workshops played a major role in arming the ghetto. They made bottle fire bombs and repaired arms brought from the "Aryan" side. Jonas Turkow[28] and Dorka Goldkorn[29] describe these workshops in more detail. But it is impossible to estimate, based on existing source material, the amount of arms that were produced in the ghetto. Edelman writes that there were 4–5 Molotov cocktails per ZOB soldier.[30] This would mean that thousands of these weapons had been made.

Another source of supplies for the ghetto military organizations was to purchase arms on the "Aryan" side and smuggle them into the ghetto. To some extent these purchases were made through contacts established through the Home Army and the People's Guard. There were also other sources. J. Turkow writes of contact with a group of Poles who delivered to the ghetto a few rifles, pistols, hand grenades and ammunition. Since this group had connections with the arms factory at Radom, it was possible to buy pistols with ammunition.[31]

Just as there is little documentation in regard to armament and homemade arms, the same difficulties apply to ascertaining the order of magnitude of arms purchases. It is likely that most firearms were acquired in this way. Home Army sources correlate the soaring prices of weapons on the black market in the spring of 1943 with the growing needs in this regard of the ghetto military organizations.[32] In reality, the rising prices for arms reflected not

25. Mark, *Walka i zaglada warszawskiego ghetta* [Struggle and destruction of the Warsaw ghetto], pp. 345–46.
26. Edelman, *Getto walczy* [The ghetto in struggle] (Warsaw, 1945), pp. 47–48.
27. C. Lubetkin, *Ostatni na murze* [The last at the top of the wall] (Ein Harod, 1946), p. 36.
28. J. Turkow, *Tak bylo* [That's how it was] (Buenos Aires, 1948), p. 465.
29. D. Goldkorn, *Wspomnienia uczestniczki powstania w getcie warszawskim* [Memoirs of a Warsaw ghetto fighter] (Warsaw, 1951), p. 14.
30. M. Edelman, op. cit., p. 50.
31. J. Turkow, op. cit., p. 410.
32. "*Polskie sily zbrojne…*," [The Polish military forces…], p. 326.

only the ghetto's growing needs as it prepared for the uprising, but also the same growing needs of the National Resistance.

In considering the question of arms purchases, it should not be forgotten that the prices paid by the ghetto were much higher than those paid by the underground organizations on the "Aryan" side. These prices did, in fact, have to reflect the risk in crossing over into the ghetto with them and the pure and simple risks involved in doing business with Jews during the Nazi occupation. The ghetto Resistance paid 10–20,000 zlotys for a pistol, 1–1,5000 zlotys for a hand grenade, 20–25,000 zlotys for a rifle and 40,000 zlotys for a machine gun.[33] During the same period, the maximum amount paid by the Home Army went from 4,000 zlotys for a pistol to 12,000 zlotys for a heavy machine gun.[34] Obviously, in the face of such high prices, the possibilities of procuring arms through purchases were extremely limited due to the limited financial resources of a ghetto that had already been thoroughly pillaged.

None of these means – help from Polish organizations, arms purchases, homemade weapons – could allow the ghetto to acquire a sufficient amount of arms. The most optimistic calculations made on the basis of existing source material allow us to establish the following estimate for the armament of the Jewish military organizations on the day the uprising broke out on, April 19, 1943:

The ZOB had, per soldier, at most, one handgun with 10–15 cartridges, 4–5 grenades and 4–5 Molotov cocktails. This means that the ZOB's total armament consisted of a few hundred pistols and a few thousand grenades and incendiary bottles. In addition, the ZOB had 10 rifles, 1 submachine gun and 15 mines.[35]

It is immediately evident that the types of weapons are not appropriate. A high percentage of these weapons are made up of handguns, which are particularly ineffective in regular warfare in an urban environment because of their limited range and accuracy.

---

33. Ringelblum, "*Stosunki polsko-zydowskie w czasie* II *wojny swiatowej*" (Polish-Jewish Relations during the Second World War), *Biuletyn ZIH*, no. 30 (1959), p. 58.
34. "*Polskie sily zbrojne*..." [The Polish military forces...], p. 327.
35. Edelman, op. cit., p. 51.

Anielewicz's remark in a letter to his second-in-command, Cukierman, who was on the "Aryan" side, is particularly telling in this regard: "Don't forget, handguns are useless for us now. We rarely use them. What we really need is grenades, rifles, machine guns and explosives."[36]

The ZOB had no submachine guns or light machine guns, which were more appropriate for urban combat. The only weapons it possessed in any significant quantity were grenades and Molotov cocktails. Although the range of such weapons is limited (20–25 meters), the extent of their impact made them much more useful than handguns.

It cannot be ruled out that the ZZW was better armed. According to B. Mark, the ZZW unit on Muranowska Street had about 300 grenades, eight submachine guns, one light machine gun and a heavy machine gun, and several thousand rounds of ammunition. Mark also mentions that the ZZW donated a certain amount of arms to the ZOB on the eve of the insurrection.[37] The total armament of the ZZW units probably comprised pistols, about 20 submachine guns and eight machine guns, and a large quantity of grenades and Molotov cocktails.

The so-called "wildcat" groups also had a certain amount of weapons. Still, we do not have the data that would allow us to make a quantitative estimate. Undoubtedly they had handguns, knives, etc., or in other words, the least effective kind of weapons. It is equally clear that these arms could not be used during the first days of the uprising when there was regular warfare in the streets. They were used only during the subsequent phase of the insurrection, the assaults and the defense of private bunkers.

In total, taking into account the high estimates, it can be argued that the ghetto's armament consisted of:

– a few thousand grenades and Molotov cocktails

36. Mark, *Powstanie w getcie warszawskim* [The Warsaw ghetto uprising], p. 262.

37. Ibid., p. 38.

– a few hundred handguns – definitely less than 2,000
– 25 submachine guns
– 20 rifles
– 10 machine guns
– 20 mines

In addition to the Jewish military organizations, all the Polish underground military organizations took part in the ghetto uprising, except for those who belonged to the far right.

The People's Guard carried out five combat operations outside the ghetto walls on April 20th, 21st, 23rd, the night of April 28th and May 10th. The following forces were deployed in those operations:

– April 20th: a special GL unit of five people.
– April 22nd: assault groups of undetermined composition.
– April 23rd: three assault groups of four persons each.
– April 29th and May 10th: smaller combat groups whose mission was to evacuate ZOB units from the ghetto.[38]

The Home Army carried out four combat actions on April 19th and 23rd and smaller-scales actions on the following days. On April 19th, a 25-person unit fought under the command of Captain Pszenny. On April 23rd, there was fighting outside the ghetto walls involving a seven-person unit of the diversion company under the command of Captain Lewinski and another unit under the command of warrant officer Stalkowski. Another, larger-scale operation carried out by the Home Army during the uprising was the liquidation of the SS post on Zakroczymska Street by a unit of eight people under the command of Lieutenant Kern-Jedrychowski.[39]

A KB unit comprising 18 people under the command of Cap-

38. J.B. Garas, *Oddzialy Gwardii Ludowej i Armii Ludowej 1942–1943* [The units of the people's guard and the people's army] (Warsaw, 1963), p. 25.
39. Bartoszewski, "*Akcje zbrojne pomocy Zydom*" [Military operations to aid the Jews], *Tygodnik Powszechny*, 27/4/1958.

tain Iwanski carried out a number of operations in support of the ghetto uprising. On April 27th, that unit entered the ghetto and fought there for a time. Further, combat operations at the outskirts of the ghetto were carried out by a PPS militia unit under the command of Wladyslaw Andrzejczak, a unit of the Socialist Combat Organization under Leszek Raabe, and a Szare Szereg [*Gray Ranks, a Polish Scouts organization*] group commanded by Marian Senger.

CONCLUSION

The information cited allows us to conclude, without falling into serious errors, that from the first day of the uprising, the Nazis enjoyed a superiority over the insurgents in terms of firearms and automatic weapons – without counting the handguns which were not very useful in regular warfare in the streets – on the order of at least 27 to 1. But the actual Nazi firepower was immeasurably superior to this order of magnitude. In fact, we should also take into account the ammunition in the hands of both sides.

We do not have conclusive data regarding the amount of the ZOB and the ZZW's respective supplies of ammunition. We only know that the ZOB had 10–15 cartridges per pistol. It is very likely that the supply of ammunition for the very few rifles and automatic weapons was a few dozen cartridges per weapon.

When it comes to the ammunition supplies of Stroop's combat group, we can make a far more precise estimate based on the standard number of rounds per reserve detail in the rear. For these details, the number of rounds per weapon was the following:[40]

– pistol	16 cartridges
– rifle	20 cartridges
– submachine gun	512 cartridges
– automatic rifle	2,505 cartridges

40. Handbook on German Military Forces, op. cit., p. VI-21.

– heavy machine gun 4,750 cartridges

Of course, the Nazi troops that entered the ghetto had at least the number of rounds stipulated in the cited standards and could top off their ammunition supply every day. It is equally obvious that there was more ammunition for one single Nazi heavy machine gun than for all the insurgent combat groups put together (without counting handgun cartridges).

Once the difference in ammunition supplies has been factored in, clearly we must double or triple the order of magnitude of 27 to 1 given above to obtain the exact balance of firepower. If, furthermore, we take into account the German's use of tanks, artillery and aviation, without exaggeration, we can speak of a Nazi firepower 100 times greater than that of the insurgents.

In these estimates, because of their short range, I have not taken into consideration the weapons, such as grenades and Molotov cocktails, which the insurgents had in very large quantities. This does not fundamentally alter the situation, because the Nazis certainly had an incomparably bigger supply of grenades than the insurgents and the firepower of the incendiary bottles was far less than that of the explosives used by the Nazi sapper details.

The Nazis' obviously superior level of training was also not a negligible factor. It is known that the majority of ZOB and ZZW soldiers were young people whose only combat training was in the ghetto camp.

One can even go so far as to say that no one has ever dared to accept the challenge to fight in the face of such an enormously disproportional balance of forces, and, furthermore, that it was theoretically impossible to fight under such conditions. Although they did not expect in any way to succeed, the Warsaw ghetto decided to fight to protest, arms in hand, against the greatest barbarism in human history, the Nazi genocide.

Nevertheless, there were factors that made it possible to engage the enemy in battle, despite his 100 to 1 superiority in firepower. These factors were the following: (1) Fighting carried out in a very dense urban environment prepared in advance, and (2) the extraordinary determination of the insurgents.

During the period leading up to the uprising, the ghetto's inhabitants succeeded in constructing more than 630 bunkers and underground hideouts.[41] Some of these bunkers were used by the ZOB and the ZZW to carry out combat operations. Many other bunkers were built so as to be able to resist the Nazis if they were discovered. Of course, without such preparations, it would not have been possible to sustain such difficult fighting for several weeks. The balance of firepower as it existed would have made it impossible to sustain combat for even an hour if the terrain had not been prepared for resistance.

The extraordinary determination of the insurgents was an even more important factor. It has been referred to by many Jewish and Polish sources, in accounts given by combatants and witnesses, the underground press and occupation diaries. It must be emphasized that this powerful determination to fight was accompanied by an awareness that defeat was inevitable, an awareness that usually leads to the rapid collapse of fighters' morale.

This determination has been confirmed by Nazi sources. Stroop wrote in the introduction to his report, "Repeatedly, fighting groups of 20 to 30 or more Jewish youths, aged 18 to 25, accompanied by a corresponding number of females, unleashed new resistance. These fighting groups had orders to offer armed resistance to the last person and, if necessary, to commit suicide to escape capture."[42] And further, "The resistance offered by the Jews and bandits could be broken only by the energetic and relentless night and day commitment of our assault units."[43]

Stroop himself becomes an unwilling witness to the heroic conduct of the insurgents in writing, "During the armed resistance, females belonging to the fighting groups were armed just like the

41. *Stroop Report*, p. 52.
42. Ibid., p. 15.
43. Ibid., p. 16.

men. Some of them were members of the He-halutz movement. Not infrequently, these females fired pistols from both hands. Repeatedly, they concealed pistols or hand grenades (oval Polish grenades) in their underpants to use at the last minute against the men of the Waffen-ss, Police or Wehrmacht."[44] The heroic attitude of these women during the fighting has been confirmed by Stroop's superior, General Kruger, who during a conversation with Hans Frank, said about the Jewish women, "Everyone knows that they are stronger than the men. We could see that during the liquidation of the Warsaw ghetto. This operation was very difficult. This strength became clear as the Jewish women fought against the ss soldiers and the police with arms in hand down to the last woman."[45]

The heroic attitude demonstrated in battle is not the only evidence of the tremendous determination of the insurgents. Under the conditions that existed in the ghetto, the long months of preparations for battle – the formation of a disciplined military organization, the preparation of the terrain where operations were to take place, the acquisition of a minimum quantity of arms and material – required a far from negligible spirit of sacrifice and will. Without these long and arduous preparations, there could have been no armed insurrection against units equipped with automatic weapons, artillery and tanks.

There was no way that the ghetto could have been armed in a way that would have allowed it to hold out better and create sufficient conditions to save a greater number of its inhabitants from deportation. The Warsaw ghetto uprising could not be powerful enough to force the Nazis to give up or limit their genocidal intentions toward the Warsaw Jews. Still, even under particularly difficult conditions, it was possible to create the requisite balance of forces sufficient to force the Nazis to engage in an inauspicious

---

44. Ibid.
45. *The Diary of Hans Frank*, quoted in Stanislaw Piotrowski, *The Odyl Globocnik Mission*, pp. 54–55.

battle in a place with the importance of Warsaw. It should also be recalled that the Warsaw ghetto uprising was the most important military insurrection in occupied Central Europe, both in terms of its duration and the forces engaged.[46] The Warsaw ghetto was also the first quarter of a major city in the occupied territories where the Germans were chased out, and over whose roofs there flew, however briefly, inaccessible to the Nazis, the flags of the combatant nations. The great importance of this was emphasized by the PPR newspaper *Gwardzista*, May 20, 1943, in an article entitled "The Ghetto in Struggle": "The ghetto's heroic struggle has already lasted a month. This is the biggest and longest act of armed resistance in the occupied territories. (Except in Yugoslavia where the fighting went over to insurrection.)"[47]

This fact could only have a great impact throughout occupied Europe. It also could not fail to influence the general struggle against Nazism. This remains the principal factor in the Warsaw ghetto uprising. This aspect was explained by the eminent military historian General Kirchmayer, who wrote, "The Warsaw ghetto uprising has fallen but the idea of armed struggle in the name of which this insurrection was carried out has spread beyond the ghetto walls, survived and witnessed the victory. This idea was disseminated in the forests by those who escaped from the ghetto and went to reinforce the partisan units. In fact, since the April uprising, we see Jews in nearly all the partisan units, and even constituting their most combative element, the most dedicated to the armed struggle. Further, the idea of armed struggle has won over a number of Poles who were confronted with the struggle in the

46. By way of comparison, it could be added that lesser Nazi forces were engaged in the two major partisan battles that had taken place in Poland during the first half of 1943. Thus, in the counterattack during the battle for the Zamojsc region that took place February 2–11, 1943, the Nazi battle group comprised 1,910 soldiers. In Operation "Ostersegen" in the forest region of Parczew, which took place April 22–24, 1943, a Nazi assault group of 1,630 men participated. See also K. Radziwonczyk, "*Niemieckie sily zbrojne w okupowanej Polsce*" [The German military forces in occupied Poland], *Wojskowy Przeglad Historyczny*, no. 4 (1962), p. 84.

47. *Gwardzista*, no. 18, 20/V/1943.

Zamojsc region or in the Warsaw ghetto […]. The military significance of the Warsaw ghetto uprising thus resides principally in its reverberations among the Polish population."[48]

It would have been impossible to achieve such results if it had not been possible to furnish the ghetto with a certain quantity of arms, minimal of course, but sufficient to do battle. The lack of these weapons was the main factor that made it impossible to organize armed resistance during the period of deportations from the ghetto in the summer of 1942 and during the deportations in other ghettos.

48. Jerzy Kirszmayer, *Wojskowe znaczenie powstania warszawskiego* [The military significance of the April uprising], AZHP, file number 76/III-335, p. 78.

BIBLIOGRAPHY

BOOKS

Apfelbaum Emil. *Maladie de famine: Recherches cliniques sur la famine exécutées dans le ghetto de Varsovie en 1942* [Famine-related diseases – clinical studies of famine, conducted in the Warsaw ghetto in 1942]. Warsaw: American Joint Distribution Committee, 1946. (Quotations translated from French edition.)

Assuntino Rudi, and Wlodek **Goldkorn**. *Straznik: Marek Edelman opowiada* [The guardian – Marek Edelman speaks]. Cracow: Znak, 2000.

Bartoszewski Wladyslaw. *1859 dni Warszawy* [The 1,859 days of Warsaw]. Cracow: Znak, 1974.

———. *Warszawski pierscien smierci 1939–1944. Wydanie drugie rozszerzone* [The deadly noose in Warsaw. Second enlarged edition]. Warsaw: Wydawnictwo Interpress, 1970.

———, and Marek **Edelman**. *Zydzi Warszawy, 1939–1943* [The Jews of Warsaw, 1939–1943]. Lublin: Towarzystwo Naukowe, 1993.

———, and Zofia **Lewinowa**. *The Samaritans: Heroes of the Holocaust.* New York: Twayne Publishers, 1970.

———, and Zofia **Lewinowa**. *Ten jest z ojczyny mojej: Polacy z pomocą Żydom 1939–1945* [This is my homeland: Polish help to Jews 1939–1945]. Cracow: Znak, 1967.

Bauman Zygmunt. *Modernity and the Holocaust.* Oxford: Polity Press, 1989.

Bednarczyk Tadeusz. *Obowiazek silnejszy od smierci: Wspomnienia z lat 1939–1944 o polskiej pomocy dla Zydow w Warszawie* [A duty stronger than death – memoirs of Polish aid to the Jews in Warsaw, 1939–1944]. Warsaw: Krajowa Agencja Wydawnicza, 1986.

———. *Walka i pomoc* [Struggle and assistance]. Warsaw: Iskry, 1968.

———. *Zycie codzienne warszawskiego getta: Warszawskie getto i ludzie (1939–1945), jakimi ich znalem* [Daily life in the Warsaw ghetto: The Warsaw ghetto and people (1939–1945), as I knew them]. Warsaw: Ojczyna, 1995.

Berenstein Tatiana, Artur **Eisenbach**, and Adam **Rutkowski**, eds. *Eksterminacja Zydow poskich w okresie okupacji hitlerowskiej* [Extermination of the Polish Jews during the Nazi occupation]. (Compiled documents and commentary.) Warsaw: Zydowski Institut Histryczny, 1957.

Borwicz Michel. *L'insurrection du ghetto de Varsovie* [The Warsaw ghetto uprising]. Paris: Gallimard, 1966.

———. *Ecrits des condamnés à mort sous l'occupation nazie (1939–1945)* [Writings by those condemned to death under the Nazi occupation]. Paris: Gallimard, 1973.

———. *Vies interdites* [Forbidden lives]. Paris: Casterman, 1969.

Cukierman Icchak [see also **Zuckerman** Yitzhak for English version]. *Nadmiar pamieci (Siedem owych lat): Wspomnienia 1939–1946* [Overflowing memories (those seven years): Memoirs 1939–1946]. Warsaw: PWN, 2000. (Translated from Hebrew; originally published by Kibbutz Lohamei Hagettaot, 1991.)

Czerniakow Adam. *Dziennik getta warszawskiego 6/IX/1939–23/VII/1942*. Warsaw: PWN, 1983. French translation: *Carnets du ghetto de Varsovie 6 septembre 1939–23 juillet 1942*, trans. Maria Elster, Jacques Burko and Jean-Charles Szurek. Paris: Editions La Découverte, 1996. English translation: *The Warsaw Diary of Adam Czerniakow: Prelude to Doom*, edited by Raul Hilberg, Stanislaw Staron, and Joseph Kermisz. Briarcliff Manor, NY: Stein and Day, 1982.

Edelman Marek. *Getto walczy: Udzial Bundu w obronie getta warszawskiego* [The ghetto in struggle: The Bund in the defense of the Warsaw ghetto]. Warsaw: Bund Central Committee, 1945.

Eisner Jack. *The Survivor of the Holocaust*. New York: Kensington Books, 1980.

Fuks Marian. *Z dziejow wielkiej katastrofy narodu zydowskiego* [On the history of the great catastrophe that befell the Jewish people]. Poznan: Sorus, 1999.

———. *Zydzi w Warszawie* [The Jews in Warsaw]. Poznan: Sorus, 1992.

Grupinska Anka. *Ciagle po kole: Rozmowy z zolnierzami getta warszawskiego* [Still in the circle: Interviews with the soldiers of the Warsaw ghetto]. Warsaw: Wydawnictwo Twój Styl, 2000.

Grynberg Michal. *Ksiega sprawiedliwych* [The book of the just]. Warsaw: PWN, 1993.

———, ed. *Pamietniki z getta warszawskiego* [Warsaw Ghetto Memoirs]. Warsaw: PWN, 1993.

Gutman, Israel, ed. *Encyclopedia of the Holocaust.* New York: Macmillan, 1990.

———. *Resistance: The Warsaw Ghetto Uprising.* Boston: Houghton Mifflin, 1994.

———. *Zydzi warszawscy 1939–1943* [The Jews of Warsaw 1939–1943]. Warsaw: Rytm, 1993. English translation: Gutman, Yisrael. *The Jews of Warsaw, 1939–1943: Ghetto, Underground, Revolt.* Bloomington, IN: Indiana University Press, 1982.

———, and Shmuel **Krakowski.** *Unequal Victims: Poles and Jews during World War Two.* New York: Holocaust Library, 1986.

Hilberg Raul. See **Czerniakow** Adam.

Kaczynska Alicja. *Obok piekla* [Next door to hell]. Gdansk: Marpress, 1993.

Kermisz Josef. *Powstanie w getcie warszawskim 19 kwietnia–16 maja 1943* [The uprising in the Warsaw ghetto, April 19–May 16, 1943]. Lodz: Centr Zydowska Kom, 1946.

Krakowski Shmuel. *The War of the Doomed: Jewish Armed Resistance in Poland 1942–1944.* New York: Holmes and Meier, 1984.

Kurzman Dan. *The Bravest Battle: The Twenty-eight Days of the Warsaw Ghetto Uprising.* New York: Putnam, 1976.

———. *Mala encyklopedia wojskowa* [Little Military Encyclopedia], vol. 3. Warsaw: Wydawnictwo Ministerstwa Obrony Narodowej, 1971.

Lazar Litai Chaim. *Masada shel Varsha: HaIrgun HaTzevai HaYehudi Be-Mered Geto Varsah* [The Masada of Warsaw: The ZZW in the Warsaw ghetto uprising]. Tel Aviv: Jabotinsky Press, 1963. English translation: *Muranowska 7: The Warsaw Ghetto Rising.* Tel Aviv: Massada-PEC Press, 1966.

Mark Bernard. *Powstanie w getcie warszawskim: Czesc druga, Dokumenty i materialy* [The Warsaw ghetto uprising: part two, documents and resource material]. Warsaw: Żydowski Instytut Historyczny, 1953. English translation: *Uprising in the Warsaw Ghetto.* New York: Schocken, 1975.

———. *Walka i zaglada warszawskiego getta* [Struggle and destruction of the Warsaw ghetto]. Warsaw: Wydawnictwo Ministerstwa Obrony Narodowej, 1959.

Matusak Piotr. "*Zwiazek Walki Zbrojnej i Armia Krajowa w AK cji pomocy*

Zydom" [The armed combat organization and the home army in the activities to aid the Jews]. In *Spoleczenstwo polskie wobec martylorogii i walki Zydow w latach II wojny swiatowej* [Polish society in the face of the martyrdom and struggle of the Jews during World War Two], edited by Krzysztof Dunin-Wasowicz. Warsaw: Instytut Historii Polskiej Akademii Nauk, 1996.

Meed Vladka. *On Both Sides of the Wall.* Washington, DC: Holocaust Library, 1993.

Minczeles Henri. *Histoire générale du Bund* [General history of the Bund]. Paris: Denoël, 1995.

Moczarski Kazimierz. *Rozmowy z katem.* Warsaw, 1978. English translation: *Conversations with an Executioner.* Englewood Cliffs, NJ: Prentice-Hall, 1981.

Najberg Leon. *Ostatni powstańcy getta* [The last ghetto rebels]. Warsaw: Żydowski Instytut Historyczny w Polsce, 1993.

Polskie sily zbrojne w II-giej wojnie swiatowej, vol. 3, *Armia Krajowa* [The Polish Armed Forces during the Second World War, vol. 3, The home army]. London/Warsaw: Instytut Historyczny im. gen. Sikorskiego, 1999.

Prekerowa Teresa. *Konspiracyjna Rada Pomocy Zydow w Warszawie 1942–1945.* Warsaw: Panstwowy Instytut Wydawniczy, 1982. French translation: *Zegota, commission d'aide aux juifs* [Zegota, the committee for aid to the Jews]. Translated by Marian Apfelbaum. Monaco: Editions du Rocher, 1999.

Ringelblum Emanuel. *Notes from the Warsaw Ghetto: The Journal of Emanuel Ringelblum.* Edited and translated by Jacob Stern. New York: McGraw-Hill, 1958.

———. *Stosunki polsko-zydowskie w czasie drugiej wojny swiatowej.* Warsaw: Czytelnik, 1988. English translation: *Polish-Jewish Relations during the Second World War.* Edited by Joseph Kirmisch and Shmuel Krakowski. Translated by Dafna Allon, Danuta Dabrowska, and Dana Keren. New York: Howard Fertig, 1976.

Rotem Simha (Kazik). *Memoirs of a Warsaw Ghetto Fighter: The Past Within Me.* New Haven/London: Yale University Press, 1994.

Sakowska Ruta. *Ludzie z dzielnicy zamknietej* [The people of the closed quarter], 2nd rev. ed. Warsaw: PWN, 1993.

Seidman Hillel. *The Warsaw Ghetto Diaries.* Translated by Yosef Israel. Southfield, MI: Targum Press, 1997. French translation: *Du fond de l'abîme: Journal du ghetto de Varsovie* [From the bottom of the abyss: Warsaw ghetto diary]. Paris: Plon, 1998. (Hebrew edition, 1946)

Skarzynski Aleksander. "*Cele polityczne 'Burzy' o sprawie wybuchu powstania warszawskiego*" [The political objectives of 'Burza' and the question of the outbreak of the Warsaw uprising]. In *Najnowsze dzieje Polski 1939–1945* [Recent Polish history, 1939–1945], vol. 2. Warsaw: Instytut Historii Polskiej Akademii Nauk, 1959.

Sobczak Kazimierz, ed. *Polski ruch oporu 1939–1945* [The Polish resistance 1939–1945]. Warsaw: Wydawnictwo Ministerstwa Obrony Narodowej, 1988.

Stroop Jürgen. *The Stroop Report: The Jewish Quarter of Warsaw Is No More.* Translated by Sybil Milton. New York: Pantheon, 1979. [See appendix 3.]

Szapiro Pawel. "*Problem pomocy dla walczacego getta w publicystyce Polski Podziemnej*" [The question of aid to the ghetto struggle in the Polish underground press]. In *Holocaust z perspectywy polwiecza...* [The Holocaust fifty years after...], *Konferencja* ZIH, March 29–31, 1993. Warsaw: ZIH, 1994.

Szpilman Wladyslaw. *Pianista* [The piano player]. Cracow: Znak, 2000. English translation: *The Pianist: The Extraordinary Story of One Man's Survival in Warsaw, 1939–1945*. London: Picador, 1999. (Originally published as *Smierc miasta* [Death of a city], Warsaw, 1946.)

Tomaszewski Jerzy. *Najnowsze dzieje Zydow w Polsce* [Recent history of the Jews in Poland]. Warsaw: PWN, 1993.

Turski Marian, ed. *Losy zydowskie: Świadectwo żywych* [Jewish destinies]. Warsaw: Nakladem Stowarzyszenie Zydów Kombatantów i Poszkodowanych w II Wojnie Światowej, 1996.

Tyszka Leon. *Sukcesy i kleski jednego zycia* [A life's success and defeats]. London: Poets and Painters Press, 1984.

Wdowinski David. *And We Are Not Saved.* New York: Philosophical Library, 1963.

Wood E. Thomas, and Stanislaw M. **Jankowski.** *Karski: How One Man Tried to Stop the Holocaust.* New York: John Wiley and Sons, 1994.

Zarski-Zajdler Wladyslaw. *Martyrologia ludnosci zydowskiej i pomoc spoleczenstwa polskiego* [Martyrdom of the Jewish population and aid from Polish society]. Warsaw: ZBoWiD, 1968.

Zuckerman Yitzhak [see also **Cukierman** Icchak for Polish edition]. *A Surplus of Memory: Chronicle of the Warsaw Ghetto Uprising.* Translated and edited by Barbara Harshav. Berkeley, CA: University of California

Press, 1993. (Translated from Hebrew; originally published by Kibbutz Lohamei Hagettaot, 1991.)

JOURNALS AND PERIODICALS

Biuletyn ZIH [Bulletin ZIH] is a publication of the Jewish Institute of History (ZIH).

Bartoszewski Wladyslaw. "*Polska podziemna a walka getta warszawskiego: Wybrane zagadnienia*" [Underground Poland and the struggle of the Warsaw ghetto: Selected questions]. *Biuletyn ZIH*, nos. 2–3 (1973): 86–87.

Bednarczyk Tadeusz. "*Poklosie 35 rocznicy powstania w getcie warszawskim*" [Anthology on the occasion of the 35th anniversary of the Warsaw ghetto uprising]. *Kwartalnik Historyczny*, no. 2, R86 (1979).

———. "*Wina i kara*" [Blame and punishment]. *Prawo i Zycie*, no. 8 (May 15, 1962).

———, alias "Bednarz," and Kalmen **Mendelson,** alias "Kalmyk." "*26 lat temu*" [Twenty-six years ago]. *Kronika* 8, no. 15 (April 19, 1969): 328.

Berman Adolf. "*O ruchu oporu w getcie warszawkim: Refleksje*" [The Resistance in the Warsaw Ghetto: Reflections]. *Biuletyn ZIH*, no. 29 (1959).

Biuletyn ZIH, nos. 71–72 (July–December 1969).

———, no. 74 (April–June 1970).

———, no. 75 (July–September 1970).

———, nos. 3–4 (1972). [Article about Adam Czerniakow.]

Datner Szymon. "*Wspolna walka*" [Common combat]. *Tygodnik Demokratyczny*, no. 17 (1968).

Fuks Marian. "*Pomoc Polakow bojownikom getta warszawskiego*" [Aid given by Poles to the Warsaw ghetto fighters]. *Biuletyn ZIH*, no. 1 (1989): 149.

———. "*Powstanie w getcie warszawskim*" [The Warsaw ghetto uprising]. *Biuletyn ZIH*, nos. 2–3 (1973).

———. "*W 40 rocznice powstania w getcie warszawskim*" [On the occasion of the 40th anniversary of the Warsaw ghetto uprising]. *Biuletyn ZIH*, nos. 1– 2 (1983): 126.

Gross Netty C. "Why Did God Do This to Us?" *Jerusalem Report* 11, no. 1 (May 8, 2000).

Hochberg Leo. "*Powstanie w getcie warszawskim w literaturze swiatowej*" [The Warsaw uprising in world literature]. *Biuletyn ZIH*, nos. 2–3 (1973).

Iwanski Henryk. "Czy *mozna bylo ratowac ludzi…? Mowi major 'Bystry'*"

[Could we have saved people…? Commander 'Bystry' here]. *Kultura* 6, no. 16 (April 21, 1968): 254.

———, et al. "*Dyskusja*" [Discussion]. *Biuletyn* ZIH, nos. 2–3 (1973): 86–87.

Jaworski Michal. "*Plac Muranowski 7: Fragment wspomnien*" [7 Muranowski Square: Fragments of a memoir]. *Biuletyn* ZIH, no. 2 (1974): 90.

———. "*Refleksje w 50 rocznice powsatnia w getcie warszawskim*" [Reflections on the occasion of the 50th anniversary of the Warsaw ghetto uprising]. *Wojskowy Przeglad Historyczny*, no. 1 (1993): 143.

Krakowski Stefan. "*Stosunek sil w powstaniu w getcie warszawskim*" [Balance of forces during the Warsaw ghetto uprising]. *Biuletyn* ZIH, no. 62 (1967).

Lazar Chaya. "The Jewish Military Organization (ZZW) in the Warsaw Ghetto Uprising: Fifty Years since the Uprising 1943–1993." *Publications of the Museum of the Combatants and Partisans* 7, no. 77 (April 1993).

Mark Bernard. "*Ruch oporu i powstanie w getcie warszawskim*" [The resistance and the Warsaw ghetto uprising]. *Biuletyn* ZIH, nos. 45–46 (1963).

———. "*Problemy badan nad ruchem oporu w gettach.*" *Biuletyn* ZIH (1950).

Mark Edwarda. "*Stosunek Polskiej Partii Robotniczej do sprawy zydowskiej w okresie okupacji hitlerowskiej. Wybor dokumentow*" [The Polish Workers Party and the Jewish question during the Nazi occupation]. *Biuletyn* ZIH, no. 41 (1962).

Mendelson Kalmen. "*Ci, ktorzy byli z nami…*" [Those who were with us…] *Argumenty*, no. 15 (April 15, 1973): 775.

———. "*Historia powstania* ZZW" [History of the founding of the ZZW]. *Kronika*, no.18 (May 2, 1970).

———. "*Oni byli z nami*" [He was with us]. *Rzeczywistosc* 3, no. 14 (April 3, 1983): 76.

———. "*Rozwoj i dzialanosc* ZZW" [The development and activities of the ZZW]. *Kronika*, no. 19 (May 9, 1970).

———. "ZZW *w walce*" [The ZZW in the struggle]. *Kronika*, no. 20 (May 16, 1970).

Niewiadomski Teodor. "*Sceny z getta*" [Ghetto scenes]. *Wiez*, nos. 4–5 (1982).

———. "*Z pomoca dla warszawskiego getta*" [Aid to the Warsaw ghetto]. *Kultura*, no. 161 (April 21, 1968): 254.

———. "*Ze wspomnien konspiracyjnych pracownika* ZOM" [Fragments of the clandestine memoirs of a ZOM worker]. *Kronika Warszawy* 3, no. 2, (1972).

Pelczynski Tadeusz. "*Opor zbrojny w ghettcie warszawskim 1943*" [The armed resistance in the Warsaw ghetto]. *Bellona* 45, no. 1–2 (1963).

Piasecki Henryk. "*Ruch oporu i powstanie w getcie warszawskim w prasie podziemnej*" [The resistance and the Warsaw ghetto uprising in the underground press]. *Biuletyn ZIH*, no. 2–3 (1973).

Ringelblum Emanuel. "*Notatki luty-maj 1941*" [Notes February–May 1941]. *Biuletyn ZIH*, no. 1 (January–June 1952): 3. [See English translation in books above.]

Sobczak Kazimierz. "*Powstanie zbrojne w getcie warszawskim, 19/4–16/5/1943*" [The armed uprising of the Warsaw ghetto, April 19–May 16, 1943]. *Wojskowy Przeglad Historyczny* 33, no. 1 (1988).

Stroop Jürgen. "*Raport Stroopa o likwidacji getta warszawskego w 1943 roku.*" Documents compiled by J. Gumkowski, K. Leszczynski. *Biuletyn Glownej Komisji Badania Zbrodni Hitlerowskich w Polsce* [Bulletin of the Central Commission for the Study of Nazi Crimes in Poland], no. 11 (1960). [See English translation in books above.]

Strzembosz Tomasz. "*Pomoc zbrojna polskiego podziemia dla walczacego getta*" [The Polish underground resistance's armed aid to the ghetto struggle]. *Wiez*, no. 4 (1973).

———. "*Tragedia i chwala warszawskiego getta*" [Tragedy and Glory of the Warsaw Ghetto]. *Wiez*, no. 4 (1979).

Szpakowski Zdzislaw. "*Getto ginace*" [The ghetto dies]. *Wiez*, no. 5 (1973).

———. "*Getto walczace*" [The ghetto in struggle]. *Wiez*, no. 4 (1973).

Zalewski Ireneusz. "*Muranowska 6*" [6 Muranowska Street]. *Trybuna*, no. 72 (March 26, 1999).

———. "*Muranowska 7/9*" [7–9 Muranowska Street]. *Trybuna*, no. 66 (March 19, 1999).

Zarski-Zajdler Wladyslaw. "*Ostatni transport.*" *Express Wicczorny*, no. 95 (April 20–21, 1968).

———. "*Pomoc walczacym*" [Aid to the fighters]. *Za wolnosc i lud*, no. 8 (April 16–30, 1968): 11, 14–15.

———. "*Wypad do getta: Fragment walk na placu Muranowskim*" [A ghetto escapade: On the battle of Muranowski Square]. *Za wolnosc i lud*, no. 8 (April 16–30, 1962): 173.

ARCHIVAL DOCUMENTS

The cited documents (unpublished) are from the following archives:

Archiwa Zydowskiego Instytutu Historycznego (Archives of the Jewish Institute of History – ZIH)

Jabotinsky Institute Archives

Archiwa Akt Nowych (Archives of New Records Actes Nouveaux – AAN)

Lohamei Hagettaot Ghetto Uprising Museum

Bednarczyk, Tadeusz. "*Getto warszawskie i ludzie – jakimi ich znalem: Wspomnienia 1939–1945; Wybitniejsze jednostki getta – Inzynier Adam Czerniakow – przewodniczacy Gminy Wyznaniowej Zydowskiej w Warszawie*" [Warsaw ghetto and people – as I knew them: Memories of 1939–1945; The most remarkable individuals of the ghetto – Engineer Adam Czerniakow – president of the Jewish community in Warsaw]. ZIH Archives, no. 5809.

———. "*Na fali wspomnien powstanczych*" [On the wave of uprising memoirs]. ZIH Archives, no. 5810.

———. "*Oswiadczenie o Niewiadomskim*" [Statement on Niewiadomski]. August 16, 1969. ZIH Archives, no. 6575.

———. "*Wyciag z zarysu AK cji pomocy OW-KB dla ZZW...*" [Excerpts from the essay on the OW-KB's activities to aid the ZZW...]. November 22, 1961. ZIH Archives, no. 5808.

Celmajster Jozef. "*Oswiadczenie*" [Statement]. Jabotinsky, W (8) R 6.

Iwanska Maria. "*Oswiadczenia o I.M.*" [Statement on I.M.]. May 24, 1967. ZIH Archives, no. 6364.

———. "*Oswiadczenie*" [Statement]. May 25, 1967. ZIH Archives, no. 6364.

Iwanski Henryk. "*Droga Kolezanko Lywio*" [Dear colleague Lywia]. Lochamei Hagettaot Ghetto Uprising Museum, Israel, no. 6708. (Letter found by Chaya Lazar.)

———. "*Zaswiadczenia o I.H*" [Attestation concerning I.H.]. ZIH Archives, no. 5792:

A. Tarnawa-Petrykowski i E. Wilk Biernacki, January 20, 1958.

Kancelaria Rady Panstwa, May 10, 1965.

ks. Czarnecki, parafia sw. Katarzyny, August 21, 1963.

K. Mendelson, December 2, 1959.

L. Hermelin z dn., September 4, 1957.

ZIH (B. Mark), June 12, 1958.

Wl. Zajdler, January 3, 1960.

Biskup Karol Niemira, August 15, 1957.

———. "*Zeznanie*" [Minutes], October 30, 1961, ZIH Archives, no. 5792.

———. "*Zeznanie*" [Minutes], November 13, 1961, ZIH Archives, no. 5792.

Jaworski Bronek. *Informacje Bronka Jaworskiego* [Information provided by Bronek Jaworski]. Jabotinsky, W (8), no. 41 and ZIH Archives, no. 5016.

Ketling-Szemley Janusz Cezary. "*Przyczynek do historii mojej walki i wspolpracy z Zydowskim Zwiazkiem Walki Wyzwolenczej na terenie ghetta warszawskiego w latach okupacji*" [Contribution to the history of my struggle and my collaboration with the ZZW in the Warsaw ghetto during the occupation]. Jabotinsky, W (8) 25.

———. "*Wspomnienia z walk i dzialalnosci* ZZW..." [Memoirs of the struggle and work of the ZZW...]. ZIH Archives, no. 4469.

Kowalska Helena. "*Oswiadczenie*" [Statement]. September 27, 1965. ZIH Archives, no. 6159.

Kowalski. "*Oswiadczenie, o 'Sepie' Marianie Kowalskim i Helenie Kowalskiej*" [Statement on "Sep" Marian Kowalski and Helena Kowalska]. ZIH Archives, no. 6159.

Landau David John. "Statement 11/7/94." Jabotinsky, W (8) R, no. 7.

Lazar Chaya, ed. "David-Yakov Landau, The Man Who Fought the Germans in Their Military Uniforms." *Publications of the Museum of the Combatants and Partisans*. Tel Aviv, Nissan 5755, April 1995. Jabotinsky, vol. 10, p. 80.

Lejewski Jozef. "Oswiadczenie" [Statement]. December 2, 1959. ZIH Archives, no. 5794.

Lohamei Hagettaot. "*Relacja Renszomsla*" [Eyewitness account]. Jabotinsky, W (8) R 4.

Mark Bernard. "*Kolekcja dokumentow*" [Documents]. ZIH Archives, KBM 265.

"*Meldunki sytuacyjne dzienne z powstania w getcie, 20, 21, 22, 23, 25, 28 kwiecien 1943*" [Daily files of the ghetto uprising, 20, 21, 22, 23, 25, 28 April 1943]. AAN Archives, file 202/XV-2.

Mendelson Kalmen. "*Oswiadczenie*" [Statement]. 1960. ZIH Archives, no. 5792.

———. "*Oswiadczenie*" [Statement]. 1968. ZIH Archives, no. 6516.

Mirski Bronislaw (Frydman). "*Zeznanie*" [Minutes]. June 6, 1951. ZIH Archives, no. 5006.

"*Odezwa* ZOB *z 4/7/1942*" [July 4, 1942, call of the ZOB]. ZIH Archives, file number 230/113.

"*Odezwa* ZZW *z 1943*" [1943 call of the ZZW]. ZIH Archives, file number 230/113.

"*Relacja o* AK *cji likwidacyjnej ne terenie szopu Többens 23/4/1943*" [Chronicle of the unfolding of the liquidation operation in the Többens shop]. ZIH Archives-AAN, file number 202/XV, vol. 2, pp. 314–15.

Ringelblum Emanuel. "*Archiwa osobiste*" [Personal archives]. ZIH Archives, file number Ring. II/333.

Szopinski Stanislaw. "*Relacja*" [Relation]. July 20, 1969. ZIH Archives, no. 6514.

Teksty "*komunikatow dziennych* ZKN: 19–22/4/1943, 27/4/1943, 29/4/1943" [ZKN daily communiqués, April 19–22, 1943; April 27, 1943 and April 29, 1943]. ZIH Archives-AAN, file number 202/XV-2.

Tyszka Leon. "*Wspomnienia o Czerniakowie*" [Memories of Czerniakow]. ZIH Archives.

"*Ulotka* ZOB *z 18/1/1943*" [ZOB leaflet of January 18, 1943]. ZIH Archives.

Walewski Ryszard. "*Protokol*" [Minutes]. November 25, 1948. Jabotinsky, W (8) R5.

———. "*Relacja na procesie Stroopa: Warszawa 1951*" [Eyewitness account of the Stroop trial: Warsaw 1951]. Jabotinsky, W (8) R5.

INDEX